Odense University Studies in History and Social Sciences vol. 193

Interdependence Versus Integration

Interdependence Versus Integration

Denmark, Scandinavia and
Western Europe, 1945-1960

Edited by Thorsten B. Olesen

Odense University Press

The publication of this volume was made possible by the generous support of
the Danish Research Council for the Humanities.

© The authors and Odense University Press, 1995
Printed in Denmark by Special-Trykkeriet Viborg a-s

ISBN 87-7838-177-0
ISSN 0078-3307

Previously published in the research project *Danish Politics in Transition 1945-85*:
Birgit Nüchel Thomsen, Tage Kaarsted og Niels Thomsen (red.): Dansk Politik under forandring 1945-1985. Forskningssekretariatet 1987.
Tage Kaarsted: Regeringen, vi aldrig fik. Regeringsdannelsen 1975 og dens baggrund. Odense University Press 1988.
Poul Nyboe Andersen: Det umuliges kunst. Erindringer fra dansk politik 1968-77. Odense University Press 1989.
Birgit Nüchel Thomsen (red.): Retten til viden. Om adgang til den offentlige forvaltnings arkiver. Odense University Press 1990.
Carsten Due-Nielsen, Johan Noack og Nikolaj Petersen: Danmark, Norden og NATO 1948-82. I samarbejde med Dansk Udenrigspolitik Institut. Jurist- og Økonomforbundets Forlag 1991.
Johs. Nordentoft og Søren H. Rasmussen: Kampagnen mod Atomvåben og Vietnambevægelsen 1960-1972. Odense University Press 1991.
Johan Peter Noack: Det sydslesvigske grænsespørgsmål 1945-47. I samarbejde med Institut for Grænseregionsforskning 1991.
Flemming Just: Landbruget, staten og eksporten 1930-1950. I samarbejde med Sydjysk Universitetscenter 1992.
Birgit Nüchel Thomsen (red.): The Odd Man Out? Danmark og den Europæiske integration 1948-1992. Odense University Press 1993.
Birgit Nüchel Thomsen (ed.): The Odd Man Out? Denmark and European Integration 1948-1992. Odense University Press 1993.
Søren Eigaard: Idealer og Politik. Historien om Grundloven af 1953. Odense University Press 1993.
Birgit Nüchel Thomsen (red.): Temaer og brændpunkter i dansk politik efter 1945. Odense University Press 1994.
Poul Nyboe Andersen: Thorkil Kristensen. En ener i dansk politik. Odense University Press 1994.
Jens Kragh: Mellem socialismens velsignelser og praktikable fremskridt. Odense University Press 1995.

Contents

Foreword	7
Thorsten B. Olesen: Introduction	9
Richard T. Griffiths: The National and International Ramifications of Post-war Europe	24
Vibeke Sørensen: Nordic Cooperation - A Social Democratic Alternative to Europe?	40
Karl Molin & Thorsten B. Olesen: Security Policy and Domestic Politics in Scandinavia 1948/49	62
Monika Dickhaus: The Functioning of the European Payments Union (EPU) 1950-1958	82
Wendy Asbeek Brusse: European Trade and Commercial Policies. Quotas, Tariffs and the OEEC	96
Hans Branner: Denmark and the European Coal and Steel Community, 1950-1953	115
Flemming Just & Thorsten B. Olesen: Danish Agriculture and the European Market Schism, 1945-1960	129
Thomas Rhenisch: The Political and Economic Foundations of the Rome Treaties	147
Richard T. Griffiths: The United Kingdom and the Free Trade Area: A Post Mortem	167
Erik Bloemen: A Problem to Every Solution. The Six and the Free Trade Area	182
Johnny Laursen & Mikael af Malmborg: The Creation of EFTA	197
John Pinder: The Influence of European Federalists in the 1950's	213
Notes on contributors	245

Foreword

During the warm and sunny summer days of June 1992 thirty European scholars and researchers convened to discuss aspects related to the theme, »Denmark, Scandinavia and European integration, 1945-1960«. The conference was held at the beautiful Meilgaard Castle, near Aarhus. It was a joint-venture project between the Depts. of History and European Studies (Aarhus University), the Dept. of History and Civilization (European University Institute, Florence) and the Danish Research Council Project, »Danish Politics in Transition 1945-1985«. The greatest financial contribution was made by the Danish Research Academy.

The conference covered a broad variety of topics related to the general theme. Unfortunately, not all of these could be fitted into the present book. The articles which constitute this book are based on papers presented at the Meilgaard-conference. They have been re-written and edited to meet the requirements of publication.

The book is subsidized by and appears in the publication series of the Research Council Initiative, »Danish Politics in Transition 1945-1985«. This research initiative was launched by the Danish Research Council of the Humanities in 1988. The purpose of the project has been to stimulate research into Danish post-war political decision-making. Research has centred on political processes, political institutions and single policy issues.

Beside participating in the present project, »Danish Politics in Transition« has arranged and financed several other research activities within the field, Denmark and international cooperation. In May 1990 the Initiative in cooperation with the Danish Foreign Policy Institute held a conference on Danish participation in Western security cooperation. Based on the papers from this conference the Initiative in 1991 published the book: *Danmark, Norden og NATO 1948-1962* (»Denmark, Scandinavia and NATO 1948-1962«) edited by Carsten Due-Nielsen, Johan Peter Noack & Nikolaj Petersen. In 1992 another conference was arranged at Christiansborg, the house of the Danish Parliament, dedicated to Danish participation in European economic cooperation. The results of this conference has been published in *The Odd Man Out. Danmark og den europæiske integration 1948-1992* (a shorter English version was published under the title: *The Odd Man Out. Denmark and European Integration 1948-1992*) edited by Birgit Nüchel Thomsen (Odense 1993).

Concerning the present book we would like to thank the Danish Research Council for the Humanities for granting the necessary means for publication. We are also grateful to professor Niels Thomsen, University of Copenhagen, and professor Bent Jensen, Odense University, who reviewed and recommended the book for publication. Our gratitude also

Foreword

covers Profs. Henning Poulsen and Uffe Østergård, Aarhus University, for their cooperation on setting up the Meilgaard-conference, and Jan Ifversen for great help in making all ends meet at Meilgaard. We are greatly indebted to Stephanie Thomas and James Heenan who provided indispensable linguistic expertise, and to Stefan Andersen at Odense University Press for all his support. Special thanks go to Prof. Richard Griffiths for his active and dedicated involvement in the project from start to end. Last, but not least we would like to thank all the authors for their cooperative spirit and tolerance towards the whims of the editor.

Thorsten B. Olesen
Dept. of History
Aarhus University

Birgit Nüchel Thomsen
Chairman, the Danish Research
Council Initiative:
»Danish Politics in Transition 1945-1985«

Introduction

By Thorsten B. Olesen

"Europe's odd man out", "the reluctant European", "the Euro-sceptic" are just a few of the most popular images resorted to by journalists, historians and political scientists when describing Danish attitudes towards European integration. Such descriptions capture an essential element of the Danish engagement with the European integration project of the Six as represented by the European Coal and Steel Community and the EEC during the period of the Cold War. Pointing to the Maastricht experience many observers eagerly maintain that the above images also convey a great deal of truth about Danish attitudes to the present day European agenda.

The last claim would need qualification to be accepted. After all, Denmark joined the Common Market in 1973, she has a record of a relatively high degree of compliance with Community legislation and regulations (she is presently the country which has converted most of the 282 Single Act directives into national legislation) and she played a constructive role throughout the Maastricht negotiations. If one takes a closer look at the Danish and French 1992 referendums on the Maastricht treaty, the "no" vote (50,7% in Denmark compared to 48,95% in France) hardly stigmatizes Danish attitudes as radically different from those of the French. And even if Denmark to some extent may be termed a foot-dragging EU-sceptic, this designation, as we all know, fits equally well – or even better – a handful of other western European countries.

These qualifications are important. Not in order to rid Denmark of the burden of unfounded accusations. Rather, because they reveal an essential fact about Danish attitudes to European integration in most of the postwar period. At the top decision-making level the supranational approach to European cooperation was never favoured. However, it has been accepted as a necessity, as a rule of the game in order to obtain other ends. The same holds true for the Danish population at large, when from the beginning of the 1970s it was allowed a say in determining the course of Danish European policy. Even yes-voters of the 1972 referendum had severe reservations about the political aspects of EEC membership and about the power of the Community institutions in Brussels. It was the economic perspectives of joining which convinced the Danish voters.[1] In other words, opposition to the political and supranational aspects of the European integration has not been strong enough to prevent Denmark from taking an active interest in that process.

Contrary to conventional wisdom this also holds true for the early phase of western European integration – the phase between 1945 and

1960 to which the present book will limit its focus. In contrast to the other Scandinavian countries Denmark took an interest in the European customs union plans of 1947 associated with the Marshall plan. Again, in contrast to the Norwegian and Swedish, but also the British government, for a brief period in 1952-53 the Danish government seriously considered joining the European Coal and Steel Community (ECSC). When the EEC became a reality, strong pressure groups centred around Agriculture opted for Danish membership, an attraction which even prominent Social Democratic ministers of the time found hard to resist, not least because the eventual alternative, EFTA-membership, had very few advantages to recommend it from a Danish point of view.

Nevertheless, Denmark did not join neither the ECSC, nor the EEC during this period. One obvious explanation is that both these constructions did not embrace Great Britain. Britain had traditionally been Denmark's largest trading partner and even by the mid-1950s 1/3 of total Danish exports and nearly 50% of Danish agricultural exports were shipped across the North Sea. Thus, to join a market arrangement not including Great Britain seemed hazardous. All the same, Agriculture was the first major pressure group to advocate Danish membership in the EEC. There were several important reasons for that, but one very important belonged to the fact that West Germany took the position as Denmark's second largest trading partner, receiving 1/3 of total agricultural exports. And whereas the British market was a declining market for Danish exporters, the German market was expanding. The creation of two separate market blocs within western Europe, the EEC and EFTA, placed Denmark in a serious dilemma. No matter which option she chose, she would exclude one of her two main trading partners. Conservative reasoning would induce the Danish government to follow Great Britain whereas following Germany would be a more radical choice. In the event the Social Democratic led coalition government chose to be conservative.

The government chose the minimalist intergovernmental approach to western European cooperation even though this type of cooperation, as exemplified by the OEEC, had been a rather disappointing experience.[2] The OEEC trade liberalization programme initiated in 1949 was designed in a way that collided directly with Danish trade interests. Administering a small open economy Denmark belonged to the European low tariff club, and consequently relied on quota restrictions as the dominant form of trade protection. The OEEC programme operated the other way around, demanding the dismantling of quota restrictions before a tariff reduction programme would be considered.

As a consequence it goes without saying that the Danish home market was exposed to maximum competition. Even worse, the prospect of a compensatory gain on the export markets did not look promising either. The problem was that agricultural products made up no less than 60% of total

Danish exports during the period 1950-1953[3]. And precisely a great part of trade in agricultural products was exempt from the OEEC liberalizing programme as the programme only covered trade on private account and not the so-called state trade. This problem was repeated when in 1956 Britain, in a counter-move to the Common Market plans of the Six, proposed a Western European Free Trade Area covering all OEEC members, but excluding trade in agricultural products. The OEEC Free Trade Area never saw the light of day, but when her amputated sister, EFTA, was finally established in 1960, agricultural products had still not found their way into the agreement. This further feature also accounts for the restrained nature of the Danish government's decision to join EFTA.

On an general western European level the OEEC trade liberalization programme was functioning with better results. Denmark was a special case, with a foreign trade composition resembling that of a developing satellite economy, a high export quota of unprocessed, agricultural products (albeit produced by a very modern, efficient and competitive farm sector), and a high dependency on a few export markets. In this sense Denmark may be termed "Europe's Odd Man Out".[4] But precisely this oddity goes a long way towards explaining why Denmark eventually showed a much greater inclination to consider the prospect of EEC membership than did the other Scandinavian countries. The great advantage of membership in this market arrangement consisted of the fact that it included agricultural trade.

However, the market schism, UK versus West Germany, still persisted. But other factors also militated against Danish EEC membership. Probably the greatest problem for Denmark's potential membership in the Six lay in the fact that none of the other Scandinavian countries intended to join. The consequence of Danish EEC membership would have been to downgrade Nordic cooperation. And Nordic cooperation was one of the primary, if not *the* primary, priority of Danish foreign policy during the early post-war period.

By the mid-1950's Norway and Sweden together constituted the third largest Danish export market, and as the EFTA experience eventually was to prove, held the potential for further expansion. Furthermore since 1947, and on an intensified basis since 1955, the Nordic countries were striving to create a customs union of their own. Whether these efforts would have been crowned with success if developments on the European scene (the launching of the EEC initiative by the Six and the British counterproposal of a European Free Trade Area) had not effectively undermined them is by no means certain. The strength of Nordic cooperation in the post-war period occurred on the informal and low-institutional level whereas the grand schemes involving transference of national power and sovereignty all failed.[5] However, the point to stress here is that it would have been extremely difficult for any Danish government during the period 1945-1960 to have opted for a solution which could have been interpreted as delivering the death blow to Nordic cooperation.

The high foreign policy priority invested in Nordic cooperation was not only pragmatic motivated by an economic cost-benefit approach. Nordic cooperation and the tendency to coordinate international policy responses with the other Nordic countries also originated in concerns of a broader political nature. The occupation of Denmark by Germany during the War stimulated political interest in developing Nordic cooperation. Dedication to this goal came from all political quarters with the exception of the Communists whose primary political point of reference was Moscow and not Stockholm and Oslo. The leading Social Democrat of the period 1945-55, Hans Hedtoft, displayed a very strong and emotional commitment to Nordic cooperation. Even if Nordism was something of a catch-all ideology, the labour movement seemed to subscribe to it disproportionately. The political leverage of Labour was great in Scandinavia, but it was most pronounced in Norway and Sweden. For the Danish Social Democrats, therefore, it was tempting to regard Nordic cooperation as a lever for Social Democracy within Denmark. Europe of the Six, on the contrary, did not hold this appeal, dominated as it was by Christian Democracy.

Nordic cooperation had another very strong asset. It was mot only at the political top level that Nordism was alive. It exercised a very strong attraction for the population at large. The Danish branch of the European Movement never gained a membership to speak of, whereas the Danish Norden Association in 1960 counted a paying membership of app. 65.000.[6] The various cultural grass root initiatives of the Norden Association were accompanied by a proliferation of Nordic contacts between professional organisations, between political parties and movements and between public institutions. Tangible results of Nordic intergovernmental cooperation such as the Nordic passport union, the common Nordic labour market, mutual social rights for Nordic citizens etc., had a strong popular appeal and were generally supported without reservation.[7]

The contrast to present day EU-attitudes is striking. Whereas during the early post-war period there was complete harmony between the government's Nordic policy and public opinion, no such harmony exists on EU policy today. In 1992 5/6 of the members of parliament endorsed the Maastricht treaty; all the same, a slim majority rejected the treaty when it was presented to the electorate in the first referendum.[8]

Whether the Nordic enthusiasm would have survived if the grand Nordic schemes had materialized (say a Nordic defence union in 1949 or a customs union in the 1950's) belongs to the realm of contrafactual questioning. However, it seems safe to expect that such schemes would have had a more binding character and demanded national sacrifice in the form of higher defence budgets, increased competition in certain sectors of the economy, a general transference of national sovereignty to Nordic institutions etc.. Nordic cooperation, then, would have taken a different path from the one it actually followed. The consensual intergovernmentalism so characteristic of Nordic cooperation could hardly have escaped a harsher supranational discipline. Seen from this perspective there are good reasons to believe that the continued Danish enthusiasm for Nordic solutions may in fact reside in the paradox that the grand schemes always failed. This has preserved Nordic cooperation, at least at the popular level, as an utopia-like totem which can be mobilized in the fight against too strong Danish involvement in European integration.

However, in the first years after World War II high-ranking decision-makers also considered Nordic cooperation both a desirable and realistic alternative to Atlantic or western European cooperation. The Social Democratic government's policy during the Scandinavian defence negotiations of 1948-49 proves this. The period 1945-1949 was a period of flux and uncertainty, not unlike the situation in Europe after 1989. Seen from a contemporary perspective it is hardly surprising that a small country like Denmark had difficulty in adopting a foreign policy suited to the occasion. The neutrality formula which had regulated Danish foreign policy for nearly a century had been stigmatised by the war experience. The new formula, politically acceptable to most political parties in Denmark, was to support the collective security system of the UN. The UN, however, quickly proved too weak to run such a system once the East-West conflict undermined its foundation. Instead, bloc-creating policies came to the forefront in Europe and elsewhere. The newly appointed Danish Social Democratic government, for political and strategic reasons, was unwilling to accept this development. When the Swedish government proposed negotiations on the feasibility of creating a Scandinavian defence arrangement in April 1948, the Danish government, therefore, did not hesitate one second in confirming its positive attitude. There were two reasons motivating this positive reponse by the Danish government. First, a joint Scandinavian defence arrangement was a way of escaping involvement in a western bloc; or alternatively, if this option proved impossible to maintain, it was a way of ensuring that all Scandinavian states became mutually involved in such a bloc. Second, the Swedish initiative might serve as the long sought catalyst for Nordic cooperation in other fields as well.

The failure to establish a Scandinavian defence union and Norway's and Denmark's entry into NATO was a fatal blow to the government's Nordic ambitions, and from then on there was a growing realization among top Social Democrats that Nordic cooperation did not represent a universal solution to the problems Denmark was facing. The Nordic orientation of Danish foreign policy was still of prime importance, but Nordic cooperation was increasingly viewed as a means to an end rather than an end in itself.

In 1950 the young Minister of Trade, Jens Otto Krag, who was destined to become Prime Minister in 1962, already had a clear vision of the relationship between Nordic cooperation and European cooperation. In front of a labour movement audience in Oslo he made it clear that Nordic postwar cooperation had been disappointing. Despite all good intentions nothing substantial had materialized, Krag maintained. Rather, Nordic cooperation had been "smothered in kindness at a hundred joyful conferences". According to Krag, the Nordic results looked particularly meagre compared to international developments. But this comparison also offered the key to understanding why binding Nordic cooperation was so difficult to achieve:

> "However, the answer to why international, or European or European-American cooperation seem so much more successful than Nordic cooperation is not hard to find. We must look among ourselves, among our own economic problems. The simple fact is, that the economic problems of the Nordic countries today must and only can be solved on an international basis."[9]

J.O. Krags understanding of Denmark's and Scandinavia's position within the international economy's division of labour was probably more advanced than that held by most of his fellow Social Democratic collegues in Denmark. Nevertheless, the collapse of the Scandinavian Defence Union plans helped bring about the realization that Denmark should not base all her international commitment on 'would-be' Nordic cooperation. The obvious consequence was that Denmark had to take a more profound interest in other kinds of international cooperation.

This realization, however, was painful and only partial. Many rank-and-file Social Democrats as well as substantial segments of the trade union movement never fully acknowledged this logic, at least not when such international cooperation involved a choice between, say, a Nordic or a European orientation. This potential conflict within the party and the labour movement did not create great havoc during the 1950's. After all, during this period Denmark only participated in intergovernmental types of international cooperation together with the other Nordic countries. And when the dilemma became acute in the second half of the decade, even pro-Europeans like J.O. Krag did not advocate Danish membership in the EEC without British participation. However, this conflict has haunted the party from the first British and Danish applications for membership in 1961 to the present day.[10]

The Liberal and Conservative parties, on the other hand, never viewed Nordic cooperation as an alternative to European or international cooperation. They generally supported all kinds of Nordic initiatives, but it is also highly suggestive that the initiative to create a Danish branch of the European Movement originated within these parties, with Thorkil

Kristensen (Minister of Finance 1945-47 and again 1950-1953) from the Liberal party, Venstre, as its first chairman. It goes without saying that the ideological appeal of a united Social Democratic Scandinavia did not stimulate interest in Nordic cooperation in these quarters. The reasoning here was more along the lines presented by J.O. Krag above. Nordic cooperation was important, but it was not an alternative to dealings with western Europe. As the political representative of the dominant part of Danish Agriculture, Venstre, for instance, supported the view of Danish farmers that the Nordic countries neither wished nor were able to function as the primary outlet for Danish agricultural exports. Consequently Denmark had to actively engage in the discussions on future market regulations in western Europe. As indicated above, from 1956-1957 on this conviction prompted Agriculture and Venstre as the first leading political faction to recommend an outright separation of Danish European policies from their dependency on considerations of preserving unity within Scandinavia. The proof was the two groups open recommendation that Denmark join the EEC.[11]

It is clear the pro-EEC stance of Venstre and Agriculture, and also the more guarded, balanced, but still rather positive attitude displayed by Krag and a few other leading Social Democrats, were based on economic considerations. The political aspects of joining the EEC played a marginal role for those who sincerely considered the prospect of Danish membership. There is nothing indicating that the federal or 'unionist' aspects written into the Rome Treaties were viewed as more than political paraphernalia. And the supranational features were a constant source of worry, a bitter pill to swallow, before flying the EEC colours.

This attitude among the more pro-EEC wing in Denmark reveals, in fact, just as much about the overall Danish scepticism of supranational cooperation as the strength of the outright "no" position does. It is revealing that the leading representatives of Agriculture were against the supranational aspects inherent in several of the plans being discussed during the so-called Green Pool negotiations in the early 1950s on regulating European production and trade in agricultural products. Only when Agriculture realized that a limited transfer of sovereignty was the price to be paid in order to secure Danish agricultural products access to continental markets did it soften its opposition towards supranational organization.[12]

It is tempting to connect the widespread Danish scepticism towards supranationality to her recent national experience as a small country at the border of Europe's most unsettled great power which constantly pushed her into the sphere of conflicting great-power interests. Since the Danish defeat in the second Schleswig-Holstein war of 1864-65 the neutrality concept had guided Danish foreign policy. In concrete terms this policy had been based on an impartial and inconspicuous policy conduct in an effort to retain a maximum degree of independence and freedom of action. And even though impartiality had been difficult to maintain on several occasions, a study of Danish foreign policy during the 1930's, and even during the subsequent German occupation period, will demonstrate that Danish decision-makers had been willing to go to substantial lengths to defend the credibility of that policy conduct.[13] However, the German occupation shattered some of the illusions about the practicability of a neutrality policy, and Danish NATO-membership in 1949 might be seen to signal a definitive break with the traditions of the past. But in reality it was a break of form more than of substance. Within the alliance Denmark continued to pursue a policy inspired by neutrality concepts.[14] In a recent book this line of continuity between the policies preceding and following 1949 has been stressed by labelling Danish NATO policy, "latent neutrality". Likewise, Poul Villaume in the most penetrating study to date of Danish NATO membership of the 1950s, strikes a similar note when employing the title, "Allied with reservations".[15]

Borrowing the two concepts of "abandonment vs. entrapment" from Nikolaj Petersen[16], Villaume inserts his analysis of Danish NATO policies into an interesting interpretive framework which may also be extended to the study of Danish attitudes to European integration as well. According to Villaume, Denmark faced a alliance dilemma in her search for the highest level of security.[17] The reason for that was that this goal conflicted with another fundamental foreign policy goal, securing the maximum degree of national independence. In fact a negative correlation existed between the two goals. If the highest possible level of security could only be obtained through full integration into the Atlantic structures, then maximum security would only be achieved at the cost of losing the capacity for independent national manoeuvring, i.e. the danger of "entrapment". If, on the other hand, priority were given to safeguarding national independence, the result might well be a more exposed security position, i.e. the danger of "abandonment".

Danish European polices during the same period may be seen to have been caught in a similar dilemma. Joining the Continental market schemes of the Six would have meant a recognition of the principle of supernationality. Or in other words: Market access granted on the basis of political concession. Here rested the entrapment danger. However, despite this danger important sections of Danish society and the body politic continued to show an interest in the various continental integration schemes. Fear of losing out on international markets motivated this interest. Here we encounter the abandonment danger inherent in the Danish market dilemma.

The two concepts, alliance dilemma and market dilemma, are useful tools when analyzing Danish foreign policy during this period because they encapsulate the most vital considerations connected to the Danish choice of direction in international politics: Security versus national independence in the first case; national welfare (or group interests) versus sovereignty and independence in the second. However, they are descriptive frameworks which do not explain where on the continuum of the dilemma Denmark is positioned. They do not enlighten us regarding, for example, why Denmark entered NATO, but stayed outside the EEC. And on a comparative basis they do not furnish us with answers to why Denmark and The Netherlands have chosen radically different approaches to European integration, or why the approaches of the Scandinavian countries have varied. Concentrating on the difference between Denmark and the Netherlands even suggests that the dilemma framework is not based on mere objective criteria. Rather, it seems to depend on political perceptions and mental structures. Whereas Danish decision makers seemed to be convinced that a negative correlation existed between integration and national self-determination, Dutch political leaders do not seem to have viewed integration in that light. On the contrary, in their view integration also seemed an instrument to strengthen Dutch political leverage within Europe[18]. A comparison with Sweden reveals another example, which like the Dutch case, should warn against treating the dilemma framework as an approach to understanding small state behaviour in general. The ruling Swedish Social Democrats definitely shared all the Danish political doubts about entering into too heavily committed forms of international cooperation. But during this period, at least, Sweden was not seen to be confronted by a dilemma. In the Social Democratic view there were no compelling reasons why Sweden should join a security arrangement like NATO or sacrifice national independence on the alter of western European integration. This perception as we all know has changed dramatically in recent time.[19]

In summation there seem to be two distinct but connected questions to concentrate on when discussing the character of Danish European policy between 1945-1960. First, why did Denmark apparently take a more positive attitude to European integration than did the other Scandinavian countries? To answer that in full requires more detail and sophistication than can be presented in this introduction. However, the Danish 'Odd-Man-Out' position goes a long way towards explaining this difference. Second, why must Denmark be termed an integration sceptic, that is a sceptic of western European cooperation on a supranational basis as embodied by the ECSC and the EEC? Again there is more to the picture than can be illuminated here. The neutrality tradition of Danish foreign policy, fear and animosity against the Germans in the wake of World War II, reluctance to join a Christian Democratic club etc. were all aspects reducing the attraction of cooperating with the Six. These aspects also reflect why it is important to bear in mind the dilemma framework in this context. Economic reasons also played an important role. The market schism, lack of compelling incentive to join the ECSC, and pressure group opposition to join the EEC (in contrast to Agriculture Danish Industry feared competition within the Common market) militated against joining the Six. Last, but not least, it should be stressed that the desire to preserve unity among the Nordic states played a crucial role. Even those decision-makers who had relinquished the thought of Nordic cooperation as an alternative to other forms of international cooperation found it difficult to openly recommend a solution which entailed a political and economic division of Scandinavia.

However, to look for the finer details necessary to answer the two questions posed above, the reader will have to proceed to the articles within this anthology. In this respect Vibeke Sørensen's article (pp. 40-61) is a fine place to start. In her contribution she analyzes the Nordic orientation of Danish Social Democracy seen in the light of the country's foreign policy tradition, her economic structure and her small state position.

Using a different focus and limited to a more restricted period of time, Karl Molin and Thorsten B. Olesen discuss the relationship between domestic policy and foreign policy in Sweden and Denmark (pp. 62-81). The period under scrutiny is 1948-49 when Scandinavian security cooperation was proposed under the influence of the escalation of the Cold War. The article demonstrates how differences in the domestic political situation are an important key to explaining the clear differences in attitude towards the proposed Scandinavian Defence Union between the Social Democratic governments in the two countries.

For years the fact that the Danish Liberal-Conservative government of 1950-53 took an active interest in the development of the European Coal and Steel Community and even considered the prospect of membership has remained unnoticed. Hans Branner's contribution (pp. 115-128) based on Danish Foreign Ministry archive material brings this interesting intermezzo into the light. His findings lead him to conclude that Danish attitudes to European integration were more open-minded than is often maintained.

Agriculture was the first prominent pressure group to advocate full Danish membership in the EEC. The background for this fact is presented in a joint article by Flemming Just and Thorsten B. Olesen (pp. 129-146). The article is a political economy analysis tracing the position of Agriculture within the Danish productive structure and outlining its vital importance for Danish foreign trade. Danish Agriculture had strong political clout on the domestic scene and was successful in its fight against Social Democratic plan economy experiments during the immediate post-war period. However, international trade developments of the 1950s undermined its position providing an important driving force behind Agricultures early interest in the continental cooperation schemes of the Six.

However, this book does not only deal with European cooperation from

Introduction

a Danish perspective. The introduction has concentrated exclusively on this perspective because the Danish angle is strongly represented within the book. In addition Richard T. Griffiths in his article, "The National and International Ramifications of Post-War Europe", presents a general introduction to, and interpretation of, the general dynamic factors initiating the early western European integration process (pp. 24-39). Thus, the main thrust of Richard T. Griffiths' article is to explain why the new, supranational approach to European cooperation was introduced in 1950, and how it was shaped through a complex interplay of national and international developments.

The intention of this book is not only to examine European cooperation in its supranational, integration variant. The intergovernmental side of the western European intercourse is also analyzed. One of the most successful components of this type of cooperation was undoubtedly the European Payments Union initiative established within the framework of the OEEC in 1950. Monika Dickhaus has undertaken a major study of the operation of the EPU during the 1950's. In her article (pp. 82-95), she demonstrates how difficult it was to make the complicated but vital monetary cooperation system within the EPU work. However, it did function despite the absence of any supranational discipline. The best indication of that is that the EPU by 1958 was dissolved after having accomplished its major task, securing full convertibility of the western European currencies.

The EPU was not the only success for the intergovernmental type of cooperation within the OEEC. According to Wendy Asbeek Brusse in her penetrating study (pp. 96-114), also the trade liberalizing programme – despite all its shortcomings – must be termed a relative success although she warns against attributing the spectacular rates of economic growth and trade within western Europe of the 1950's to "the miraculous workings of the OEEC". She points out that it is important to acknowledge that the OEEC reforms had a different impact within different nation states. Precisely this realization prompts her to underline that only a research method flexible enough to catch both international trends and national particularities can explain why in the event a group of OEEC members decided to leave the well known territory of intergovernmental cooperation in exchange for a more sophisticated, but less tried experiment with supranational organization.

Taking the national approach Thomas Rhenisch in his contribution analyzes the domestic political compromises which allowed France, West Germany and the Netherlands to agree on forming a Common Market with supranational structures (pp. 147-166). It is a revealing study demonstrating that it was hard to reach the necessary compromise within the national context in all three countries, and indicating that generally it was easier to mobilize support for the project at the political level than among the dominant economic pressure groups. The article also demonstrates the

19

interesting, but well-known insight, that a common goal in international organization is achievable even though national motivations differ.

Political perceptiveness and statesmanship are important ingredients to make international cooperation work. In his second contribution to this book Richard T. Griffiths reveals that these qualities were in severe demand in Great Britain during the late 1950s (pp. 167-181). The article takes its point of departure in a post-mortem exchanged between high-ranking British civil servants in 1959 on the reasons for the failure of British policy-making in securing the creation of an OEEC Free Trade Area. The post-mortem represents a valuable additive to the normal archival record of British policy-making because of its quasi-official and evaluative character. Beneath the surface of this evaluation of what went wrong in British European policy we are introduced to the basic concepts of politics and to the images of Europe animating the top-echelons of British decision-making. As Richard T. Griffiths unmercifully unravels, these concepts and images were in flagrant contradiction with establishing a strategy able to impose British points of view on European developments.

However, it must be admitted that the challenge faced by British decision-makers of the second half of the 1950s was particularly daunting. This is the essence emerging from Erik Bloemen's article, which analyzes the British Free Trade initiative from the perspective of the Six (pp. 182-196). Already his imaginative title, "A Problem to Every Solution", points to the reluctance of Continental Europe to consider the British proposal. French decision-makers in particular were convinced that the British proposal was nothing more than a counter-proposal to torpedo the EEC-initiative. Even though such an interpretation held a great deal of truth, this should not rule out that a Free Trade compromise could have been reached between the Six and the rest of the OEEC once the Rome Treaties had been signed. However, this was not to be the case. As Erik Bloemen demonstrates, each proposal for a compromise was met by new sets of potential problems rendering this possibility unachievable.

As a consequence of this failed opportunity for reaching a compromise, the European Free Trade Association (EFTA) was set up in 1960 by seven of the 'non-Six' members of the OEEC. The creation of EFTA is the topic treated by Johnny Laursen and Mikael af Malmborg (pp. 197-212). Once again it is demonstrated that it took a lot of hard work and compromise to reach a mutual agreement of this sort. Organized on intergovernmental principles and excluding trade in agricultural products, EFTA was a more restricted and less committed type of cooperation compared to the customs union arrangement of the Six. It was also a more fragile and less powerful organization compared to the EEC, with Britain as the only European great power to participate. According to Laursen and Malmborg this is precisely mirrored in article 42 of the Stockholm Convention (The EFTA equivalent to the Rome Treaties). This article stated that any member state had the right to withdraw from EFTA on 12 months notice. A concession – one has to admit – which was a far cry from the "ever closer union" rhetoric of the preamble of the Rome Treaties.

The "ever closer union"-perspective was eagerly pursued by European federalists. This book ends with an analysis of the influence of European Federalists during the 1950s carried out by the insider expert, John Pinder (pp. 213-244). The thrust of this book leans in the direction of explaining European cooperation and integration in terms of national interests. In his lucid and highly informative article John Pinder reminds us that we should not overlook the influence of European Federalists in initiating and retaining the topic of integration on the European agenda. Moved by various idealistic, ideological and political motives European Federalists, in Pinder's view, were able to maintain a great public interest centred around European issues. Even more important, through the often very influential administrative and political posts held by people connected to the federal movement, federalism was able to leave an important stamp on the concrete design and content of European integration.

The last words of this introduction will be dedicated to a commemoration of our dear colleague and co-writer of this book, Vibeke Sørensen. It was a shock to us all when Vibeke suddenly died earlier this year. She is sadly mourned by friends and colleagues alike at the University of Copenhagen where she commenced her studies in European cooperation and integration; at the European University Institute in Florence where she defended her PH.D on Denmark and the Marshall Plan, and at Rijksuniversiteit Groningen where she worked as a Jean Monnet professor. Vibeke was loved and admired for her unfailing interest in the people surrounding her, for her dynamic academic style, and for the inventiveness and hard work she invested in her research. On the behalf of all those who worked together with Vibeke in contributing to the project which resulted in this book, I express our deepest grief at the loss of a beloved fellow-historian and friend.

Notes

1. For an analysis of the Danish 1972 referendum, see P. Hansen. M. Small & K. Siune: "The Structure of the Debate in the Danish EC-Campaign: A Study of an Opinion-Policy Relationship", in *Journal of Common Market Studies*, vol 15(2) 1973, pp. 93-129.
2. This was not true, however, for monetary cooperation within the OEEC administered European Payments Union (EPU). The credit facilities within the EPU served Denmark well.
3. The figures are taken from Ann-Christina Lauring Knudsen: *Denmark and the*

OEEC, 1949-1956. A case study of the limitations to western European economic co-operation, un. publ. MA thesis, Dept. of History, Aarhus University 1995, table II.10 p. 22.
4. The Danish 'oddity' has inspired the title of a recent collective volume dedicated to the topic, Denmark and European integration, see Birgit Nüchel Thomsen (ed.): *The Odd Man Out. Danmark og den europæiske integration 1948-1992*, Odense 1993. A shorter English version also exists under the title: *The Odd Man Out. Denmark and European Integration 1948-1992*, Odense 1993.
5. There exists a considerable amount of literature analyzing and discussing Nordic post-war cooperation. Here it must suffice to point to a recent double-volume of the periodical, *Den jyske Historiker*, dedicated to this topic, see "De Nordiske Fællesskaber. Myte og realitet i det nordiske samarbejde", vol 69-70, 1994. Especially the contributions by Johnny Laursen: "Fra nordisk fællesmarked til Helsingfors konvention – nordisk økonomisk samarbejde 1945-1962", pp. 179-200, and by Bo Stråth: "Nordiska Rådet och nordiskt samarbete", pp. 201-212, are discussing the general features of Nordic cooperation. See also Vibeke Sørensen's article in this book where further references to the literature on Nordic cooperation may be found.
6. Jan A. Andersson: *Idé & verklighet. Föreningerna Norden genom 70 år*, Stockholm 1991, p. 111.
7. The results and character of Nordic cooperation are treated in detail in: Frantz Wendt: *The Nordic Council and Co-operation in Scandinavia*, Copenhagen 1959, and ibid.: *Cooperation in the Nordic Countries. Achievements and Obstacles*, Stockholm 1981.
8. Based on elctoral surveys the two Danish referendums on the Maastricht Treaty in 1992 and 1993 have been thoroughly scrutinized in two books by K. Siune, P. Svensson & O. Tonsgaard: *Det blev et nej*, Århus 1992, and: *Fra et nej til et ja*, Århus 1994. For shorter presentations in English, see K. Siune & P. Svensson: "The Danes and the Maastricht Treaty: The Danish EC Referendum of June 1992", in *Electoral Studies*, 12:2 1993, pp. 99-111; P. Svensson: "The Danish Yes to Maastricht and Edinburgh. The EC Referendum of May 1993", in *Scandinavian Political Studies*, vol 17(1) 1994, pp. 69-82; K. Siune, P. Svensson & O. Tonsgaard: "The European Union: The Danes said 'No' in 1992 but 'Yes' in 1993. How and Why", in *Electoral Studies*, 13:2 1994, pp. 107-116.
9. "Skandinav. og intern. øk-samarb", speech notes for speech in Oslo 18.2.1950, at J.O. Krag's archive, box 17, at Arbejderbevægelsens bibliotek og Arkiv (The Labour Movement's Library & Archive) Copenhagen.
10. For general treatments of the Social Democratic conflict between Nordic co-operation and European integration in the period 1955-1972, see the contributions by Vibeke Sørensen and Thorsten B. Olesen & Johnny Laursen to Tom Swienty (ed.): *Danmark i Europa 1945-1993*, Copenhagen 1994.
11. Johnny Laursen: "Mellem fællesmarkedet og frihandelszonen. Dansk markedspolitik 1956-1958", in Birgit Nüchel Thomsen: op. cit..
12. Vibeke Sørensen: ""Free Trade" Versus Regulated Markets: Danish Agricultural Organisations and the Green Pool, 1950-1954", in B. Girvin & R.T. Griffiths (eds.): *The Green Pool and the Origins of the Common Agricultural Policy*, (forthcoming).
13. For the Danish foreign policy during the 1930's, see Viggo Sjøqvist: *Danmarks udenrigspolitik 1933-1940*, Copenhagen 1966 and Susan Seymour: *Anglo-Danish Relations and Germany 1933-1945*, Odense 1982. Susan Seymour's analysis also covers the period during the German occupation of Denmark. For this period, see also Hans Kirchhoff: *Kamp eller tilpasning. Politikerne og modstanden 1940-1945*, Copenhagen 1987, and Henning Poulsen's bitter-sweet interpretation:

"Dansk modstand og tysk politik", in "(Besættelsen & Befrielsen) 50 år efter", *Den jyske Historiker*, vol. 71 1995, pp. 7-18.
14. Among scholars the Danish decision to join The Atlantic Pact in 1949 and the character of Danish NATO-membership has triggered off a debate about rupture and continuity in Danish foreign policy. The 'break-interpretation' is most strongly represented in the works by Nikolaj Petersen, see a.o.: "Optionsproblematikken i dansk sikkerhedspolitik 1948-1949", in N. Amstrup & I. Faurby (eds.): *Studier i dansk udenrigspolitik*, Århus 1978, pp. 199-235, and: "Atlantpagten eller Norden. Den danske alliancebeslutning 1949", in Carsten Due-Nielsen et al. (eds.): *Danmark, Norden og NATO 1948-1962*, Copenhagen 1991, pp. 17-42. The continuity aspect has been stressed by Martin Heissler: "Denmark's Quest for Security. Constraints and Opportunities Within the Alliance", in Gregory Flynn (ed.): *NATO's Northern Allies. The National Security Policies of Belgium, Denmark, the Netherlands & Norway*, London & Sydney 1985, pp. 57-112, and by Hans Branner: "Vi vil fred her til lands. En udenrigspolitisk linie 1940-1949-1989?, in *Vandkunsten*, vol. 3 1990, pp. 47-90. See also Thorsten B. Olesen: "Jagten på et sikkerhedspolitisk ståsted. Socialdemokratiet og holdningerne til sikkerhedspolitikken 1945-1948", in Birgit Nüchel Thomsen (ed.): *Temaer og brændpunkter i dansk politik efter 1945*, Odense 1994, pp. 15-54.
15. The expression "latent neutrality" is coined by Carsten Holbraad in: *Danish Neutrality. A Study in the Foreign Policy of a Small State*, Oxford 1991, p. 108 ff.. The full title of Poul Villaume's book is: *Allieret med forbehold. Danmark, NATO og den kolde krig. En studie i dansk sikkerhedspolitik 1949-1961*, Copenhagen 1995.
16. Nikolaj Petersen: "Abondonment vs. Entrapment. Denmark and Military Integration in Europe 1948-1951", in *Cooperation and Conflict*, vol. XXI 1986, pp. 169-186.
17. Poul Villaume: op. cit., p. 26 ff.
18. For the Dutch position on supranationality, see Joris J.C. Voorhoeve: *Peace, Profits and Principles. A Study of Dutch Foreign Policy*, Leiden 1985, p. 160 ff.
19. For an extensive treatment of Swedish attitudes to western European integration, see Mikael af Malmborg: *Den ståndaktiga nationalstaten. Sverige och den västeuropeiska integrationen 1945-1959*, Lund 1994.

The National and International Ramifications of Economic Reconstruction in Post-war Europe

By Richard T. Griffiths

Integration, European style, seems to head the list of many countries' foreign policy aspirations whether through adhesion to the European Union, as aspired to by the former Soviet satellites in Eastern Europe, or through emulation, as witnessed by the proliferation of experiments in North America, the Pacific basin, Africa and the ex-Soviet Union itself. Yet, it was not always so that 'integration' ranked so highly in academic and popular esteem. For virtually a century before the Second World War, the focus of the intellectual elite was upon multilateral free trade rather than upon the coalescence of groups of nation states. One could go further and observe that from the middle of the last century, or at least from the 1860's, few new initiatives were taken towards the disappearance of nation states. It was as though governments had learned to harness the forces for nineteenth century integration, namely communications and capital movements, and to direct them towards strengthening integration within the separate nation states. This trend intensified and culminated during the Depression of the 1930's, which was characterised by economic autarky and totalitarianism and which led to the bloodiest conflict in modern World history.[1] This particular manifestation of human folly is often supposed to have acted as the catalyst for a profound reorientation in political perspectives. The traditional nation states of Europe had proved singularly inept at fulfilling their functions and had become as much anachronisms as the patchwork of feudal princedoms, kingdoms and dukedoms they had replaced centuries earlier. The obvious solution lay in dissolving meaningless frontiers and ultimately creating a Western European federal state.[2] History is rarely so simple and events are susceptible to different interpretations.

The lessons drawn by federalists from prewar history represent one stream in the discussion. Another, earlier and potentially more powerful reassessment of the recent past was forged by an examination of the limitations and failures of the international economic system. The analysis and the lessons drawn from that analysis were assimilated into the plans developed by the Allies during the war years themselves. Since the Americans were undisputably the strongest power, these plans also bore the stamp of their particular preoccupations and hobbyhorses. Nonetheless, underpinning them all is a faith that, with more and more effective safeguards, the restoration of a global, multilateral World order was possible. These plans, one must remember, moved beyond the drawing board and took on a definite institutional form. Indeed, all of them are still with us today. However, it was a mark of their failure, either to analyse the past accurately or to anticipate properly future problems, that regional solutions were necessary.

In explaining the Great Depression, American policy-makers placed much emphasis on the breakdown of the international monetary system. They focussed particularly on two aspects. The first was the tide of international speculation in 1931 that toppled the banking systems of Austria, Germany and other Central European countries and that led to the widespread imposition of exchange control. Movements of "hot money", as we would now call it, culminated in September 1931 in the devaluation of sterling and, by the end of that year, of 32 other currencies dependent upon it. These events destroyed the fragile economic stability of the early months of 1931 and altered a sharp but painful readjustment after the Wall Street Crash into a deep and persistent depression. The second American fixation was with the phenomenon of "competitive devaluation", fixed into the collective psyche by the experience in 1933-34 when the depreciation of the dollar was shadowed continuously by sterling. As a result both currencies plunged by about 40 per cent before reaching a new equilibrium. Whether this incident really deserved the attention paid to it in subsequent policy planning is open to question.[3] Nevertheless, the innovations incorporated into the Bretton Woods system can be traced back to these two factors. By contrast very little was to be found of UK concerns that lack of international liquidity creation had been a major contributing factor in the Depression.

The Bretton Woods system was little more than the restoration of the gold-exchange standard of the 1920's, itself a product of a misinterpretation of the late 19th century monetary system, but with extra safeguards. It was based upon the dollar and sterling maintaining free convertibility into each other and into gold. An International Monetary Fund (the IMF) was introduced to provide resources that private speculators, hopefully, would be unable to match and so to forestall the prospect of countries being forced to suspend convertibility against their will. Moreover, IMF rules enshrined the principle of fixed exchange rates and placed limitations upon countries' freedom to devalue. All provisions, of course, were temporarily suspended in the immediate aftermath of the War. This was just as well because in 1945 there was not a country in Europe that was not practising exchange control and many had not one but several rates of exchange, varying according to the necessity of the product or the hard currency losses involved in each transaction.[4]

Richard T. Griffiths

The IMF proved utterly incapable of meeting the challenge. Its funds were totally inadequate to supplement reserves sufficiently to permit the elimination of currency controls and it lacked the authority to impose its rules. The extent of the problem, and equally of the failure to anticipate it, was revealed by the sterling convertibility fiasco of 1947. In the space of six weeks, the American/Canadian loan to facilitate the restoration of sterling convertibility, and thus the establishment of one of the foundations of the Bretton Woods system, was exhausted.[5] Thereafter the IMF provisions were suspended until 1958 when, eventually, Western Europe officially established convertibility on commercial account. Meanwhile, as we shall see below, Europe's problems were resolved on a European basis.

American international analysis of the 1930s extended equally to trade. In this area, one of the main targets was the quantitative trade restrictions (QRs; i.e. quotas and licenses), increasingly imposed in the early 1930s as price falls rendered tariff protection ineffective. If tariffs were imposed without discrimination amongst trading partners, as the "most favoured nation" (MFN) clause implied, they at least allowed market forces to determine trade volume and supplier. By contrast, QRs allowed governments to discriminate on both counts. Moreover, whereas tariffs were usually the outcome of parliamentary procedures, QRs were increasingly imposed and manipulated by closed bureaucratic decisions. In a fair world trading system both the arbitrary and discriminatory nature of QRs made them less desirable instruments of trade control than tariffs. Trade restrictions were originally imposed to insulate national economies from the effects of deflationary forces emanating from abroad but later they served to mute the international expansionary effects of national recoveries, or else to restrict the impact within discriminatory trading blocs. Herein, American policy found economics coalescing with political prejudice against empires and imperialism. Although the British would have distinguished between their own healthy imperial preference system and the predatory nature of the Nazi trade drive, the League of Nations was even-handed in condemning both.[6]

American postwar planning made room for an International Trade Organisation (the ITO), based on global non-discriminatory trade, as the commercial counterpart of the IMF. Not unexpectedly, it placed severe limitations on QRs, promoted tariffs as the principle instrument for trade regulation and tried to provide a context for lowering those as well. Although the US was unable to prohibit imperial trading arrangements, it successfully prevented their extension with a "no new preference" rule. This rule, together with the existing MFN clause, ran the risk of preventing nations that wanted to promote mutual trade, from reducing their tariffs towards each other in order to do so. Thus the ITO allowed discriminatory tariff reductions if the object was to reduce mutual tariffs to zero as part of an operation to create a customs union or a free trade area. In that case, however, any new external tariffs should be no higher than the average of the old.

The picture of commercial exchanges in Europe in the immediate postwar years dwarfed anything experienced in the 1930s. Scarcely a good crossed a frontier on the continent that was not licensed in one way or another. So tight were controls that many tariffs were suspended. Yet, the extent of the ITO's failure is apparent by the fact that it was never created. The bill was never ratified by the US Congress and a much weaker General Agreement on Trade and Tariffs (the GATT) came in its stead. The GATT, having registered a general increase in postwar tariffs in 1949, succeeded in massaging them downwards in 1950. Thereafter it had very little effect on tariff levels until the Dillon and Kennedy Rounds in the 1960's. Its contribution to the elimination of QRs was still less. Again it was in a European context, and one that discriminated against the US, that these problems were solved.[7]

American-inspired attempts to revive an almost late nineteenth century internationalism, albeit under better and stronger regulation, may always have been utopian. However, they all implied a philosophy that Europe's problems were World problems and were better resolved in a worldwide framework. In the event, the institutions created proved unequal to the challenges of postwar reconstruction. By 1947 it was becoming apparent that the solution of Europe's problems was a precondition for the smooth functioning of the international arrangements constructed after the war.

Within Europe there emerged a somewhat different analysis of the nature of the problems and a radically different solution. The European federalists saw the essential problem in the anachronistic nature of the European nation state itself. The Depression had demonstrated the impossibility of isolating domestic economies; certainly without grave social and political penalties. Moreover, there were doubts whether Europe's fragmented national markets could meet the challenge of mass production already posed by the United States and latent in the USSR. Worse still, these small nation states had shown an alarming proclivity for wars; at least two of which, in the space of less than half a century, had extended far beyond the continent. The harsh memories of dole queues, fascist marches, mutilation, destruction and death provided fertile ground for those who felt that the nation state had proved itself incapable of providing for the welfare of its citizens or the security of its borders. Just as the shock of defeats by Napoleon had made nonsense of the patchwork of small states that were destined to become modern Germany, so World War II demonstrated the bankruptcy of the nation state concept for post-1945 Europe.[8]

John Pinder's article in this book traces the development of the federalist movement and I will therefore be relatively brief on this point. History will doubtless judge the success of the gradualists, but the prescriptions offered by the one-step federalists were also doomed. This was already apparent in the failure to win significant powers for the Council of Europe in 1949. Although the blame for that and for subsequent rebuffs could be attributed to the voting majority of the so-called functionalists, there were more deep-seated reasons for their lack of success. This became apparent in 1953/54 when they failed to win support of the six ECSC countries, that had already demonstrated their willingness to accept supranational solutions, for their draft European constitution for a European Political Community (EPC). It is wrong to see this failure as merely a by-product of French reluctance to accept a European army; there was deep disquiet among the other states too over the EPC treaty itself. By the time they had finished their examination of the treaty, carefully reinstating the nation state controls avoided by the federalists, there was precious little left of the original concept. If there was one thing upon which the governments were agreed, it was never again to hand over so important a matter to a group of parliamentarians.[9]

The error of the one-step federalists was to underestimate the power of the nation state. Having seized the key positions in drafting the treaty, they failed to anticipate the objections that governments would raise. It was elitist policy-making of the same kind that characterised the lack of parliamentary feedback with the Maastricht treaty. It is possible that to have incorporated the objections at source would have been to surrender without a struggle. Besides, it is in the nature of national governments to hang on to national power. In this way, they may have hoped for more support from parliaments and public opinion had the treaty been submitted for ratification. That prospect too, however, was far from certain. Amid all these might-have-beens, which good historians should avoid, lies concealed the fact that we should not be talking at this level. In early federalist analysis, the nation state was doomed. Yet, by the early 1950s it was more powerful than ever. Far from having lost all credibility among its citizens, it was more than ever the focus of their aspirations. Through democratic mass parties and elections, the nation state regularly mobilised more support than federalists of all hues could muster.

That the nation state was not ready to fall was evident within a couple of years of the end of the War. As was the case with American planners, the one-step federalists were selective in their analysis of the past but, more to the point, they failed to grasp the realities of the immediate postwar period. At first sight one could hardly blame them. The politicians who returned to power were faced with the blights of shortages and destruction, with the dislocation of the trading system and often with winning the allegiance of populations that had been subjected to years of occupation. These were problems that seemed capable of submerging even well-established regimes. But national governments had also been learning lessons from the 1930s and the War.

One lesson all national governments had learned during the Depression was how to operate the commercial and monetary instruments of frontier control. If we take a country like the Netherlands, which in the 1930s remained more old-fashionably liberal for longer than most, this process can be clearly seen. When the Great Depression hit the country, it did not even have the national accounts necessary to know how severe the damage had been. The minister of economic affairs at the end of the 1920s, had described the ministry as a "sweet shop"; a decade later it was more like a gigantic candy store. It administered a panoply of QRs and the distribution systems they in turn required, managed the bilateral trade agreements with countries like Germany, overlooked the wage cuts demanded in return of business subsidies and, at the end of the decade, was venturing into state investment banking. His colleague in agriculture was, after 1933, running the entire sector as a virtual national corporation. The war years simply reinforced these trends. Employment in the Dutch economics ministry more than doubled as mechanisms of distribution and control permeated all areas of the economy. In countries with more interventionist policies, this process started earlier and penetrated more deeply still. For all states, post-war reconstruction began with domestic and frontier controls already in existence and with long experience in their use. If the immediate tasks appeared daunting, the nation state was certainly the best equipped for dealing with them.[10]

This fortuitous match of goals and instruments could lend the nation state only a transient allegiance. However, the politicians and governments that returned in European states were not the neo-classical or even the muddle-through interventionists of the 1930s. All governments accepted with alacrity that they were the only agencies in place that were capable of mobilising the resources necessary for the immediate tasks of relief and reconstruction. Many governments also believed that their duty lay beyond the pragmatic intervention required to put economies and societies back on their feet and extended to correcting deficiencies in economic structures. This was motivated by a desire either to tap existing economic potential, or to adjust to perceived changes in world trade or to provide future employment opportunities. Most governments, although with various degrees of enthusiasm or commitment, also assumed more ambitious long-term programmes of welfare distribution. Social democratic or christian democratic, their reforms usually embraced improved health care programmes, better unemployment and pension facilities and higher family benefits. Finally, several governments brought with them a belief in new remedies against economic collapse and poverty and the political extremism that accompanied them. At its simplest, there was a general belief that governments had responsibility for maintaining high levels of economic activity. A few, usually social democratic governments, went further and accepted the tenet that by adjusting levels of government expenditure they could avoid the recessions. Such Keynesian beliefs permeated the European body politic throughout the 1950s, although it was only in the 1960s that the illusion gained ground that deep cyclical downturns were a thing of the past.[11]

All these activities required an acceptance of more state intervention in national economies and, if necessary to accomplish these ends, increased control at the frontiers. Unlike the federalist lessons, these convictions were not the exclusive property of a political elite or even the unarticulated reflection of a swathe of the population. Rather they formed the core of a new political appeal in an age of mass parties and mass politics. It was upon such beliefs that postwar democracy was re-established and from which political parties derived their new legitimacy.

If the new orthodoxy was couched in essentially national terms, the question arises why a measure of integration occurred at all. Part of the answer lies in the fact that even the most autarkic European countries were required to resort to international trade to fulfil their domestic requirements. At the depths of the Depression, larger countries such as Germany and France still satisfied over 10 per cent of their requirements through imports, and for smaller countries the figure was higher still. Self-sufficiency was not an option in the postwar world; nor had it been in the 1930s. Rather than see the Depression in terms of autarky, it would be more accurate to describe international commerce as a quest for bloc-forming whereby trade was deliberately deflected into channels that provided security of supplies and, more often than not, that saved on scarce resources of foreign exchange. What happened in Europe after the War was a continuation, or even an intensification, of these same trends and it was caused by essentially the same type of circumstances.[12]

The War had disrupted the European trading pattern in three important respects. First, the defeat of Germany and the determination of the Allies to repress its economic potential had the effect of removing from the scene a major component in European trade. Although it is a cliché to describe Germany as "the power house of Europe", it is true that, before the Depression, for most countries in Western Europe it had been either the first or second most important trading partner. There was simply no other European supplier capable of filling the gap in terms of energy and a range of manufactured goods and little immediate alternative to the United States as a source of supply. National industrialisation programmes developed as a response to this situation; as an opportunity to displace German suppliers from domestic markets and as a necessity to conserve scarce reserves of hard currency. Second, the devastation in Eastern Europe and the deflection of its trade towards the Soviet Union removed from the system an important supplier of foodstuffs, particularly cereals. At a time when Western Europe was having to turn to the USA to meet its reconstruction, it also became increasingly dependent on the North America for its food supplies. This, too, had to be paid in dollars. The possibility of earning dollars was further diminished by a third factor. Traditionally, Western Europe had run substantial trade surpluses with the primary producers in the Third World and these, in turn, had run surpluses with North America. There existed what could be described as a 'trading triangle'. However, where these Third World areas had been directly involved in the hostilities, the devastation had been, if anything, worse than that experienced in Western Europe. These areas were incapable of resuming their role as net exporters to the United States, and therefore of generating demand for traditional imports from Europe. In areas not affected by hostilities the effect of being cut off from traditional industrial suppliers had, as had the first World War, stimulated domestic industrialisation based on import substitution. Their own industrialisation programme precluded a return to the earlier reliance on European imports. Whatever the cause, Europe proved incapable of reviving the triangular trade and the dollar deficit widened accordingly.[13]

Now, throughout the interwar period Europe had had a trade deficit with the United States, but the factors mentioned above aggravated the imbalance. In such circumstances, Europe had two alternatives; either to increase direct exports to the United States or to attempt to diminish its own dependence on American imports. The first option, however, was effectively closed by the supply constraints on European production, the product mix of European exports and, most importantly, by the incipient protectionism of the US Congress. This left the second option, which had the added advantage of dovetailing with the industrialisation programmes developed by postwar governments. It also impelled states to attempt to deflect commerce into currency-saving trading blocs.

A typical example of this process is afforded by the case of the Benelux customs union. Launched in 1944 by the governments-in-exile of Belgium, the Netherlands and Luxembourg, it provided for the elimination of internal trade barriers and the creation of a common external tariff. Between the wars the Netherlands had relied on Germany for between 20 and 30 per cent of its imports and between 17 and 24 per cent of its exports. Belgian's export package promised the fulfilment of some of these needs, particularly in the area of basic metals, construction materials, chemicals and certain semi-manufactures. This arrangement offered Belgium the opportunity to expand its industrial base and the Netherlands to reduce its dependency on dollar imports. The latter, however, was only at the cost of increasing its dependency on Belgium. This could only take place as long as the Belgian government was willing to extend commercial credits, which it did since it provided the chance to supplant German producers. For the Netherlands there remained the problem of what to do with the economic capacity devoted to exports it had traditionally sent to Germany. For the shipping services, upon which it had usually earned a surplus, Belgium had no need, and it could only absorb Dutch agricultural surpluses at the expense of domestic output. The result was an imbalance between the treatment of industrial and agricultural products that was only partially resolved in 1947 by a protocol whereby the Netherlands became a preferential foreign supplier of Belgian agricultural imports.[14] The impact of this was dramatic. The share of Dutch imports from the BLEU rose from 11.4 per cent in 1938 to 18.4 per cent in 1950, the share of exports increasing from 10.2 to 13.5 in the same period. The picture for the BLEU is the mirror image of this, its share of exports destined for the Netherlands rising from 12.2 to 22.4 per cent between 1938 and 1950 whilst its imports derived from there edged upwards from 9.8 to 10.2 per cent.

If Belgium had an impelling logic in the construction of the Benelux, this could equally have been true for France. The French industrialisation plans were geared towards supplanting German heavy industry in its own market and they would equally have benefitted from making inroads into the markets of Belgium and the Netherlands. In 1938 France had derived 6.8 per cent of its imports from the BLEU but had sent 13.7 per cent of its exports there, making it France's third export market behind Algeria and the UK. If France could have obtained a share in the 11-12 per cent of imports Belgium had traditionally derived from Germany, it would considerably have expanded its market base. Such considerations underlay French diplomatic manoeuvres to join the Benelux agreement in 1944, before it was signed, and its efforts in 1945 and 1946, whilst the customs union had still to be effectuated, to break open the agreement. Had such plans been realised, the resulting customs union would probably have been protected by high tariff barriers, certainly higher than the Benelux levels, directed primarily against Germany. It was for this reason that it proved unattractive to the Benelux countries in general and to the Netherlands in particular. The latter would have found itself penalised in acquiring many of the semi-manufactures on which its industrialisation was based and would have found France even less likely than Belgium to absorb the agricultural exports traditionally destined for Germany. Dutch policy became directed at securing Germany's economic rehabilitation, in order to restore its trading links, before deciding on any further bloc membership.[15]

When in June 1947, in the course of the Paris negotiations on the acceptance of Marshall Aid, the French repeated the appeal, directed primarily at Benelux, to form a customs union, the offer was again rebuffed. However, to forestall an outright refusal, the Dutch connived at the creation of a Customs Union Study Group to investigate the prospects for a pan-European customs union. These efforts eventually floundered on the coolness of the British response and on the inability of countries to commit themselves to any binding commercial agreements whilst the future of West Germany was still uncertain.

The Customs Union Study Group was Europe's gesture in the face of American wishes to see a closer degree of integration in Western Europe. The Americans were determined that dollar aid would not be squandered on competitive European programmes that served merely to entrench the autarkic tendencies already present. They demanded a coordinated European plan for the distribution of Marshall Aid, leading to the creation of the Organisation for European Economic Cooperation (OEEC) in 1948. Beyond that, they had very little idea of how to effectuate their plans for closer European unity. The Customs Union Study Group soon lost all drive and direction and was eventually wound up in 1950. Instead of co-ordinated planning the Americans received a jointly written document, which was not the same thing. Commercial arrangements among European states were conducted largely along bilateral lines which cemented into place layer upon layer of mutual preference and mutual discrimination.[16]

By the middle of 1949, American policy-makers began to despair at the lack of progress and resolved to use their political leverage by tying the continuation of aid to significant progress in the area of European integration. It is possible that economic forces within Europe may independently have led to the same result but, as it turned out, America did provide the agenda and the funds for lubricating the way to a solution. US pressure was rewarded by two initiatives. A European Payments Union (EPU) was designed to prevent bilateral balance of payments considerations from inhibiting the expansion of European trade. If each pair of trading relationships had to balance, trade between the partners would tend towards the lower import requirement. Whatever could be done to allow a deficit in one set of trading relationships to be offset against surpluses elsewhere would obviously raise the overall level of trade. The EPU, therefore, allowed for the pooling of surpluses and deficits and provided for a degree of automatic credit to debtor countries. The system was funded by a loan of $ 350 million from Marshall funds. In the American strategy, it made little sense to free intra-European payments if trade were to remain strangled at international frontiers by a network of arbitrary regulations and quantitative restrictions (QR's). Thus, in parallel to the EPU, the US encouraged a trade liberalisation scheme providing targets for the removal of QR's on private trade. Although the exemption of state trade was a major flaw in the scheme, by the end of 1950 most countries had achieved 75 percent trade liberalisation of private trade. Both the EPU and the OEEC's liberalisation scheme were designed to relieve the dollar gap by stimulating intra-European commerce and by tolerating a degree of discrimination against the United States. These efforts were reinforced by the acceptance, in September 1949, of a series of devaluations against the dollar. Both schemes provided the institutional framework for the rapid expansion of trade and economic growth that took place in the 1950s. In the same month in which the Federal Republic of Germany regained sovereignty and became a full member of both schemes, its industry, however, still remained under international control, although the capacity of the Allies to enforce these measures of control had still to be tested. At the time, a major source of concern lay in the potential in Germany afforded by its idle steel capacity and the question whether with independence Germany would still deliver the coal required by the heavy industry in neighbouring countries. These questions became actual in the spring of 1950, when, in response to the change in the strategic balance created by the Soviet atomic tests, the Americans resolved to press for the removal of restraints of German industrial production.[17]

One of the greatest bottlenecks experienced during the reconstruction had been the need to acquire coal and basic iron and steel products. This shortfall had been caused partly by the increased reconstruction demands but mostly because western Germany, prewar Europe's major supplier, had not been allowed to reassert its traditional position. With the other major supplier, the United Kingdom, deflecting its own output increasingly to the domestic market, imports could only be acquired at high prices but were also often determined in hard currency. Those countries that had coal and steel supplies available, found themselves enjoying all the benefits of a sellers' market.

Both buyers and sellers, therefore, had every motive to include an expansion of indigenous coal and steel production as an inherent part of their reconstruction plans, either to conserve their own hard currency supplies or to move into a lucrative and growing international market. The absence of the Ruhr industrial complex as a competitor served only to make this logic more compelling. Although the Allied Occupation Authorities had originally aimed at the de-industrialisation of Germany, they were nevertheless compelled to maintain minimum levels of output in order to prevent the total collapse of European trade. Ceilings, however, were imposed on basic steel output whilst compulsory coal deliveries were guaranteed to fuel deficient areas. What did this mean in practice for a country like France? The fact that German steel production was held at 12 million tons whilst potential output could have reached 18 million provided French planners with the opportunity both for import substitution and for the chance of conquering new export markets. French planning therefore envisaged the doubling of steel output between 1947 and 1950 to nearly 12 million tonnes, almost 30 per cent higher than the peak interwar level. The problem lay in the fact that prewar Lorraine and Saar production had been dependent on supplies of Ruhr coal and that any increased French steel capacity would merely aggravate the dependence. French planning, therefore, relied both upon having at least a breathing space before German production ceilings were raised and upon being guaranteed high levels of coal supplies. These conditions were fulfilled until 1949 by the Allied High Commission but in that year three new developments undermined the certainty that such controls could long continue. Firstly, the costs of limiting German production were serving not only to 'punish' the vanquished but were also penalising the victors who found themselves having to subsidise the German economy as a result. Secondly, the intensification of the Cold War dictated a raising of German employment levels and living standards if potential social unrest were to be avoided, and this could only be done by realising German industrial potential. Moreover, only by utilising latent German capacity could the pace of Western rearmament be accelerated without damaging the achievements of four years of reconstruction. Finally, in September 1949 West Germany gained the status of sovereign nation-state and it was questionable for how long it would still accept international controls. One such control was the International Ruhr Authority, upon which the three Western Allies were represented, which was designed to regulate the output and direction of German heavy industry. Already in the early months of 1950, however, German steel output had climbed above the ceilings stipulated.[18]

The dangers that these developments posed to French, and other reconstruction plans were manifold. Firstly and most obviously, the restoration of approximately 8 million tons of steel capacity at a time when the demand was visibly beginning to slacken risked causing a collapse in international prices and a new trade war. It also threatened to undermine the vital supplies of fuel upon which reconstruction plans had been based. This occurred because many of the German coal mines were owned by German steel companies which were likely to satisfy their own needs before fulfilling the obligations to customers and competitors. Moreover, remaining German coal sales were concentrated in a single monopoly sales organisation that was already resorting to the practice of differential pricing whereby domestic consumers were charged considerably less than those abroad. These developments formed the backdrop for a meeting of the three Western Allies in London on May 10, 1950. A major item on the agenda was the future of the International Ruhr Authority.

It was France rather than the UK or the US that stood to risk most from these developments and French planners sought a way to neutralise the dangers. Since the unilateral imposition of controls on German industry could not last forever, perhaps the solution lay in the acceptance of equal obligations and conditions by both Germany and France under the auspices of an institution independent from national authority. This assumption underpinned the proposal for a coal and steel pool worked out by Jean Monnet at the Commissariat au Plan and announced by Foreign Minister, Robert Schuman, in a radio speech on May 9; one day before the crucial London meeting of the Western Allies. The Schuman Plan would mark the first step towards the creation of a supranational organisation within Europe. It would also make a contribution to the prevention of any future war between France and Germany. And finally, it provided a framework for the successful organisation of the western European market in coal and steel.[19]

The postwar European nation state was not a rotten fruit ready to fall from the branch. Indeed, the needs of reconstruction endowed it with new functions and a new legitimacy. Nonetheless, national priorities were still determined by the leeway afforded by the international environment which both served to aggravate the problem of reconstruction but also to clear several barriers that had stood in the way of alternative political solutions in the 1930s. Thus the road was opened for experiments in small economic bloc forming, in pan-European economic collaboration and in experiments in supranational sectoral organisation within the economic core of Continental Europe. In each of these areas there was a remarkable shift away from the introverted perspectives of the interwar years. To concentrate purely on the supranational aspects of this new dawn in the regulation of international financial and commercial relations is not only to distort the history of the immediate reconstruction period but also to miss the institutional mainsprings for the unprecedented transformation of European economies in the subsequent decade.

Notes

1. See R.T.Griffiths (ed.), *Economic and Monetary Unions in the past. From Continental System to Common Market*, London, Forthcoming.
2. The classic exponent of this line of reasoning was the late Walter Lipgens: W. Lipgens, *European Federation in the Political Thought of Resistance Movements during World War II*, The Hague, 1980; W. Lipgens and W. Loth, *A History of European Integration, Volume 1: 1945-1947, The Formation of the European Unity Movement*, Oxford, 1982; W. Lipgens (ed), *Documents on the History of European Integration, Volume 2. Plans for European Union in Great Britain and in Exile 1939-1945*, Berlin/New York, 1986; W. Lipgens and W Loth, (eds), *Documents on the History of European Integration, Volume 3. The Struggle for European Union by Political Parties and Pressure Groups in Western European Countries 1945-1950*, Berlin/New York, 1988; W. Lipgens and W. Loth (eds), *Documents on the History of European Integration, Volume 4. Transnational Organizations of Political Parties and Pressure Groups in the Struggle for European Union, 1945-1950*, Berlin/New York, 1991. See also W. Loth, *Der Weg nach Europa: Geschichte der europäischen Integration, 1939-1957*, Göttingen, 1990.
3. H.W. Arndt, *The Economic Lessons of the 1930s*, London, 1944; W.A. Brown,

The International Gold Standard Reinterpretted, 1914-1934, New York, 1940; J.B. Condliffe, *The Reconstruction of World Trade*, New York, 1940; H.S. Ellis, *Exchange Control in Central Europe*, Cambridge Mass., 1941; M.S. Gordon, *Barriers to World Trade: A Study of Recent Commercial Policy*, New York, 1941; League of Nations, *Commercial Policy in the Inter-war Period. International Proposals and National Policies*, New York, 1942. League of Nations, *Commercial Policy in the Post-War Period*, Geneva 1945; League of Nations, *The Course and Control of Inflation*, Geneva, 1946; League of Nations, *Economic Instability in the Post-War World*, Geneva, 1945; League of Nations, *Trade Relations between Free Market and Controlled Economies*, New York, 1943; League of Nations, *Industrialization and Foreign Trade*, Geneva, 1945; League of Nations, *Quantitative Trade Controls. Their Causes and Nature*, Geneva 1943; League of Nations, *Report on Exchange Control*, Geneva 1938; W.A. Lewis, *Economic Survey, 1919-1939*, London, 1949 et seq.

4. E.M. Bernstein, "The Evolution of the International Monetary Fund" in A.L.K. Acheson, J.F. Chant and M.F.J. Prachonney (eds) *Bretton Woods Revisited*, Toronto/London, 1972, 51-65; W. Diebold, *Trade and Payments in Western Europe*, New York, 1952; A.E. Eckes, *A Search for Solvency: Bretton Woods and the International Monetary System, 1941-1971*, Austin, 1975; R.N. Gardner, *Sterling-Dollar Diplomacy: Anglo-American Collaboration in the Reconstruction of Multilateral Trade*, Oxford, 1956; J.K. Horsefield (ed) *The International Monetary Fund 1945-1965: Twenty Years of International Monetary Cooperation*, Washington, 1969; E. Somaini, "I rapporti monetari internazionali nel secondo dopoguerra" in *Rivista di Storia Contemporanea* Vol 4. No 2. 1975, 241-275.

5. Acheson, Chant, Prachonney (eds) *Bretton Woods Revisited*; S.W. Black, *A Levite Among Priests: Edward M. Bernstein and the Origins of the Bretton Woods System*, Bolder, 1991; R. Clarke, *Anglo-American Economic Collaboration in War and Peace, 1942-1949*, Oxford, 1982; A.S. Milward, *The Reconstruction of Western Europe, 1945-1951*, London, 1984; S. Newton, "The Sterling Crisis of 1947 and the British Response to the Marshall Plan", in *Economic History Review* Vol 37. 1984, 391-408; R.A. Pollard, *Economic Security and the Origins of the Cold War, 1945-1950*, New York, 1985.

6. R.T. Griffiths, "The Economic Disintegration of Europe. Trade and Protectionism in the 1930s" in R.T. Griffiths (ed.), *1992 and the Heritage of History; Economic and Monetary Unions in the Past*, forthcoming; League of Nations, *International Currency Experience, Lessons of the Interwar Period*, Princeton, 1944.

7. W.A. Brown, *The United States and the Restoration of World Trade. An Analysis and Appraisal of the ITO Charter and the General Agreement on Tariffs and Trade*, Washington, 1950; G. Curzon, *Multilateral Commercial Policy*, London, 1965; K.W. Dam, *The GATT Law and International Economic Organisation*, Chicago, 1970; W. Diebold, *The End of the ITO*, Princeton, 1952; K. Kock, *International Trade Policy and the GATT 1947-1965*, Princeton, 1966.

8. W. Lipgens, *European Federation in the Political Thought of Resistance Movements*; Lipgens and Loth, *A History of European Integration, Volume 1*

9. R. Cardozo, "The Project for a Political Community (1952- 54)" in Pryce, R. (ed) *The Dynamics of European Union*, London/Sydney/New York, 1987, 49-77; P. Fischer, "Die Bundesrepublik und das Projekt einer Europäischen Politischen Gemeinschaft" in L. Herbst et al (eds), *Vom Marshall-Plan zur EWG. Die Eingliederung der Bundesrepublik Deutschland in die Westliche Welt*, Munich, 1990, pp 279-299; R.T. Griffiths, "The Beyen Plan" in R.T. Griffiths (ed.), *The Netherlands and the Integration of Europe 1945-1957*, Amsterdam, 1990, 165-182; R.T. Griffiths and A.S. Milward, "The Beyen Plan and the European Political Community", in W. Maihofer (ed.), *Noi si mura. Selected Working Papers of the Euro-*

pean University Institute, Florence 1986, 595-621; D. Preda, *Storia di una speranza. La battaglia per la CED e la Federazione Europea nella carte della delegazione italiana (1950-1952)*, Milan, 1990.

10. P.A. Blaisse, "De Nederlandse handelspolitiek" in P.B. Kreukniet (ed.) *De Nederlandse volkshuishouding tussen twee wereldoorlogen*, Utrecht/Antwerp, 1952; J.L van Zanden and R.T. Griffiths, *Economische geschiedenis van Nederland in de 20e eeuw*, Utrecht, 1989.
11. M. Abramovitz, *Thinking About Growth and Other Essays on Economic Growth and Welfare*, Cambridge, 1989; A. Maddison, *Dynamic Forces in Capitalist Development; A Long-Run Comparative View*, Oxford, 1991; A.S Milward, *The European Rescue of the Nation-State*, London, 1992; G. Peden, *Keynes, the Treasury and British Economic Policy*, London, 1988; N. Rollings, "British Budgetary Policy, 1945-1954; a 'Keynesian Revolution'?", in *Economic History Review*, Vol. 41, 1988; A. Shonfield, *Modern Capitalism. The Changing Balance of Public and Private Power*, London, 1965; H. van der Wee, *Prosperity and Upheaval; The World Economy 1945-1980*, London, 1986.
12. Griffiths, "The Economic Disintegration of Europe, 1929-1939".
13. Milward, *The Reconstruction of Western Europe*.
14. A.J. Boekestijn, "Een nagel aan Adam Smiths doodkist. De Benelux-onderhandelingen in de jaren veertig en vijftig" in E.S.A. Bloemen (ed) *Het Benelux-effect. België, Nederland en Luxemburg en de Europese integratie, 1945-1957*, Amsterdam, 1992, 143-168; R.T. Griffiths, "The Stranglehold of Bilateralism", in Griffiths (ed.), *The Netherlands and the Integration of Europe*, 1-26; J.L. van Zanden, "De economische ontwikkeling van Nederland en België en het 'succes' van de Benelux, 1945-1958" in Bloemen, *Het Benelux-effect*, 13-32.
15. R.T. Griffiths and F.M.B. Lynch, "L'échec de la 'Petite Europe'? Les négociations Fritalux/Finebel, 1949-1950", in *Revue historique*, no. 274, 1985, 159-193.
16. W. Asbeek Brusse, *West European Tariff Plans, 1947-1957; From Study Group to Common Market*, Ph.D., Florence, 1991; W. Diebold, *Trade and Payments in Western Europe*, New York, 1952; A.S. Milward A.S., "OEEC and the Origins of the Customs Union" in W. Lipgens, *The Origins of European Unity, Part I, 1945-47*, Oxford, 1981.
17. M. Dickhaus, "The European Payments Union" in Griffiths (ed.) *Explorations in OEEC History*, forthcoming; K.F. Flexner, "The Creation of the European Payments Union: An Example in International Compromise", in *Political Science Quarterly* Vol. 72, No 2, 1957; S. Godts-Peters, "La rôle des belges dans l'élaboration d'un système de paiements en Europe, de 1947 à l'Union européenne de paiments", in M. Dumoulin (ed) *La Belgique et les débuts de la construction européenne de la guerre aux traités de Rome*, Louvain-la-Neuve, 1987, 87-102; J.B. Kaplan and G. Schleiminger, *The European Payments Union: Financial Diplomacy in the 1950's*, Oxford, 1989; G.L. Rees, *Britain and the Postwar European Payments System*, Cardiff, 1963.
18. J. Gillingham, "Die französische Ruhrpolitik und die Anfänge des Schuman Plans", in *Vierteljahreshefte für Zeitgeschichte* Vol. 35, 1987, 1-25; F.M.B. Lynch, "Resolving the Paradox of the Monnet Plan: National and International planning in French Reconstruction" in *Economic History Review* Vol 37. 1984, 229-43; Milward, *The Reconstruction of Western Europe*, P. Mioche, *Le Plan Monnet. Genèse et Elaboration 1941-1947* Paris, 1987; I. Turner (ed) *The Reconstruction of Post-war Germany. British Occupation Policy and the Western Zones, 1945-1955*, Oxford, 1989.
19. W. Diebold, *The Schuman Plan: A Study in Economic Cooperation, 1950-1959*, New York, 1959; P. Gerbet, "Les origines du Plan Schuman: Le choix de la méthode communautaire par le gouvernement français" in R. Poidevin (ed)

Origins of the European Integration, March 1948-May 1950, Brussels, 1986; J. Gillingham, *Coal, Steel and the Rebirth of Europe, 1945-1955*, Cambridge, 1991; R.T. Griffiths, "The Schuman Plan" in Griffiths (ed.), *The Netherlands and the Integration of Europe*, 113-135; K. Schwabe, (ed) *The Beginnings of the Schuman-Plan*, Baden-Baden, 1988; I. Warner, *The Deconcentration of the German Steel Industry 1949-1953*, PhD, Florence, 1991.

Nordic Cooperation – A Social Democratic Alternative to Europe?

By Vibeke Sørensen

Since the 1950s the Scandinavian Social Democratic (SD) parties have found it difficult to adjust their national economic strategy to European integration. While their continental fellow-parties have all seen their national welfare strategies as inseparable from, or even dependent upon, the development of an integrated Europe, the Scandinavian SD parties have tended to view their national welfare model and European integration as separate and often conflicting issues.[1] This more hesitant approach to European integration is usually explained by reference to the SD parties' preoccupation with national sovereignty, that is, their wish to retain a certain political autonomy in face of economic interdependence. However the SD parties' more positive attitude towards Nordic cooperation indicates that there is no defined level or point at which interdependence will be seen to jeopardize national sovereignty. The free movement of labour and capital and a certain harmonization of social security policies which has played such an important role in the SD parties' critique of the EC, has been implemented in Scandinavia under SD leadership without provoking similar concerns over national sovereignty. The different attitude to Nordic and to European integration suggests that there is a close connection between attitudes to integration and the organisation of the national polity and that the explanation of why the Scandinavian SD parties have tended to see their national development as separate from European integration should be sought in the political particularities of 20th century Scandinavia.

It is generally assumed that small countries like the Scandinavian only have marginal room for pursuing independent political strategies to safeguard national interests and therefore will reap maximum benefit from fitting into an international system based on more institutionalised co-operation with larger nations.[2] This is most obviously expressed in realist thinking on military security, but small countries are also seen to be highly vulnerable to economic interdependence and without any real choice with respect to their national economic development. There is no doubt that providing adequate national security in a bipolar world has been particularly difficult for small countries, but the general assumption that small countries also have very little choice with respect to their international political and economic environment seems to fit very badly with the realities of Scandinavian foreign policy formulation in the 20th century. Their negative attitude to European integration and the conscious attempt to maintain a certain political distance from Western Europe, despite a rapidly increasing economic interdependence, clearly indicates the option of choice in Scandinavian foreign policy. In the case of European integration, foreign policy has been determined almost exclusively by domestic policy priorities and in order to understand why it is necessary first to take a closer look at the particular development of the national polity in the three Scandinavian countries.

"The Scandinavian Model"

Both political scientists and economists have identified separate political and economic development paths in Scandinavia. They base their analysis on a variety of variables which they see as particular to the organisation of political and economic life in Scandinavia. The sum of these variables is referred to generally as "the Scandinavian model". This concept is highly contested within the social sciences but will be used in this analysis because it provides a structured framework for understanding the connection between domestic policy and foreign policy choices. The fact that this concept is explained to a large degree by Social Democratic dominance should be kept completely separate from the parties' own concept of a special Scandinavian Social Democratic model.

Crucial to the social science understanding of the Scandinavian model is the notion of reformed capitalism and a high level of working-class mobilization as a basis for national political organisation. The formation of the Scandinavian working-classes as collective actors is seen to have strengthened their ability to strike and define political compromises with private business under the leadership of strongly reformist SD parties. Esping Andersen has showed how historical circumstance encouraged the growth of democratic cross-class "red-green" alliances in the 1930s between representatives of the reformist working class and small independent farmers based on a social policy package of agricultural subsidies, employment support and social reform.[3] By adding a social dimension to traditional liberal democracy, the Scandinavian SD parties constructed a new basis for national political organisation which was able to attract the allegiance of much broader sections of the population than liberal democracy previously had been capable of. This domestic development had important implications for foreign economic policy. The new action programme for national development represented an alternative to the automatic adjustment to international market forces which earlier had dominated economic policy in Scandinavia. In all three countries the new political alliances rested on the exports sectors' acceptance that the link between the domestic economy and world markets should be managed on the macro-economic level with a certain consideration for the social effects of international market forces. In a world like the 1930s this economic policy was unlikely to incur retaliation from trading partners, but after 1945 such policies appeared to be less sustainable. This raised the important question of how to adapt the Scandinavian model to the post-war world without jeopardizing national consensus.

In 1945 the Scandinavian countries were also faced with a particular problem of industrial restructuring. Historically the Scandinavian countries' role in the European division of labour has been to supply the industrialised economies with processed raw materials in exchange for capital and consumer goods, an economic structure which has encouraged a trade pattern based on complementary trade. In contrast to the rest of Western Europe, the Scandinavian countries were still, in 1945, highly specialised in a few dominant export staples based on a natural comparative advantage – in Sweden and Norway timber, paper, iron, steel and fish, in Denmark butter and bacon. In the post-war period these export staples have continued to play an important role because they earn foreign exchange to pay for the imports of capital and consumer goods needed for mass consumption. However, since the 1930s these sectors have employed a decreasing share of the working population; a problem which has had a destabilising effect on economic development and which has focused political attention on the creation of employment. In other words, economists suggest that until the mid-1960s the Scandinavian countries had particular problems in managing their economies because of their industrial structures which were skewed more towards inter-industry trade based on differences in factor endowments than towards intra-industry trade based on product differentiation which dominated in the rest of Western Europe.[4]

The new post-war international economy was therefore a considerable challenge for the Scandinavian model. In varying degrees, all three countries faced a catching-up problem with respect to the European division of labour which posed a serious long-term risk for employment and welfare. How could the three countries adapt themselves to the European liberalisation of trade without disrupting domestic consensus? And how could they develop and sustain the new industrial sectors which were necessary for the long-term preservation of economic growth in the face of strong competition from the rest of Western Europe? A traditional protectionist response in order to protect domestic consensus and support industrial growth like that undertaken in post-war France was never a viable long-term option in Scandinavia. The openness of the economies and the high trade dependency, which set very narrow limits for the use of tariffs to protect domestic industry, has been emphasized as another characteristic of the Scandinavian model.[5] Although Norway consistently used tariffs for industrial protection after 1945, its average tariffs, like those in Sweden and Denmark, remained low in comparison with the rest of Western Europe. Domestic industry was therefore mainly protected by quantitative restrictions, a policy instrument which was gradually outlawed by the OEEC during the 1950s.[6]

These different elements of Scandinavian development illustrate a certain separateness between Scandinavia and Europe. In Scandinavia the political basis for the development of the modern nation state was laid down already in the 1930s and resulted in a certain withdrawal from Europe. The economic and political disintegration of Europe in that decade helped strengthen popular support for the new economic policy. The political consensus of the 1930s was the basis from which the Scandinavian SD parties expected to further consolidate their power in the post-war period. In Denmark the consensus had already broken down in 1945 when the Social Democrats presented their post-war programme setting out their strategy for a full employment welfare state based on new modern export industries. Fear of state planning and intervention brought the Liberal and the Conservative parties together in a tenuous post-war alliance. The breakdown of the pre-war consensus had profound impact on post-war politics in Denmark; neither the Liberal party nor the SD party were able to form coalition majority governments until 1957. But in Norway and Sweden the 1930s consensus survived intact and became the post-war foundation for a very ambitious Social Democratic government policy which often served as an inspiration and model for the less successful Danish Social Democrats, in particular the new ambitious generation of young economists who were to become so influential in the post-war period.

Seen in this perspective, the Scandinavian model was quite different from the socio-economic model which developed on the Continent during the 1950s. There the reconstruction of the nation state developed under the direction of the new Christian Democratic parties. A new political consensus was gradually built up around the 'politics of productivity', the notion that the politically controversial question of income redistribution could be overcome by the pursuit of high economic growth.[7] Rapid increases in productivity combined with an expansion of international trade were seen as a crucial precondition for economic growth. New research on the history of the European Community suggests that it was this ideology of economic growth rather than federalist ideals, which provided the real impetus for European integration in the 1950s.[8] This research also demonstrates the growing political awareness of the importance of intra-European trade for national economic growth and sees the upswing in this intra-European trade between 1954 and 1957 as an important precondition for the creation of the Common Market in 1957. In this period the German Federal Republic emerged not only as the largest exporter of manufactured products, but also as the largest market for these products in Western Europe. This was a clear indication of the potential of the German economy and the development of a new intra-European trade structure based on mutual exchange of highly differentiated industrial products.

Like the rest of Western Europe, Scandinavia experienced a rapid increase in its trade with Germany during the 1950s. But while the Benelux countries, for example, saw this trade as so crucial to domestic growth and welfare that they actively sought to encourage it through political and economic integration with Germany, the Scandinavian countries were for a number of reasons much more ambivalent about such integration. In Denmark and Norway, considerations of industrial development and fear of German industrial power persuaded governments to closely monitor and control bilateral trade. But economic relations with the new German republic were also cause for concern in the larger and more industrialised Sweden, where the rapid growth of trade with Germany in the early 1950s was seen to have a destabilising effect on the weak balance of payments.[9] The strategy of industrial modernisation together with the fear of German industry and the balance of payments problems did not speak in favour of a Scandinavian opening towards Europe in the 1950s. But economic policy as it was conducted on the continent also helped to strengthen the negative attitude towards Europe: German economic policy under Ludwig Erhard was seen as an example of the kind of economic policies that would prevail in an integrated Europe. Adjustment to international market forces via deflation, wage restraints and high interest rates were certainly irreconcilable with Scandinavian SD policy objectives.

The perception of the need for larger scale industrial development together with the importance of providing a certain protection of industry had already persuaded Social Democrats and trade unions early in the post-war period to consider Nordic cooperation. The many plans to create a Nordic customs union between 1947 and 1957 were to a large degree a Social Democratic project constructed for the international advancement of this industrial objective, although wrapped in ideological cliches about Scandinavian unity. In 1948/49 the project had been couched in integrationist terms to please the American Marshall Plan administration, but the institutional arrangements planned for projected Scandinavian customs union were in fact wholly intergovernmental. Throughout this period the Norwegian SD government wavered in its commitment to the Nordic project which it feared would expose domestic industry to competition from the more advanced industries of Sweden and Denmark, an ambivalence which has lead most scholars to question the viability of the Nordic project. It is the purpose of this paper to show that in the 1950s the Danish SD government saw a Nordic customs union as a viable international strategy for the pursuit of the SD domestic policy objectives.

Danish Social Democrats and Nordic Cooperation 1945-54

The Danish SD Party was, together with the Radical Party, the most pro-Nordic of the Danish parties. Until early 1949 the party was firmly committed to the idea of a Nordic region as a 'third force' between the two superpowers and the continuation of the policy of neutrality within the framework of a Scandinavian defence union formed the basic guideline for SD post-war foreign policy. It was generally assumed that the defence union would create a basis for an extended economic and political co-operation between the three countries.[10] The defeat of the defence union project in early 1949 and the subsequent membership in NATO was a traumatic event for the SD party, and also influenced the belief in the Nordic economic project. When the Norwegian government in a bid to obtain a larger share of Marshall aid re-launched the Nordic economic project in October 1949, the government supported the proposal, but remained sceptical about Norwegian intentions. When negotiations disclosed that the Norwegian government was only prepared to consider a Nordic free trade arrangement for a few commodity sectors, the government for a while turned its attention to the OEEC and the negotiations to create a European payments scheme which it hoped would provide a workable international financial framework for the support of Danish recovery policies.

But the prospects for the Danish economy were to change very rapidly during 1950. The devaluation in September 1949 meant a serious deterioration in terms of trade which gradually began to be felt during the spring of 1950 in the form of increased import prices. At the same time, a shift in the United States' European policy, away from reconstruction towards trade liberalisation, was rapidly changing the external conditions for Danish recovery. In October 1949, the OEEC decided on a timetable for the dismantling of import restrictions establishing that 60% of the participating countries' imports should be liberalised by July 1950. The OEEC programme's focus on import restrictions rather than tariffs was the first real indication that tariffs were regaining their old position in Western Europe as legitimate instruments of commercial policy; a development which clearly was not anticipated by Danish policy makers. On the contrary, during the 1947 and 1949 GATT negotiations Denmark, like other small countries, had agreed to keep a very large part of its tariffs low which left the government totally dependent on the import restriction system for the protection of domestic industry. Considering the protectionist tariff policy introduced in several of the larger European countries in the late 1940s, the Danish belief in the ability of GATT to abolish tariffs seems overly optimistic, but strong domestic opposition to use of tariffs as protectionist measures and the need to secure access to foreign markets for its agricultural exports might have forced the government's hand. Whatever the reason, the decision to bind a series of industrial tariffs in 1947 and

1949 served to constrain Danish options with respect to trade liberalisation and thus had a profound impact on Danish foreign economic policy in the early 1950s.

By 1950 both the United States and Britain were pressing ahead with an OEEC programme which left tariffs aside and concentrated exclusively on the dismantling of import restrictions. The OEEC programme discriminated against low tariff countries like Denmark in several ways. First of all, it ignored existing tariff disparities among the member states which meant that Denmark would expose its domestic industry to foreign competition without being able to increase its share of foreign markets which remained safely protected by high tariffs. Secondly, the programme did not include agricultural products which prevented agricultural producers like Denmark from expanding their share of European markets. In the Danish case, this posed a serious threat to future foreign currency income as well as to agricultural incomes. Dismantling of import restrictions also threatened to eliminate the only domestic policy instrument available for the implementation of the government's industrial policy.

In November 1949 only 33% of Danish imports were exempt from control, and the prospect of increasing that percentage to 75% by 1951 was indeed a daunting prospect for a government committed to full employment and welfare.[11] The Foreign Minister complained bitterly in the OEEC over the programme's unfair discrimination against Denmark, but over the next six months the government gradually increased the liberalisation percentage to 53%, mainly by increasing raw material imports. This modest liberalisation, combined with the delayed effects of the 1949 devaluation, had an immediate impact on the balance of payments which deteriorated rapidly during the summer, and in August the government finally decided to reactivate import controls. The balance of payments crisis in August 1950 represented a dramatic change in economic progress compared to the previous five years and was the first warning of the structural balance of payments deficit that was to dictate economic policy throughout the 1950s. The economic crisis also demonstrated the deep disagreement between the Social Democrats and the opposition over the question of trade liberalisation. In November 1950 a new Liberal/Conservative government (1950-53) initiated a tight economic policy in order to keep up with the OEEC liberalisation programme but even to the most ardent supporters of trade liberalisation it was obvious that Denmark would not be able to meet the new OEEC target of 75% by 1951.

The general setback for the OEEC trade liberalisation programme in 1951 under the impact of the Korean War provided a temporary relief from this policy conundrum but did little to solve the Danish balance of payments problem. On the contrary, the Korean War raised the new question of how to finance the growth in defence expenditures demanded by NATO without resorting to further cutbacks in economic activity. The pervading agricultural protection in Europe indicated that agricultural foreign currency receipts were unlikely to increase in the near future, and it was gradually realized that extraordinary policy measures were now needed to boost industrial development. But in 1952, the prospects for industrial growth looked bleaker than at any time since 1932: industrial investments lagged far behind those of other countries and the predominance of small domestic market orientated firms was thought to prevent Danish industry from breaking into Western European markets dominated by large mass producing industrial plants. Even more important, potential industrial markets in Western European would remain closed unless a solution could be found linking tariff reductions to quota-dismantling.

It was in this situation that the Social Democrats seriously began to reconsider the Nordic customs union. The direction taken by the OEEC trade liberalisation programme since 1949 made it increasingly unlikely that the SD post-war policy objectives of industrialisation and social reform could be successfully pursued within the Western European policy framework. During 1952/53 Denmark took an active part in the low-tariff countries' attempt to link the dismantling of import restrictions in the OEEC to tariff reductions in the GATT and launched repeated specific complaints in the OEEC over tariffs preventing Danish industrial exports from entering European markets.[12] The high-tariff countries' rejection of these initiatives demonstrated how little real influence Denmark had on OEEC policy-making and was seen as a clear indication that growing interdependence with Western Europe could be at the cost of further losses of employment and welfare. A regional arrangement like the Benelux was seen to offer better opportunities for industrial development: a smaller preferential trading area would provide a certain industrial protection as well as opportunities for expanding growth sectors like chemicals, machinery and pharmaceuticals.

The early negotiations for a Nordic customs union had been buried in January 1950, but an inter-governmental committee had continued working with new instructions to investigate the possibilities for a Nordic free trade arrangement. In 1951 the Scandinavian trade unions had already proposed the creation of a Nordic common market and a Nordic investment bank to support industrial development, and in 1954 the Nordic inter-governmental committee delivered its report.[13] At a government conference the following October, the Danish, Norwegian and Swedish governments appointed an ad hoc committee, the Nordic Economic Cooperation Committee (NECC), to investigate the conditions for the creation of a customs union.

Vibeke Sørensen

The Economic Benefits of a Nordic Customs Union

Research into Nordic cooperation has concluded that the customs union negotiations were primarily a means to achieve a better position for the Scandinavian countries in European trade negotiations in the 1950s.[14] According to this literature, none of which is based on government archives, the Nordic negotiations were motivated by external policy considerations rather than by the economic advantages of cooperation. European developments obviously were an important incentive after 1956/57 when Nordic cooperation within the negotiations of a European free trade area was politically conditioned by the wish to create a better bargaining position for the Scandinavian countries. But research in government archives now suggests, at least in the case of Denmark, that it was the economic motivations which were the driving force behind the country's support for the Nordic plans in the early 1950s. The source most revealing of these economic motivations is the Nordic white papers published by the NECC during the 1950s which are economic studies of the benefits of larger markets, larger units and technological know-how.[15] These white papers point specifically to the structural problems arising from the high dependence in Scandinavia on a few raw material based export staples and the need to enter new high value-added industrial production. In the case of Denmark, a customs union was seen as providing both a larger market for industrial expansion and a preferential trading arrangement that could compensate for the insulation from the German economy which was thought necessary. Research into Nordic cooperation has also ignored the powerful political motive; a cooperation of this kind between Social Democratic parties might build an international framework for the establishment of a new political alliance between labour and industry as a basis for the preservation of the Scandinavian model in the post-war period.

The existing literature, thus, is unable to explain what motivated the decision to continue the investigations into the creation of a customs union in October 1954, when the French 'no' to the European Defence Community appeared to have brought commercial negotiations between the Six to a standstill, as well as having ended the attempt to create a European Union. Scholars have emphasized the strong opposition towards the custom union in Norway and have questioned the sincerity of the Danish and Swedish commitment to the project.[16] However, seen in relation to overall economic developments in Europe, in particular the unexpected upswing in intra-European trade from the winter of 1953/54, which in Denmark immediately elicited a balance of payments deficit, the Danish and Swedish agreement to move ahead with the Nordic plans is more understandable. This upswing confirmed the rapid development of a new dynamic economic centre around Germany and consequently the necessity of accelerating industrial restructuring and development to prevent

Scandinavian industry from falling further behind in the European division of labour. The simultaneous failure of the low-tariff countries' action in GATT and the OEEC seemed to indicate that free market forces could not be relied on to provide scale and scope for such a restructuring. The existence of a catching-up problem in relation to the rest of Europe was, of course, less strongly felt in Sweden than in Denmark, but even in Sweden traditional export staples like timber, paper products, and iron and steel accounted for over 70% of exports by value in the late 1940s indicating the need for the expansion of manufactured exports.[17] Seen from this point of view there were, in fact, very good reasons to maintain the Nordic alternative in 1954 and gradually attempt to overcome opposition in Norway.

The main reason, however, why research into Nordic cooperation until now has underestimated these economic motives is the general evaluation that the economic foundations for a Nordic common market did not exist. The raw material based Scandinavian exports, such as pulp and paper, had their markets outside Scandinavia and the intra-Nordic level of trade was therefore relatively low. This has been interpreted as an indication that the potential for the expansion of intra-Nordic trade was equally limited. Seen from the liberal assumption that countries trade with each other to exploit differences in comparative advantages, this is a logical conclusion which seems to be confirmed by the relative stagnation of intra-Nordic trade in the 1950s compared to the increase in the Scandinavian countries' trade with the continent. Danish exports to Norway and Sweden, for example, accounted for a fixed share of 10-12% of total exports throughout the decade while exports to Germany alone increased from 11% in 1953 to 21% in 1959.[18]

But such a conclusion tends to overlook the fact that in the 1950s intra-Nordic trade was already dominated by the exchange of manufactures. In 1957 raw materials and semi-finished goods accounted for 30% of intra-Nordic trade, but manufactures for 44%. In 1960 exports of machinery from each of the three countries to their proposed partners were larger than their exports of machinery to the Six and the United Kingdom.[19] The Scandinavian countries, thus, had a potential for intra-trade exactly in those sectors that their governments wished to promote. This trade potential was realised in the 1960s when membership in EFTA led to a dramatic increase in intra-Nordic trade.[20] Its relative stagnation during the 1950's might actually help to explain why the early Nordic customs union was not realised before the later proposals for a free trade area and then, still later, EFTA completely changed the Scandinavian agenda. In contrast, between the Six there was a rapid increase in intra-trade supporting the creation of the customs union by demonstrating concretely its possible benefits. The Nordic project rested on a belief in an as yet unexploited intra-trade potential in manufactured products, while the interest in the free trade area was stimulated by a desire to secure the traditional Scandinavian export staples against discrimination in their European markets. The latter responded immediately to balance of payments and full employment considerations, the former to (less pressing) longer-term strategic considerations of Scandinavia's place in the European division of labour.

The economic motivations for the Nordic common market in the mid-1950's were, thus, to a large degree the same as those behind the Treaty of Rome in 1957 and the Single European Act in 1986 – namely the search for economies of scale, improved competitiveness, and technological development. Only the means and methods by which these goals were to be achieved were different. In the Nordic plans, production cooperation between producers played an important role. In order to overcome the restraints of small national markets and limited economic resources, such cooperation under a degree of state supervision, was thought necessary in order to match the modern large-scale plants being developed in the USA and Europe in industries like steel, chemicals and cars.

Nordic Cooperation 1954-58: Strategy for Industrial Development?

The NECC reports demonstrate that the Nordic project was driven by industrial policy motives similar to those which encouraged European integration on the Continent, but they say very little about the Scandinavian SD governments' actual commitment to the Nordic project. Government archives now confirm that from 1954 the Danish SD government was seriously committed to the Nordic project and continued to pursue Nordic cooperation even after the free trade negotiations in 1956/57 had changed the external conditions for regional cooperation in Scandinavia. If we look at the economic difficulties which the party faced in the early 1950s, it is not difficult to see why. The deficit on the balance of payments could only be controlled via a tight economic policy that had negative effects on industrial investment and growth, and NATO demands for increased defence expenditures further reduced finances available for industrial support. The trade unions had for some time been arguing for Nordic cooperation as means to promote industrial development and growth. A Nordic customs union could not provide an outlet for Danish agricultural exports, but these exports, which until 1954 continued to grow slowly, were not the primary concern of the Social Democrats when they returned to power in October 1953. The new government's main priority was to find new ways of encouraging industrial growth. In 1952 the Liberal/Conservative government had continued liberalisation, but the SD government had no serious intention of complying with the OEEC scheme as long it discriminated against Denmark. Industrial protection could be maintained temporarily by invoking the OEEC escape-clause but this would not facilitate the expansion of industrial exports which the government needed so badly, and by 1953/54 the Nordic customs union project began to look very attractive for exactly those reasons. While access to European markets for products like machinery and chemicals was barred by excessive tariffs, a Nordic customs union was seen to provide a smaller but more accessible market for these exports in which Danish industry could develop the large-scale industrial plants necessary to compete in European markets.

Part of the government administration now became more favourably disposed to Nordic cooperation, in particular when such cooperation seemed to present an alternative to the policy of liberalisation advocated by the Liberal party. By 1953 it was generally acknowledged that the import restriction system could not be relied on for long as a policy instrument for the direction of the economy, a problem which raised the more general question of how to regulate and direct the economy in the future. The Directory of Supplies, in charge of imports, together with the government's Economic Secretariat, played a crucial role in the coordination of economic policy and activity. In both agencies policy-making was to some extent influenced by the vision of a more independent and self sufficient Nordic region. The potential for industrial exports, as well as a reduction in scarce foreign currency expenditures inherent in a higher level of intra-Nordic trade, made the Directorate and the Economic Secretariat feel very positive towards the Nordic project and top officials from both agencies were heavily involved in the Nordic negotiations during the 1950s.[21]

A more tangible advantage of the Nordic project was that it would provide a convenient domestic excuse to adapt the low Danish tariffs to the realities of the post-war world. Tariffs were an explosive issue in domestic politics. Powerful interest groups (farmers, small-holders and wholesalers) were united in favour of low tariffs, while some domestic market industries, fearful of foreign competition, would only be persuaded to give up import restrictions if compensated by excessively high tariffs. Both government and administration were in favour of a tariff reform that would secure a certain continued protection of industry, but they also wanted to keep the average tariff levels relatively low. A common Nordic tariff would automatically mean an increase in Danish tariff levels and would provide a useful government instrument for restraining excessive tariff demands from individual industries. The Industrial Council reacted very positively towards the Nordic project which was seen to promise protection from European industry as well as possibilities for industrial growth. The Nordic common market, thus, seemed to promise a new consensus between government and industry on industrial policy.[22]

All in all, there were good reasons to support the Nordic project when the NECC delivered its report in 1954. In August the government decided to set up a special civil servant committee under the Economic Secretariat to coordinate Danish policy with respect to the Nordic customs union investigations in consultation with private industry. By October the committee recommended a Danish 'yes' to start investigations into a Nordic customs union.[23] It was recognised that participation in such a union would mean higher Danish tariffs for raw materials like steel and iron, which might meet resistance in some sectors, but it was the committee's evaluation that benefits from the common market would far exceed the costs of implementing higher tariffs for these raw materials. The committee recognised that the proposal would meet strong opposition from Norwegian industry and suggested that the best way to overcome this opposition would be to investigate the problems sector-by-sector.[24]

But the Harpsund meeting in October 1954 clearly showed the limitations of such an approach. All three countries agreed to the inclusion of sectors like wood, timber, pulp, paper and ships, in which tariffs and import restrictions played only a minor role. The Norwegian government, however, was reluctant to go any further although these sectors only covered 32% of intra-Nordic trade. Four new sectors (iron/steel, chemicals/pharmaceuticals, electronics and metals/metal goods) were therefore eventually included, which brought the percentage up to 58. This meant that the intra-trade agreed to in Harpsund was still below the 70-80% required to get the customs union recognised in GATT. More importantly, the agreement did not include the machinery sector. In Denmark the exclusion of machinery was seen to defeat the whole purpose of creating a common market.[25] The machinery sector accounted for only 11% of intra-trade but represented a important market for Danish industry. Between 1950 and 1955 Danish exports of machinery had doubled and Sweden and Norway had emerged as the largest customers for these exports. But rather than risking a breakdown of negotiations, the government decided to settle for what had been achieved and instead instructed the delegation to try more subtle forms of persuasion. At the insistence of Denmark and Sweden, the machinery sector was quietly included in the investigations six months later.[26]

Once the machinery sector had been included, both the administration and the government were very optimistic about the prospect of a customs union. Danish industry had also welcomed the Harpsund agreement. The chemical industry was already involved in extensive cooperation across Nordic frontiers and had even come up with a proposal for a common Nordic tariff. Other sectors were equally positive; the machinery industry expected considerable benefits arising from product specialisation and expansion of exports in a larger market. Only about 20% of the machinery industry, the Industrial Council predicted, would encounter initial difficulties arising from abolishment of import restrictions.[27]

Investigations of the conditions for the expansion and coordination of the Scandinavian steel industry was the other important part of the NECC's brief in 1954. The three countries had planned an expansion of their domestic steel production on an individual basis of between ten to twenty percent over the decade after 1955, which would bring the total Scandinavian production up to 4.5 million tonnes by 1965. There was very little intra-Scandinavian trade in steel; net imports into Denmark and Norway accounted for 60-80% of consumption, in Sweden for 40%. This relatively high level of dependence on the rest of Europe was felt to be more problematic after the creation of the European Coal and Steel Community (ECSC) in 1951 which, in economic terms, was perceived as a re-creation of the European steel cartel of the 1930s. An increase of intra-Scandinavian trade to cover 85% of total consumption was seen as offering benefits both in security of supplies and stabilisation of prices.[28]

Both issues were especially important in Denmark. In 1951, 74% of Danish steel imports by value came from the ECSC which, indeed, by early 1953 constituted an export cartel.[29] In 1953 a committee had already been set up under the Ministry of Trade and Industry to conduct consultations with private industry on commercial problems in relation to the ECSC. The discussion in this committee gives a relatively clear picture of how Danish officials and industry perceived their supply problems. Some industries, the steel traders in particular, hoped to continue to profit from price competition among producers, while the shipyards were more concerned with the long term security of supplies. The Directorate of Supplies and the Ministry of Trade and Industry were rather sceptical about the future possibilities of exploiting price competition. They saw the ECSC investment policy as a sign that the steel market would be more coordinated, a development that would work against price cycles and so make it more difficult for Denmark to pursue its traditional import policy. The implementation of quotas by the ECSC on exports to third countries in 1954 was seen as confirmation of this view.[30]

Danish officials complained strongly about these quotas both in GATT and to the ECSC. During 1955, the complaints were discussed several times with the High Authority of the ECSC with Denmark claiming that the prices paid by Danish industry were 15-20% higher that those paid by Community consumers. The Danish position, however, was seriously weakened by the fact that higher prices had not reduced consumption. On the contrary, Danish imports of steel had increased since October 1954 when prices started to go up. Discussions in GATT gave the clear impression that Denmark was acquiring a reputation for complaining without reason and the High Authority pointed out that Denmark could not expect to enjoy the same advantages as member countries without accepting the commitments of membership.

The Nordic plans for cooperation within their own iron and steel market elicited a response from the ECSC in 1955. This is hardly surprising considering that such a market would have been the ECSC's largest customer for coal, coke and steel and its largest supplier of iron ore (in 1954, 54% of ECSC imports). In October the Dutch member of the High Authority, Spierenburg, suggested that Denmark should consider a closer relationship with the ECSC. The proposal was that Denmark, without becoming a member, would achieve 'equal' treatment with respect to prices and supplies if it agreed to keep coal and steel imports tariff-free and in times of surplus production to implement certain restrictions on imports from third countries. The proposal was clearly aimed at obstructing the Nordic plans and was therefore, after careful investigation, rejected by the government in August 1956. Discussions with private industry showed that both the shipyards and the steel traders were now in favour of the Nordic solution to the Danish supply problems.[31]

However, this solution was not without problems. Although all three participants were small economies, they were also very different. Both Norway and Sweden produced more steel than Denmark and an important issue of disagreement was that of fixing the level of a common external tariff. Sweden wanted a tariff-rate on raw materials high enough (5-6%) to prevent dumping, while Denmark insisted on maintaining tariff freedom on such imports, although the shipyards were less adamant. The greater problem was the different production structure in the three countries. In Denmark and Norway, steel production was concentrated in two or three enterprises under a certain state guidance. Production in Sweden was highly decentralised in 43 mills, of which only five had a production capacity over 100,000 tonnes.[32] When Norway insisted on the restructuring and planning of Scandinavian steel production as a prerequisite for membership, this inevitably encountered strong opposition from private industry in Sweden. Norway and Denmark favoured a concentration of the steel production into a production cycle beginning with the blast furnace and including a few large rolling mills, with special steel and other products delegated to smaller plants. This meant restructuring of the larger Swedish industry.[33]

The political attitudes behind these disagreements are relevant. Denmark and Norway wanted to submit Swedish industry to a higher level of state control in order to strengthen an inter-governmental bargain which required a deflection of their trade away from traditional suppliers and, as long as the Swedish government was not ready to step in and overrule private industry, could not see much future in the Nordic plans for a steel market. Even so, the negotiations were continued and the proposal for a Nordic steel market made up the central part of NECC's final report in 1957. By this time, however, ambitions had been lowered; instead of state supervision and planning, cooperation among the Scandinavian steel industries was to be left to the operation of free market forces within the customs union.

The Messina conference in June 1955, marking the beginning of the customs union negotiations among the Six, did little to reduce the Danish commitment to the Nordic project. During 1955 the investigations into the customs union made slow but gradual progress and by mid-1956 a common Nordic tariff had been agreed unofficially for two thirds of the 1100 positions of the Brussels nomenclature. Despite this progress the basic disagreements remained: the Norwegian government still insisted on an extended production cooperation as a precondition for its agreement to a common tariff and had secured long transition periods for a series of products. Even so, by mid-1956 the Swedish and Danish governments were ready in principle to begin the negotiations for a treaty to be presented after the publication of the NECC's report in 1957.[34]

Failure of the Nordic Project 1957-1959

In July 1956 Britain for the first time presented its alternative to the Six's customs union, but initially the British proposal did little to change Nordic priorities. At first glance, the free trade project even seemed to be the perfect framework for the realisation of the Nordic plan. Technically, the relationship of a Nordic customs union to the free trade area would be the same as that of the Six, and a free trade area consisting of two customs unions, and the United Kingdom would eliminate the discrimination against the traditional Scandinavian exports staples which might have resulted from the Nordic project alone. But new domestic political developments eventually forced the Danish government to reconsider its commitment to Nordic cooperation. Danish farmers, concerned about protecting access to the German market, had closely followed developments within the Six and in December 1956 the president of the Agricultural Council officially demanded Danish participation in these negotiations. When in January 1957 the Liberal Party backed up this demand, Danish foreign economic policy became a politically sensitive issue in the spring election. Open government support for the Nordic project now became more difficult since such a membership would automatically exclude Denmark from membership in the Six. Officially the government now opted for postponement of a decision with respect to both projects. The Foreign Minister travelled to Brussels and achieved a vague promise that membership in the Six would remain open for Denmark if the government would decide to apply after first having investigated the option of the wider free trade area. The so-called 'open door' policy helped the government to withstand political pressure from the Liberal Party until the formation of a coalition government with the Radical Party in May 1957 secured the SD Party a parliamentary majority backing its Nordic policy.

In principle the government remained committed to the Nordic project as a regional arrangement within the wider free trade area. This, however, would require the inclusion of agriculture in the free trade arrangement, which Britain opposed. For most of 1957 the government therefore focused its attention on this problem and tried, in cooperation with the Six, to persuade Britain to include agricultural products in the free trade area. In order to withstand political pressure at home from the opposition, at a Nordic inter-governmental meeting in January 1957 the SD government declared its wish to postpone the final decision on the Nordic customs union until the fate of the free trade area had been decided.[35] At the same time, however, the government confirmed its continued commitment to the Nordic project by emphasising the advantages the Scandinavian countries could obtain in the free trade area if the removal of tariffs on industrial products was begun on the basis of Nordic rather than national tariffs. At a meeting of the Nordic Council in February 1957, all three Scandinavian Social Democratic parties spoke very strongly in favour of the creation of a Nordic customs union within the free trade area and in October the NECC presented its five volume report on the creation of a Nordic customs union.[36] Despite the postponement of the final decision until the free trade agreement had been signed, the Danish government believed this to be the most positive solution for Denmark because of its benefits for employment and industrial development.

It was only in autumn 1958 that it began to become clear that French opposition might lead to the breakdown of the free trade area negotiations. The prospect of failure and of an economic division of Western Europe rather than more widespread commercial cooperation quickly changed priorities, not only in Denmark, but also in Sweden and Norway. The gradual erection of the European Community tariff walls from 1 January 1959 was not only a threat to Danish agricultural exports, especially to Germany, but also to other Scandinavian export staples. The gloomy prospects for products like paper, aluminium, and alloy iron which made up a large part of Norwegian and Swedish exports to the Community played an important role in provoking the collapse of the free trade negotiations. With respect to these products, France claimed that Scandinavian producers had an unfair natural advantage which required tariff compensation for less fortunate producers.[37] The French insistence on this issue, as well as on the demand for a transition period for the establishment of the free trade area, placed Sweden and Norway in a very similar situation to Denmark. Even if the negotiations could be brought to a successful conclusion, the outcome might very well be a free trade area discriminating for some time and, perhaps even permanently, against the traditional Scandinavian export sectors which still were the most important earners of foreign currency.

This new threat explains several changes in the Nordic priorities during 1958. Cooperation now became more concentrated on the two issues which divided opinion within the free trade negotiations, namely agriculture and the question of the rules of origin of imports. It was the agricultural issue particularly which altered opinions in Norway and Sweden. In principle, both countries preferred a free trade agreement without agriculture, but Norway had strong fishery interests demanding access to European markets and both countries now realised that some sacrifice of protection was necessary to strengthen the bargaining power of the Scandinavian bloc. At a meeting in Saltsjöbaden in September 1958 all agreed to postpone the Nordic negotiations until an agreement on the free trade area had been reached. The statement from the meeting underlined the necessity of establishing a common Nordic policy with respect to the free trade area negotiations, in order to prevent arrangements between the larger countries which could increase discrimination against the Scandinavian export staples of fish, agriculture, timber, paper, aluminium and alloy iron. The fear was that a trade-off between the United Kingdom and the Six could result in an arrangement excluding important Scandinavian exports. In the first instance a common stand had to be found on the agricultural question which could satisfy Danish requirements.[38]

In reality, the breakdown of the free trade area negotiations in November 1958 also meant the defeat of the Nordic project. Afterwards, Sweden and Norway focused on the possibilities of creating an alternative commercial framework including the United Kingdom. Officially, the opinion that the Nordic customs union could be included in an 'outer' free trade area was maintained, but it was clear that this option now had a much lower priority in Sweden and Norway. The breakdown of the free trade negotiations and the creation of EFTA was a serious blow for the Danish government. Membership of the Six was not a realistic political option, but EFTA, like the free trade area, could not provide the necessary alternative outlet for agricultural exports and the government was now forced to give up its 'open door' policy with respect to the Six.[39]

Conclusion

The story of the negotiations of a Nordic customs union in 1950-58 indicates that small countries do indeed have more options with respect to their foreign economic policy than international relations theory would want us to believe. The negotiations also seem to confirm the hypothesis that when important economic foreign policy choices were made in Scandinavia in this period they were primarily defined by domestic policy considerations. The national choice made in the 1930s, in favour of employment, social reform and industrialisation, which had been the Scandinavian SD parties' road to power, determined their post-war attitude to the mainly Christian Democratic Western Europe which grew out of the Cold

War. For the same reasons the idea of a Social Democratic Scandinavia cooperating on defence and foreign policy held a strong attraction for all SD political leaders in the early post-war period. The realisation that a Nordic Defence Union was not feasible in a bi-polar world did not mean the rejection of cooperation on foreign economic policy; on the contrary, the Scandinavian countries continued to cooperate closely in GATT, the OEEC and the EPU. When it became clear in the early 1950s that progress in GATT was blocked by strong protectionist interests and that Great Britain and France had opted out of OEEC commitments in order to protect their balance of payments, the strategy of pursuing industrial development and expansion of trade within a Nordic regional arrangement began to look more attractive.

The Danish archives show that the SD-led governments between 1954 and 1958 were firmly committed to the Nordic project and that it was only political considerations for farmers and small-holders which prevented the government from saying so openly in 1957-58. The motivations were many and mixed but, in contrast to the earlier Nordic negotiations in 1947-1950, a strong interest in a common market for industrial products, in particularly machinery, is discernible not only within the government but also within the group of policy-making civil servants in the Economic Secretariat, the Directorate of Supplies and the Ministry for Trade and Industry. This attitude is perhaps not surprising considering that Danish industry had most to gain from a common market. Certainly the industrial gains were less clear cut in Norway and Sweden. Norwegian home market industries would be certain to suffer and the gains to the exports industries depended on their modernisation, hence the Norwegian demands for investment support and common development projects in the sectors of steel, water and electricity. The negotiations for the Nordic customs union suggest that the Norwegian government was sympathetic to the Nordic project but severely restrained by the strong opposition to a Nordic common market within domestic industry.

However, the idea that, by pooling their economic resources within a customs union, the three countries could achieve the larger freedom of action in their economic relations with Europe which would simultaneously promote industrial development, was in fact totally dependent on the attitude of Sweden which, as the largest and most industrialised economy, was designated the important role of growth pole within the Nordic project. This raises the crucial question of determining the Swedish government's commitment to the customs union. It has been suggested that the gains Swedish industry could expect from the Nordic project compared with the larger market inherent in the British free trade area proposal were far too small to justify participation in a project which Swedish industry seems to have interpreted mainly as a Social Democratic plot to extend government influence over private enterprise.[40] This argument clearly does not take into account the fact that until the autumn of 1958 it was believed that a Nordic customs union could be achieved within the free trade area; a situation in which Swedish industry could combine the preferential position within a Nordic common market with free access to the markets of Western Europe. But even if we assume that the Swedish government was fully committed to the Nordic project, it would have been reluctant to alienate powerful domestic interests in order to bring it to life. Only the opening of the Swedish archives will be able to answer the important question of the government's commitment to the Nordic project and thus determine whether Nordic cooperation in the 1950s was pursued as a realistic Social Democratic alternative to Europe.

Notes

1. Griffiths, R.T. (ed.): *Socialist Parties and the Question of Europe in the 1950s*, Leiden 1993.
2. Hansen, P.: "Adaptive Behavour of Small States: The Case of Denmark and the European Community", in: *Sage International Yearbook of Foreign Policy Studies*, vol II, 1974.
3. See among others Korpi, W.: *The Democratic Class Struggle*, London 1983 and Esping Andersen, G.: *Politics against Markets*. Princeton 1985. Their definition of a Scandinavian welfare model has been criticized for its Swedish bias. In Denmark the existence of a large group of highly competitive farmers and a strong Liberal Agrarian party meant a split within the agrarian part of the 'red-green' alliance. As a consequence the alliance has always been weaker in Denmark than in Sweden and Norway, in particular after 1945. The existence of a large Liberal Agrarian party also meant that the Danish Conservative party remained weak and limited to the cities. For a discussion of the Danish development compared to Sweden see Elder, N., Thomas, A. H. and Arter, D: *The Consensual Democracies? The Government and Politics of the Scandinavian States*, London 1988, p. 29-58.
4. Mjøset, L. "Nordic Economic Policies in the 1970s", in *International Organization*, 43(3), 1987, p. 433-56; Norway and Denmark clearly fit this model better than Sweden which is more industrialised. But as late as 1980 the raw material based export staples still made up 30% of Swedish exports. Samuelsson, K. "The Swedish Model and Western Europe", in *Journal of International Affairs*, 41(2) 1988, p. 376.
5. Katzenstein, P. J.: *Small States in World Markets*, Ithaca 1985; Senghaas, D: *Von Europa Lernen*, Frankfurt 1982.
6. In 1954 Norway and Denmark had each liberalised 75% and Sweden 92% of OEEC imports.
7. Maier, C.S.: "The Politics of Productivity: Foundations of American International Economic Policy after World War II", in P.J. Katzenstein (ed.): *Between Power and Plenty. Foreign Economic Policies of Advanced Industrialized States*. Madison 1978.
8. Milward, A.S.: *The European Rescue of the Nation State*, London 1992.
9. Fritz, M. "Schweden und der westdeutsche Markt 1945-1955", in L. Herbst, W.-Bührer, H, Sowade (eds.): *Von Marshall Plan zu EWG. Die Eingliederung der Bundesrepublik Deutschland in die westliche Welt*, München 1990, p. 115.

10. For this point, see article by Molin & Olesen in this book.
11. Sørensen, V.: *Social Democratic Government under the Marshall Plan, 1945-1950*. Ph.d.-thesis, European University Institute, Florence 1987, p. 389-426.
12. These complaints were concentrated in growth sectors like chemicals and machinery. Asbeek Brusse, W.: *West European Tariff Plans, 1947-1957*, Ph.d.-thesis, European University Institute, Florence 1991, p.105 .
13. DsF: *Nordisk Økonomisk Samarbejde*, (Copenhagen, 1952); Det fælles Nordiske Udvalg for Økonomisk Samarbejde: *Et Fælles Nordisk Marked*, Copenhagen 1954.
14. B. Haskel: *The Scandinavian Option*, (Oslo, 1976); G. P. Nielsson: "The Nordic and the Continental European Dimensions in Scandinavian Integration: NORDEK as a case study", *Cooperation and Conflict*, VI, 1971, p. 173-78; N. Amstrup, "Nordisk samarbejde – myte eller realitet?", in *Nær og fjern. Samspillet om den indre og ydre politik. Studier tilegnet dr. phil. S. Henningsen*, (Copenhagen, 1980); B, Stråth: *Nordic Industry and Nordic Economic Cooperation*, (Stockholm 1978); B. Stråth: "The Illusory Nordic Alternative to Europe", *Cooperation and Conflict*, XV, 1980, p. 102-114; N. Andren: "Nordic Integration and Cooperation – Illusion and Reality", *Cooperation and Conflict*, XIX 1984, p. 251-262. For a more varied analysis, see C. Stålvant: "Nordic Policy towards International Economic Cooperation", in B. Sundelius (ed.): *Foreign Policies of Northern Europe*, (Boulder, 1982) and B. Turner & G. Nordquist: *The Other European Community: Integration and Cooperation in Nordic Europe*, (London, 1982).
15. NECC (Det fælles nordiske udvalg for økonomiske samarbejde): *Nordisk Økonomisk Samarbejde*, (Copenhagen, 1950); NECC: *Et Fælles Nordisk Marked*, (Copenhagen, 1954); NECC: *Nordisk Økonomisk Samarbeid*, vol. 1-5, (Oslo, 1957). The arguments and results of these reports are summed up by F. Wendt: *The Nordic Council and Co-operation in Scandinavia*, 1959, p. 165-233.
16. B. Stråth: The Illusory .... op.cit., p. 111.
17. In 1980 these products still made up 30% of total Swedish exports. K. Samuelsson: The Swedish Model.... op. cit., p. 376. See also L. Mjøset, Nordic Economic Policies.... op.cit., p. 403-56.
18. The precise distribution is revealed in the table below.

Distribution of Danish Exports 1950-1990 (percent)

	Germany	UK	Sweden	Norway	rest EC
1950	17	42	6	4	–
1953	11	40	5	3	–
1959	21	25	7	5	11
1967	12	23	14	7	11
1971	12	19	16	7	10
1980	19	14	13	6	16
1985	16	12	12	7	16
1990	20	11	13	7	22

Source: H.C.Johansen, *Dansk Økonomisk Statistik 1814-1980*, (Copenhagen, 1985); *OECD Statistics of Foreign Trade*, (Paris 1985 and 1990).

19. H.C.Johansen: "A Century of Nordic Cooperation", *EUI Colloquium Papers*, 135/89, Florence, p.8.
20. J. Fagerberg, "Diffusion of Technology, Structural Change and Intra-Industry Trade: The Case of the Nordic Countries 1961-1983", in J. O. Andersson: *Nordic Studies on Intra-Industry Trade*, (Abo, 1986); J. Fagerberg: "Norden og strukturendringene på verdensmarkedet. En analyse av de nordiska lands handel med

hverandre og de øvrige OECD-landene 1961-1983", *Statistisk Sentralbyro*, 18 (1986) Oslo.
21. Directory of Supplies (Vareforsyningsddirektoratet) journal no. 586; "Nordisk Samarbejde."
22. For an analysis of the Scandinavian industrial organizations' attitudes to the Nordic Common Market, see B.Stråth: *Nordic Industry*....op. cit.
23. Minutes 20/8-54. Regeringens Økonomiudvalg (RØ). Departmentchef K. Hansens embedsarkiv, Rigsarkivet.
24. Embedsmandsudvalg vdr. et fælles nordisk marked: minutes from meeting 22/10-54. Handelsministeriet (HM): Ujournaliseret journal no. 224: "Nordisk Samarbejde" (Rigsarkivet).
25. "P.M. om et nordisk fællesmarked for maskiner 19/3-55". HM: ujournaliseret journal nr. 224 (Rigsarkivet).
26. Minutes from meeting 26/2-1955. Det danske udvalg for nordisk økonomisk samarbejde (DNS). HM: ujournaliseret arkiv nr. 224 (Rigsarkivet).
27. Minutes from meeting 10/1-55, DNS. HM: ujournaliseret arkiv nr. 224 (Rigsarkivet).
28. NECC, *Nordiske Økonomiske Samarbeid*, (speciel del: vareområderne) op.cit.
29. Udenrigsministeriets Arkiv (UMA) 74C13f: "Notat ang. Minister Bartels besøg i CECA 24-25 november 1952." (Rigsarkivet).
30. See the minutes from the committee meetings 1953-1956 in UMA: 73C13g.
31. V. Sørensen: "How to become a member of a Club without Joining. Danish Policy with Respect to European Sector Integration Schemes 1950-1957.", in *Scandinavian Journal of History*, 16 1991, p.16.
32. NECC, *Nordisk Økonomisk Samarbeid*, op.cit.
33. UMA: 74C13g: "Referat fra ekspertgruppen i jern og stål 21-22 oktober 1955"; UMA: 73C13g: "Notat om det fælles nordiske marked for jern og stål 17 november 1955."
34. "Møde mellem de nordiske samarbejdsministre 9/1-56". HM: ujournaliseret arkiv nr. 224 (Rigsarkivet)
35. "Referat af de nordiske samarbejdsministres møde 24/1-57". HM: ujournaliseret arkiv nr. 224 (Rigsarkivet).
36. See F. Wendt, *The Nordic Council*....op.cit., p. 187.
37. Paper and pulp accounted for more than 10 % of Sweden's and Norway's exports, while aluminium and alloy iron alone accounted for 10% of Norwegian exports. UMA: 73B66f: "Udenrigsministerens redgørelse i Tinget 17 februar 1959 for situationen vdr. de europæiske markedsplaner."
38. In October such a proposal was presented in Paris. UMA: 73B66f: "Referat af Udenrigsministerens møde med Erhvervsorganisationerne 5 november 1958."
39. Udenrigsministeriet: "Notits om møde mellem de nordiske samarbejdsministre om genoptagelse af forhandlingerne mellem de 17. 31/5-59." Erik Ib Schmidts embedspapirer, box 2: Nordisk Samarbejde, Budgetdepartementet (Rigsarkivet).
40. See Stråth, B.: *Nordic Industry*....op. cit.

Security Policy and Domestic Politics in Scandinavia 1948-49

By Karl Molin & Thorsten B. Olesen

Introduction

On 30 April 1948 the Swedish Foreign Minister Östen Undén informed the Danish Ambassador to Stockholm that Sweden was willing to initiate discussions on the premises for and feasibility of establishing a Scandinavian Defence Union. This move was the first of a series of talks and negotiations which dominated the agenda of all inter-Scandinavian relations for the next ten months. The process was interrupted in February 1949 when the Norwegian government revealed its intentions of seeking membership in the Atlantic Pact. As a consequence, but without much conviction, the Danish government embarked on the same route shortly after. Both countries, thus, became original signature powers of the Atlantic Pact whereas, Sweden faithful to her tradition of neutrality, stood aloof.

The Scandinavian Defence Union talks were provoked by the escalation of the East-West conflict in the first months of 1948. Especially the coup in Czechoslovakia and the Soviet proposal to Finland of a mutual 'Pact of Friendship' prompted a profound reexamination of the Scandinavian countries' security policy doctrine. The reigning non-bloc-policy came under pressure, and especially Norway seemed inclined to sacrifice the non-bloc-policy on the altar of some form of security cooperation with the West. The Swedish invitations for discussions on closer Scandinavian defence cooperation were launched in this precise situation following secret and informal treatment of the issue at various inter-Scandinavian ministerial meetings during the previous months.

The Scandinavian discussions, however, were complicated from the start. Disagreements on the character of a Scandinavian defence union – such as whether such a union should be neutral or aligned under some form with the West – delayed all progress for months. This intricate problem was reinforced by the simultaneous discussions between the Brussels Pact members and the USA and Canada on establishing a broader Atlantic defence framework. In June Denmark and Norway learned that they both were regarded as potential members of a future Atlantic defence arrangement. Thus, from the opening of the Washington Exploratory Talks in early July 1948, the Atlantic discussions acted as an external strain on the Scandinavian defence union efforts.

All the same the Scandinavian perspective gained momentum in the

Security Policy and Domestic Politics in Scandinavia 1948-49

beginning of September 1948. During a meeting in Stockholm the Foreign Ministers of the three countries agreed on the authorisation to establish a joint defence committee. The purpose of this committee, which was finally appointed in October, was to work out a report both investigating the feasibility of creating an outright Scandinavian defence union and, less ambitiously, more limited Scandinavian defence cooperation.

The committee handed in its recommendations on 14 January 1949. Progress in the Atlantic Pact negotiations had induced the Scandinavian countries to initiate the final series of negotiations before the committee had submitted its final verdict. Nevertheless, the recommendations were known in their main outline when the first round of discussions took place in the Swedish town of Karlstad on 5 and 6 January 1949. Although the Karlstad meeting seemed to increase hopes for a Scandinavian solution, the subsequent rounds of meetings during January (in Copenhagen from 22 to 24 January and in Oslo from 29 to 30 January) showed that the basic schism, neutrality versus Western alignment, still existed.

It did not come as a surprise, then, that Norway, advocate of the latter position, headed directly for NATO membership when the Scandinavian efforts had been exhausted. The Danish government had greater difficulty in coming to terms with this fact and continued for nearly one more month to strive for a Scandinavian solution. In the end Denmark also took the path of Norway. Sweden, on the other hand, did not, and in this way the new North Atlantic Treaty Organization divided Scandinavia in two separate security policy spheres. One aligned with the West, and one which at least officially claimed to defend a neutrality position.

The debate on the Scandinavian defence union plans did not stop here. For years it continued to preoccupy the minds of many politicians of the time. The failure to create a Scandinavian defence union generated a great deal of bitterness and many recriminations. Even the respective foreign ministries have been mobilised to keep a watchful eye on how events of 1948/49 are described and explained to the public in the other two countries, or have themselves taken initiatives to sponsor and publish accounts of these events. The Danish Foreign Ministry in 1966, as a prelude to the debate on the prolongation of Danish NATO membership expiring by 1970, published a two-volume book covering Danish security policy from 1948 to 1966. The Scandinavian Defence Union issue naturally plays a prominent role in the book, and those parts of the book canvassing this area were seriously discussed with the Foreign Ministries of Norway and Sweden before its publication. Similarly, the 'classic' book on Norway's road to NATO through the Scandinavian defence negotiations, Magne Skodvin's, "Norden eller NATO", was the result of the Norwegian Foreign Ministry's wish to promote such a general account based on material in its own archives.[1]

From the beginning of the 1970's the task of analysing and presenting the complicated events linked to the Scandinavian Defence Union plans has been left mainly to historiography. Or one should rather say Norwegian historiography since the predominant part of research in this field until recently has been carried out by Norwegian historians such as Magne Skodvin, Knut Einar Eriksen, Geir Lundestad, Helge Pharo and Olav Riste.[2] The very important contributions made by Yngve Möller and Krister Wahlbäck in Sweden and just as significantly by Nikolaj Petersen in Denmark cannot change the overall picture of Norwegian predominance in this field of research.[3]

This state of affairs is probably the result of three sets of circumstances. Firstly, since the publication of Skodvin's book Norway has adopted a much more liberal archive policy than that of both Sweden and Denmark thus allowing Norwegian historians access to the relevant material. Secondly, two of the main protagonists in the Norwegian drama on the orientation between Scandinavia and the Atlantic Pact, Foreign Minister Halvard Lange and his adviser Arne Ording, were themselves historians. Especially the latter, a professor at the University of Oslo, inspired his students (who in turn became professors themselves – Lundestad, Eriksen, Riste and Pharo) to take an interest in the matter. In this way a very fertile and productive environment for studies on foreign policy was created in Norway. Thirdly, the tendency among both the Swedish and Danish contemporary protagonists of the drama to 'blame' Norway for the defence union failure may have acted as a catalyst, especially for Norwegian historians, to counterbalance this tendency.

Despite all the merits of Norwegian historiography in covering Scandinavian security policy of the late 1940's, it has been a setback to research that results have been so dependent on Norwegian (together with British and American) archives. This situation has fortunately been changing over the last five years. Based on access to the archives of the Swedish Foreign Ministry and the archives of the Swedish labour movement, scholars such as Kersti Blidberg and Gerard Aalders have recently published interesting studies.[4] Denmark has been slower to follow suit, but even here archive restrictions are being attenuated.[5]

The present paper is a product of the more liberal archive policies in Sweden and Denmark. Through our work in the archives of these two countries we have felt the need to challenge and reassess some of the results and interpretations of previous research. We do not claim or intend to present an organic reinterpretation of the whole Scandinavian defence issue of 1948-49. What we would like to do here, is to focus on a perspective which has generally been neglected in the existing research on the Scandinavian Defence Union project.

The Scandinavian Defence Union project has been thoroughly studied in its traditional security policy aspects, i.e. from perspectives of foreign and defence policies, and has also been closely analysed in connection with general developments within the international system. In this article we will attempt to approach the topic from the other angle, pointing to aspects of domestic politics and of ideology as being essential for a full understanding of not only attitudes towards Scandinavian security cooperation, but also of attitudes towards membership in a broader Western defence arrangement.

To maintain that aspects of domestic policy are indispensable to a serious discussion of the history of the SDU talks, is not necessarily to claim a general priority of interior politics to foreign affairs. It is rather a matter of balancing the intricate reciprocal relationship between the two. Different aspects of this relationship will be illuminated below. Firstly, the background of the Swedish invitation to start the SDU talks will be discussed as an illustration of the national unity concept in foreign policy making. According to traditional small state theory, unanimous support behind a government's foreign policy is a prerequisite for gaining international credibility and prestige. At the same time the ability to express and represent a broad public opinion is a major asset in the competition between the parties. No party can lead the government unless it is able to rally a strong and solid majority behind its foreign policy. Such considerations are paramount for understanding the Swedish government's SDU initiative.

Secondly, the SDU project will be examined in relation to specific domestic policy conditions in Denmark. The strong support for a Scandinavian Defence Union expressed by the Danish Social Democratic Party cannot be understood solely in relation to developments in the international system, but must also be seen as a strategy to promote Social Democratic policy goals and to improve the party's power base within the Danish political system. The case illustrates, on the one hand, how international cooperation may 'spill over' into the domestic scene, and, on the other hand, how political and ideological priorities may influence foreign policy behaviour. As such this provides a striking example of the complex interaction between foreign and domestic affairs.

Sweden and the Neutrality Question, 1948-49[6]

The essence of the policy pursued by Foreign Minister Östen Undén and the Swedish government was that Sweden should remain neutral in case of war and should act in accordance with the regulations of the Hague-Convention of 1907. Swedish performance in peacetime would serve the aim of creating confidence among potential belligerent powers that Sweden would not join their opponents. Military alliances as well as any other binding commitment were consequently ruled out.

On the surface this policy of neutrality seemed to enjoy a solid backing in the Swedish political system. During the first post-war years there was a widespread belief in neutrality as the best possible means for a small country to preserve peace. The fact that neutral Sweden had remained outside two devastating world wars tended to confirm this conviction. Concerning the ideological aspects of the Cold War, on the other hand, the Swedish public opinion was not neutral. Belief in democratic values was strong and virtually undisputed. Communism was detested. Western values and Americanism were applauded. Tension between a neutrality policy and Western thinking was thus a distinctive feature of public opinion.

In the parliamentary debate this tension was less conspicuous. The demand for national unity was very important in regulating party behaviour. The widely accepted assumption was that foreign powers would only have confidence in the Swedish commitment to neutrality if it was supported by all major parties. Divided opinion would produce speculations on possible changes in Swedish foreign policy. In case of war the consequence would be that a preventive attack on Sweden could not be ruled out. This assumption exerted strong pressure on the non-government parties to conform with the foreign policy conducted by the government. Parliament adopted a routine display of unity as every major government statement was followed by declarations of support by the leaders of the opposition parties. Similarly during election campaigns security policy was treated as a non-topic. In this way foreign policy, like defence policy, was elevated above the level of party politics.

During the spring of 1948 public debate on foreign policy changed radically. In the wake of Ernest Bevin's famous speech on 22 January calling for closer Western military cooperation, the largest Swedish newspaper, the liberal "Dagens Nyheter", abandoned its traditional neutrality line and started a campaign for Sweden's association with a Western defence alliance. A few liberal papers followed suit. Simultaneously some published articles on an alternative solution to the present security dilemma: A Scandinavian Defence Union. Such a proposal presented in a Norwegian paper was favourably reviewed by the editorials of a number of liberal and conservative Swedish newspapers. "Stockholms Tidningen", a leading liberal paper, even published a series of articles in which a detailed argument for Scandinavian foreign policy and defence cooperation was presented.[7]

The communist coup in Prague and the Soviet pact-proposal to Finland in February increased anxiety in political circles. Both Prime Minister Tage Erlander and Foreign Minister Undén repeatedly stated that the policy of neutrality remained unchanged. As usual the leaders of the opposition parties did not openly challenge the government, but behind closed doors they were arguing for a modification of the official policy. It was evident there was a growing sympathy for reconsidering the policy of neutrality.

Thus, a situation developed in which anxiety and doubts were prevalent but mainly expressed at various intimate and closed gatherings. In this rather conspiratory atmosphere, government officials representing the Foreign Ministry and members of the central military staffs played important roles. They were the experts, they knew how foreign powers reacted to Swedish policy, and they had the expertise to interpret the situation in military-strategic terms. Some of them were quite outspoken in their criticism of Undén's policy. From the government's perspective this criticism was most disquieting. It was delivered by prestigious officials like Erik Boheman, Ambassador to Washington, Sven Grafström, the head of the Foreign Ministry's Policy Division and by Helge Jung, Supreme Commander of the Armed Forces. The Commander of the Joint Military Staffs and the Commander of the Air Force were also among the critics.[8]

What these influential critics wanted was essentially a stronger orientation towards the West and a more pronounced anti-communist line. They did not, for the time being, advocate formal military ties, but they were clearly inclined to explore other ways of cooperating with the West. All kinds of informal military contacts and preparations for wartime aid in the form of both troops and equipment were to be recommended. The outcome of this attempted revision of Swedish foreign policy could hardly lead elsewhere than to formal membership in a Western military alliance.

The 'revisionists' used various channels to propagate their points of view. As advisers to the Cabinet they could freely express their views and recommendations through personal conversations and private letters. So they often did, and this practice was accepted by the Cabinet as part of a normal and useful internal discussion.

Less acceptable, however, were the vigorous efforts to spread these ideas to the broader public. Although their activity was basically in the private sphere, they would occasionally, during confidential conversations with journalists and politicians, report on the unfavourable reactions abroad to Mr. Undén's statements or warn that continued isolation would lead to disaster. They would recommend a change in Swedish foreign policy as the only way to preserve peace and independence. The importance of this informal propaganda should not be underestimated. In a small country, a few well-connected, prestigious experts will easily obtain personal contact with everyone of importance within the political parties and the press.

Efforts to influence public opinion did not, however, stop at this informal level. On a number of occasions high-ranking officers publicly questioned the wisdom of the neutrality policy. In February and March 1948 several officers stated that the strategic situation of Sweden made it most unlikely that the country could, in the long run, remain outside a war. Sweden lies, they pointed out, precisely under the trajectory of an East-West conflict.[9] These statements were most inconvenient to the government and placed it in an obvious predicament. Foreign newspapers saw them as a portent of a new Swedish policy to come, and foreign ambassadors called on Mr. Undén to discover the true character of these speculations. Undén, of course, denied all rumours of an imminent change of policy and had to admit that the military leadership acted without the consent of the Cabinet.[10]

Besides giving advice to the government and trying to influence public opinion, government officials had a third remedy up their sleeve. This simply consisted of trying to modify the implementation of government decisions. As representatives of the Swedish government they were supposed to explain and defend Swedish policy to foreign colleagues. In reality they often presented a more or less distorted version of the government's policy. Diplomats defended the Swedish policy with arguments never mentioned in the Foreign Minister's instructions. The diplomats would say, for example, that Sweden remained neutral because such a remote country would not receive substantial military aid in case of an attack, thereby implying that reliable Western guarantees could change this calculation. They also indicated that a new Swedish government would launch a new foreign policy which might include Swedish membership in a Western military alliance. In a confidential conversation with the American Ambassador to Stockholm, the Supreme Commander revealed his aspirations of 'educating' Swedish foreign policy-thinking in order to make it more Western oriented. He also asked questions on conditions for American arms-deliveries, showing very little concern for the official neutrality line.[11]

These incidents reveal that there was a real ambiguity in the way Swedish foreign policy was presented. To the government it was paramount that the firmness and continuity of the Swedish neutrality line was in no way cast in doubt and therefore it strove to give the outside world the impression of a nation unanimously supporting this policy. However, as we have seen, the real picture was more blurred in practice, with the Foreign Minister pursuing one policy, and leading officers and diplomats another.

The relevance of this observation is vital for an understanding of the Swedish government's SDU initiative in April 1948. The initiative can only be fully explained against this domestic background of an unusual lack of foreign policy consensus – or of loyalty towards the policy of the government.

The SDU idea was brought to the fore by the dramatic international events during the spring of 1948. The governments in Stockholm and Oslo reacted differently to the escalation of international tension. The Swedes were determined to stick to a policy of neutrality, while the Norwegians turned to Washington for protection. Fearing the prospect of a rift in Scandinavian security policies, Undén made an inventory of his policy options. He presented his findings in a memorandum of April 2. One of the possible lines of action he scrutinised was entering into a neutral

Scandinavian Defence Union. The idea was, he wrote, worth considering, but had two major disadvantages. Firstly, as the military forces of the neighbouring countries were weak, a union would not bring any advantage for Sweden from the military point of view. Secondly, the Norwegians would not accept the idea of a union based on neutrality. The conclusion was that Sweden should continue her traditional policy of neutrality.[12]

This was Undén's assessment in the beginning of April. He presented it to his colleagues in the government who in turn approved it. A few days later it was also presented to the Social Democratic Party Executive and was once again accepted. Thereby the entire Government and the party leadership had supported the memorandum in which the idea of a Scandinavian Defence Union had been rejected. Nevertheless, a few weeks later, on 22 April, the idea of a Scandinavian Defence Union was presented to the Foreign Policy Committee of the Riksdag, where it was favourably received.

The obvious question, therefore, is: why did the government present a proposal which had been unanimously rejected by itself and the party leadership?

The answer, it seems, must be found on the domestic scene. The presentation of Undén's memorandum to the government and the Party Executive was followed by a series of foreign policy speeches by Undén himself and other prominent members of government. The purpose of these appearances was evidently to rally public support behind a continuation of the policy of neutrality. In that respect, however, they were a complete failure. Leading liberal and conservative newspapers reacted with disapproval. Words like "unrealistic", "isolationism" and "blindness" were frequently used. Diplomats displayed similar reactions.[13]

At a time when new parliamentary elections were approaching within a few months, the prospect of a deep general controversy on Swedish foreign policy must have been very inconvenient. The problem was that the opposition might rally behind the SDU concept which had a substantial backing among important factions of the press. In this situation the Social Democratic Party had an obvious self-interest in reaffirming its grip on the foreign policy debate. By presenting the SDU idea to representatives of the opposition parties, the party regained control. If the opposition turned the idea down, it could be shelved with little regret on the side of the government. If, however, the idea was accepted, the opposition had to line up behind the policy of the government and order was restored.

To sum up: the Swedish Foreign Minister and the government had a clear conception of the policy they wished to pursue. Facing considerable domestic opposition, however, they found it opportune to present an alternative policy line. Thus, at the outset the SDU idea was not regarded as a realistic, or even desirable, project, but as a means of diverting criticism away from the policy of the government in order to end up with the traditional neutrality formula again.

This conclusion does not rule out the fact that the government came to view the SDU project in a different light during the actual process of negotiation. In January 1949 the Swedish government agreed to the solidarity defence clauses coming into force from the date of signature of a mutual treaty. The argument until now had been to wait for Norway and Denmark to rearm to a level relatively equal to that of the Swedish armed forces before granting this concession. This new move was clearly designed to evade blame for the expected failure of the project. However, at the same time the Swedish government, or at least its Prime Minister Tage Erlander, began to adopt a more positive attitude towards the whole SDU idea. In a diary entry of 9 January he asked himself whether he at heart really wanted the negotiations to succeed. Would he not rather prefer a breakdown because of the Norwegian intransigence?[14] There was no easy answer to that question, he wrote. But after all and in spite of the prospect of a continuous tug of war with the Norwegians, he hoped the SDU idea would be realised. Other reflections in his diary show that Tage Erlander expected a union to increase Sweden's international – as well as his own domestic – prestige.[15] Thus, the tactical considerations behind launching the initiative did not prevent a more genuine sympathy for the idea to materialise during the phase of negotiations.

Security Policy and Social Democracy in Denmark 1948-49

Among Scandinavian historians it is generally accepted that Denmark was the country most genuinely striving to achieve a Scandinavian Defence Union. Whether such a defence union should be nonaligned following Swedish wishes or aligned with the West under some form as maintained by the Norwegians, was not crucial to the Danish Government, the dominant interpretation runs. As Nikolaj Petersen has stated it: Denmark would have accepted any solution which Norway and Sweden would have been able to agree upon. What really mattered to Denmark was to keep Scandinavia united. For that reason Denmark assumed the role of mediator between Norwegian and Swedish views[16].

Petersen's conclusion is accurate. Considerations for Scandinavian unity were paramount to the Danish Social Democratic Government. Had Sweden shown a greater disposition towards incorporating a Scandinavian Union into a wider Atlantic defence framework, Denmark would certainly not have obstructed such a solution. On the other hand, it should be stressed that the Social Democratic government tended to give a higher preference to a solution based on Swedish principles than actually emerges from Petersen's works. It should not be forgotten that the mediator-role was, to a large extent, conceived and celebrated by the Danish government itself, and that this image, true or not, served purposes of domestic policy. There is, at least, no reason to accept the claim uncritically, which the Swedish Foreign Minister, Undén, also refused to do. In September 1948 he confided to his diary that he was fed up with the Danish claims of playing the role of mediator as the Danish government had not at any time voiced a position differing in the least from the Swedish one[17].

If one takes a closer look at the Danish role during the intensive period of negotiations in January 1949, it is also quite difficult to accept the mediator-role at face value. In many ways the Danish government held the most radical views on how to realise a Scandinavian Defence Union. Already at Karlstad on 5 and 6 January, Premier Minister Hans Hedtoft was returning to a point which he had confidentially voiced to his Scandinavian colleagues several times during autumn: the road to follow was to erect a Scandinavian Defence Union as a 'fait accompli' and only afterwards to ask for American benediction and weapons. This position, which clearly contradicted an official Danish proposal from September 1948 to work for a unilateral American guarantee to a Scandinavian Defence Union, was further developed and strengthened by Hedtoft during the rest of January.[18]

To erect a Scandinavian Defence Union as an unsanctioned gesture was a drastic move which does not fit into the dominant view of Denmark being the mediator between Norwegian and Swedish points of view. Such a move ran contrary to the Norwegian strategy of maintaining Western Power backing for every step taken towards closer Scandinavian defence cooperation, and (albeit for different reasons) it was also too hazardous for the Swedish government to support. Hiding the existing differences in security policy outlook between the Scandinavian countries behind the fragile cement of a defence union quite understandably did not appeal to the Swedish government. On the premise that the Danish Social Democrats wanted a Scandinavian Union to be created at all costs, Hedtoft's plan made equal sense: a Scandinavian Union had to be a reality before Norway and Denmark received official invitations to join the Atlantic Pact. Otherwise it would never materialise.

Having said this, we shall turn away from the debate on the Danish mediator roll. Instead the following presentation will concentrate in more detail on the background and reasons for the Danish Social Democrats' attraction to a Scandinavian Defence Union. Part of this attraction, naturally, consisted of military-strategic and general security considerations.[19] It was the dominant view within Social Democratic circles, but also within the Government as a whole that Sweden was essential, in fact indispensable, for the defence of Scandinavia. In a traditional Second World War scenario (and the Danish experience with the German occupation in 1940 still constituted the decisive mental point of reference for most strategic thinking), Sweden was the only country in the late 1940's with a military strength and a proximity to Danish borders able to guarantee rapid military intervention in case of an attack on Denmark. Denmark's problem was her small size and her exposed border to Germany through which a major enemy, be it Russian or maybe once again German, would have easy access to Danish territory. The Danish government did not entertain much hope that any Western defence arrangement excluding Sweden would be able or willing to meet an attack on Denmark with immediate military intervention – a fear which, in fact, was proved justified by the first operational plans worked out within the NATO framework in the years to come[20].

Following this kind of reasoning – and leaving out the discussion of whether the Danish government and especially Prime Minister Hans Hedtoft had invested much too much faith in the capability of the Swedish Armed Forces – a Scandinavian Defence Union was considered strong enough also to function as an effective, preventive defence arrangement. A war against Scandinavia would be more than just a Sunday picnic. This view was further strengthened because the Danish government was inclined to share the fundamental position of the Swedish government that a Soviet attack on Scandinavia in any event would unleash a great war. The West would not let Scandinavia disappear into the Soviet empire without resistance.

A formal incorporation of a Scandinavian Defence Union into a Western defence framework was not ruled out by the Danish government. Swedish opposition to such an arrangement, however, rendered this option obsolete. But also within the Danish Social Democratic Party, a nonaligned Scandinavian Union was by far the preferred solution. A nonaligned Scandinavian Union was considered more flexible. By avoiding direct military entanglement in the East-West confrontation, pressure on Scandinavia was expected to diminish. There was even a belief that a nonaligned Scandinavia had a chance of escaping war in the case of conflict elsewhere in Europe. Finally, it was believed Scandinavia would retain a much better background for pursuing her traditional bridge-building and peace-keeping policies in the UN and elsewhere, if not directly attached to any of the power blocs.

Nikolaj Petersen has thoroughly analysed the importance of these strategic and general security policy aspects and considerations for shaping the Social Democratic government's attitude towards the different Scandinavian and Western options during the last half of 1948 and the first months of 1949[21]. As in Sweden, however, less emphasis has been dedicated to an analysis of this issue in the setting of domestic politics. This neglect is serious because in our view the Danish Social Democrats' preference for a Scandinavian Defence Union was equally, or even more so, motivated by general political preferences and by constraints of domestic politics as by military and strategic considerations. A striking example of this – among many others – is the way in which the Danish Government disregarded the recommendations of the Scandinavian Defence Committee in January 1949 and proceeded along lines which not even the Danish members of the Committee had recommended.

Nikolaj Petersen is not blind to the importance of these factors. He also concludes that one of the reasons why Danish Social Democrats moved closer to the Swedish position during January 1949 was the higher political identification with this position compared to an Atlantic solution[22]. In her analysis of the attitudes of the Nordic Social Democratic Parties' attitudes to security policy in the post war period, the Swedish historian Kersti Blidberg has also maintained that the Danish Social Democratic party was the most eager to achieve a Scandinavian Defence Union. According to her, a positive outcome of the Scandinavian defence negotiations functioned both as a means to obtain a higher degree of security and as a goal in itself with much more far-reaching perspectives for inter-Scandinavian cooperation[23].

Accepting this conclusion, the question immediately arises: why was that so? What generated this political preference for Scandinavia? So far historians have only dealt with these questions superficially. In order to answer them a complex research strategy is needed. Such a strategy must include a profound appraisal of Social Democratic post-war politics with attention both being dedicated to its ideological and its political economy context. The findings produced through this analytical strategy should then again be linked and evaluated in relation to the Social Democratic Party's overall position within the power structure of the Danish political system. Within such an interpretative framework the party's attitudes to the proposed Scandinavian Defence Union not only dissolve into something much more than well-defined and conventional reactions towards a strict security policy initiative. It also holds the key to explain the high political preference for a Scandinavian solution.

Here we shall limit ourselves to present two of the major political incentives stimulating Social Democratic interest in a Scandinavian defence union. The first, being of a predominantly ideological nature, may be termed the "Third Way Priority" or the "Scandinavian Model Priority", while the second, based on a power structure analysis, may be labelled the "Squeeze of Domestic Politics".

Already during the war the Social Democratic Party made it clear that Denmark had to initiate much closer cooperation with the rest of Scandinavia when peace had been restored.[24] Cooperation, thus, had not to centre exclusively on economic cooperation, but must be extended also to include broader political issues, as well as foreign policy. Nothing much came out of these plans when the war ended, however. The Soviet Union met all attempts of more formal Scandinavian cooperation with severe distrust. Denmark for her part was very vulnerable to Soviet pressure during this period. Firstly, because Soviet support was essential to the Danish desire to be accepted into the allied camp as symbolised by an invitation to join the founding conference of the UN in San Francisco. Secondly, because Soviet troops actually occupied the Danish island of Bornholm in the Baltic, until the spring of 1946. For these reasons there was a general consensus within the Danish political system not to provoke the Soviet Union unnecessarily. This effectively contributed to the shelving of all Scandinavian visions for the time being within the Danish Social Democratic Party.

The escalation of the Cold War (and the Soviet withdrawal from Bornholm), however, brought them rather quickly out into the open again. The impotence of the UN was soon evident to everyone, and the foreign policy reaction of all three Scandinavian countries to that fact was to opt for a non-bloc foreign policy orientation. The non-bloc policy, as a consequence, fuelled endeavours to promote Scandinavian cooperation in a wide range of cultural, political and economic areas.

The drive behind Scandinavian unity did not only stem from Social Democratic quarters. Especially in Denmark, Scandinavianism was a strong force within most of the political spectrum. The reasoning behind the need for closer Scandinavian cooperation was generally ascribed to the Danish war-time experience. It was felt Scandinavia should never again be divided. It was a common belief that the Scandinavian people were so homogeneous and linked by history, culture and language that it was only logical to unite as much as possible.

The Social Democrats, however, added a more specific Social Democratic tone to the reasoning behind this folkloric recommendation. Both Norway and Sweden had Social Democratic majority (or near-majority) governments, whereas the Danish Social Democrats were only able to regain governmental power in October 1947 (and then only as a quite fragile minority government). Because of the strength of the labour movement in the other two Scandinavian countries, Danish Social Democrats viewed Scandinavian cooperation as a road to the desirable 'third way' between Capitalism and Communism. Prime Minister Hans Hedtoft described this vision in a speech in May, 1948:

> "The consequence of political democracy is economic democracy. That is what we are fighting for today. Everyone can see that the system of private capitalism after this war has come to an irrevocable end and must be substituted by other forms of society. It is a bit general, but in this respect I think one can be allowed to say that the world of today is characterized by the struggle between two systems: American capitalism and Soviet coerced collectivization. The Scan-

dinavian Social Democratic Labour Movement does not accept neither."[25]

It was assumptions like this, which can be discerned behind expressions like "Our hearts are neither in Moscow nor Washington". Thus, the will to steer free of Western bloc initiatives did not only originate in a limited security policy analysis, but was also based on political preferences of a wider scope. Social Democratic Scandinavia was the promising laboratory for the new ideas of a planned economy based on demand management and an active fiscal policy. The aim was to industrialise Danish society and to avoid the cyclical fluctuations inherent in liberal capitalism. The fear was a return to the crisis-ridden societies of the 1930s which, according to Social Democratic thinking, had paved the way for Nazism.

These ideas were most clearly exemplified in the ambitious post-war programme, "The future of Denmark". In the introduction of this programme, one reads:

> "Since 1939 the world has escaped the threat of Nazism. Still functioning, however, is an economic system, which was not capable of resolving the pre-war problems. This system like the war has brought upon humanity sweat and tears, when crisis, misery and unemployment reigned ("for alvor svang pisken"). These cyclical crises greatly influenced the political convulsions of the thirties threatening Democracy and Peace and eventually giving way to Nazism and War. Before this system has been changed we have not cleared the mess neither at the top nor at the bottom. The War and the war economy have shaken this system radically. Now it must never return. It was not capable of resolving the pre-war problems, neither will it be able to meet those of the post-war period. It will be a source of more crises, more unemployment – maybe even of more Nazism and war."[26]

Even allowing for a certain amount of rhetoric and propaganda and without running the danger of overemphasising the theoretic consistency of Danish Social Democratic thinking (Danish Social Democrats were generally more pragmatic than theory minded), there cannot be any doubt that Danish Social Democrats of the first post war period were greatly committed to the ideas of reforming capitalism through a planned economy and active conjunctural policies. To Danish Social Democrats Scandinavia looked liked the perfect playground for such experiments. Therefore, the Scandinavian Defence Union was an important issue. It nourished the hopes of becoming "a lever for much wider Scandinavian cooperation", as one prominent leader, Julius Bomholt, expressed it[27].

Membership in an Atlantic organisation, on the other hand, did not promise such political advantages. To the contrary, Denmark ran the risk of joining a club in which demands for military rearmament and unbridled capitalism threatened the welfare of the working class. For reasons of both domestic and international character, these worries were rarely expressed so blatantly. But their presence is clearly demonstrated in an article written by the young Minister of Trade (and architect of "The Future of Denmark" programme), Jens Otto Krag, for the foreign policy magazine, "Fremtiden". His article was written in March 1949 when it was clear that the plans for a Scandinavian Defence Union had collapsed, and the Social Democratic Party had consequently decided to support Danish membership in NATO. It reads as follows:

> "One thing is extremely important: The Atlantic Pact must never be a pact of reaction. The Member states must have the will and economic strength to foster social progress. They must at all costs try to avoid a capitalist depression. If such an occurrence is not prevented, political conditions and propaganda will be favourable to the Communists. A conjunctural economy must be created. Intensive cooperation among the countries and great visions for the economic policy of the US will be required to achieve this. The liberal doctrines must be buried in the same museum, where the principles of isolated neutrality are now resting."[28]

As indicated by Krag, Social Democratic fears about joining the Atlantic Pact were not only rooted in traditional anti-militarism or strict considerations of security policy, but were of a much broader political nature. Similarly the attraction of a Scandinavian Defence Union – representing, so to speak, the opposite side of the coin – was based on preferences of a very broad political nature.

However, when Prime Minister Hans Hedtoft during the Karlstad-negotiations stressed that the SDU question "is of vital importance to the Danish Labour Movement", the word 'vital' probably did not only refer to the importance of Scandinavian cooperation as a catalyst for Social Democratic "third way-perspectives". More basically it also reflected the difficult situation of the government and of the Social Democratic Party on the domestic political scene[29]. Scandinavian cooperation was not only seen as an instrument to implement Social Democratic visions and policies in Scandinavia in a wider sense, but was clearly also perceived as a remedy to improve the power base of the Social Democrats within Denmark itself. Or in other words to untighten the "squeeze of domestic politics". It is very important to bear this perspective in mind when trying to explain why Danish Social Democrats seemed to invest much more faith and energy in Scandinavian cooperation than their Norwegian and Swedish colleagues.

As already mentioned, the Danish Social Democrats did not have the same political backing as their sister-parties in Norway and Sweden. Unlike the situation in these countries, Danish Social Democrats never gained an absolute majority at any parliamentary election. At the first election after the war the Social Democratic Party faced heavy defeat as the consequence of Communist success. Part of the loss was recovered in the 1947 election, but although the party took over government responsibility from the liberal party, its room for manoeuvring was precarious.

The problem was that the government needed support from both the Communist Party and the left-liberal Radical Party or the support of the liberal party, Venstre. Normally the Radical Party functioned as a coalition party. On questions of security policy, however, the Radical Party was more pacifist and neutralist in inclination than were the Social Democrats. For a long time the Radicals did not even know which position to take on the Scandinavian Defence Union issue. Not until these plans had actually foundered and it was faced with the threat of the much worse perspective of Danish membership of an Atlantic Pact, did the party come out in support of a Scandinavian Union. On matters of security policy, therefore, the Social Democrats had to reach an agreement with the two traditional bourgeois parties, Venstre and the Conservative Party. Cooperation with the Communists was, of course, ruled out in this area. The overall complexity of this political landscape was responsible for much of the specific flavour of the security policy discussions in Denmark during 1948-49.

Problems were not less intricate in other areas. In terms of economic policy the parliamentary situation did not allow much room for a planned stimulation of the process of industrialisation or for conducting expansive fiscal policies along the lines presented in "The Future of Denmark". The coalition partner, the Radical Party, did not share the visions of planning. As the representative of the small-holders, it shared some of the economic and social policies of the Social Democrats, but planning was certainly not among them. The idea of planned industrialisation was even more detested by Venstre, the representative of medium- and largesize agricultural interests. Even among the Conservatives it was not possible to obtain support for a policy of directing investments towards the industrial sector. Danish industry was overwhelmingly home-market oriented and relied nearly exclusively on self-financing. State-sponsored investment schemes held no appeal.

However, the real problem for a Social Democratic economic policy was not parliamentary, but linked to the productive structure of the Danish economy (which parliament, of course, reflected). It was the role and power of the highly developed Danish agricultural sector that proved the biggest hindrance to Social Democratic economic ambitions. Agriculture was Denmark's prime exporter, responsible for more than 70% of total exports in the late 1940's. In a period of chronic foreign currency problems this control of exports gave agriculture tremendous power within the Danish economy. This position was reinforced by the well organised structure of agricultural pressure groups. The organisational system was so elaborate that it was an official secret that even the Ministry of Agriculture was run by these pressure groups.[30]

The Social Democratic minority government found it extremely difficult to assert itself in the face of such a system. Confrontation with Venstre and the agricultural pressure groups was constant and covered all conceivable angles of economic policy making: planning for reception of Marshall aid, discussions on abolition of wartime restrictions, the setting up of state financed and controlled investment schemes for industry, trade policy, and especially the important trade negotiations with the United Kingdom, along with many others.[31]

The outcome of these confrontations normally placed the Social Democrats on the losing side. The party was forced to lead an economic policy which not only had an unsatisfactory ad hoc character, but which also failed in most of its Social Democratic objectives. Against this background it is hardly surprising that the party viewed intensified Scandinavian cooperation as a means of bolstering Social Democratic influence and power in Denmark. A successful completion of a Scandinavian Defence Union would be the first step to closer political and economic cooperation. It would be an incentive to reach a positive result on the proposed Scandinavian Customs Union and, were this to happen, the way would really be cleared for more binding cooperation, maybe even with a federal scope.

Denmark's inclusion in a strong Social Democratic framework on a Scandinavian basis, thus, would stimulate the "third way perspective" and in the process, by exploiting the strength of the labour movement of a combined Scandinavia, also promise to release Danish Social Democrats from the frustrating "domestic politics-squeeze". These were not the only considerations dictating the attitudes of the Danish Social Democrats towards the security choices of 1948-49. But they are very important for understanding how and why government and party were able to disregard, if not directly oppose, any serious and open discussion on the Atlantic perspective as long as the Scandinavian option was still an option. Only when Norway 'defected' and Denmark was forced into the choice between "two evils" – as Julius Bomholt expressed it – did the Social Democrats turn to NATO as a lesser evil than isolated neutrality.[32]

As demonstrated the Scandinavian defence union negotiations had a significance well beyond the security policy perspective. In Hedtoft's own words, their collapse represented his "greatest political defeat". This defeat, however, did not create internal divisions within the party, not even when the party leadership shortly afterwards had to recommend Danish

Security Policy and Domestic Politics in Scandinavia 1948-49

membership in NATO. Compared to the present day problems of securing a firm backing behind the Social Democratic Party's official European policy, the party in 1949 remained loyal to the recommendations of its leaders, even if the recommendation to join NATO was met with uncertainty and scepticism.

Notes

1. Udenrigsministeriet (ed.): *Dansk sikkerhedspolitik 1948-1966*, vol. I (presentation), vol. II (sources), Copenhagen 1968 and Magne Skodvin: *Norden eller NATO. Utrikesdepartementet og alliansespørsmålet 1947-1949*, Oslo 1971. The Norwegian Foreign Minister at the time Halvard Lange has also published his own account of the events: *Norges vei til NATO*, Oslo 1966 and the Swedish Prime Minister Tage Erlander dedicates much attention to the event in his memoirs, see *Tage Erlander 1940-1949*, Stockholm 1973 p. 362-401.
2. Magne Skodvin: op. cit.; Knut Einar Eriksen: *DNA og NATO. En redegjørelse for debatten og vedtakene i Det norske Arbeiderparti 1948-49*, Oslo 1972; Morten Udgaard: *Great Power Politics and Norwegian Foreign Policy. A Study of Norway's Foreign Relations November 1940-February 1948*, Oslo 1973; Geir Lundestad: *Scandinavia and the Cold War 1945-1949*, Oslo & New York 1980; Olav Riste: "Was 1949 a Turning-Point? Norway and the Western Powers 1947-1950", in O. Riste (ed.): *Western Security: The Formative Years. European and Atlantic Defence 1947-1953*, Oslo 1985, and Helge Pharo: "Scandinavia and the Cold War: An Overview", in D. Reynolds (ed.): *Origins of the Cold War in Europe*, Yale 1994.
3. Krister Wahlbäck: "Norden och blockuppdelningen 1948-49", in *Internationella Studier*, 1973 (2); "USA i Skandinavien 1948-49", in *Internationella Studier*, 1976 (5) and 1977 (7); and Yngve Möller: *Östen Undén. En biografi*, Stockholm 1991. Nikolaj Petersen's many articles on Danish security policy in 1948-49 include a.o. the following: "Optionsproblematikken i dansk sikkerhedspolitik 1948-49", in A. Amstrup and I. Faurby (eds.): *Studier i dansk udenrigspolitik*, Aarhus 1978; "Danish and Norwegian Alliance Policies 1948-49. A Comparative Analysis", in *Cooperation and Conflict*, vol. 14, 1979; "Storbritannien, USA og skandinavisk forsvar 1945-1949", in *Historie*, ny række XIV (1) 1981, and "Atlantpagten eller Norden? Den danske alliancebeslutning 1949", in C. Due-Nielsen, J.P. Noack & N. Petersen (eds.): *Danmark, Norden og NATO 1948-1962*, Copenhagen 1991. See also Mary Dau: *Danmark og Sovjetunionen 1944-1949*, Copenhagen 1969.
4. Kersti Blidberg: "Just Good Friends. Nordic Social Democracy and Security Policy 1945-1950", in *Forsvarsstudier*, no. 5 Oslo 1987; Gerard Aalders: *Swedish Neutrality and the Cold War 1945-1949*, Ph.D.-disertation, Nijmegen (NL) 1989, and "The Failure of the Scandinavian Defence Union, 1948-49", in *Scandinavian Journal of History*, vol. 15(2) 1990.
5. Based on access to Danish and Swedish archives Thorsten B. Olesen has recently presented a comparative analysis of the three Scandinavian countries' attitudes and policies in relation to the Scandinavian Defence Union intermezzo, see Thorsten B. Olesen: "Brødrefolk, men ikke våbenbrødre – Diskussionerne om et skandinavisk forsvarsforbund 1948-49", in Thorsten B. Olesen et al. (eds.): "De nordiske Fællesskaber. Myte og realitet i det nordiske samarbejde", *Den jyske Historiker*, vol. 69-70, p. 151-178, 1994 (T. B. Olesen 1994 (1)).

6. The following chapter is based on Karl Molin: *Omstridd neutralitet. Experternas kritikk av svensk utrikespolitik 1948-1950* ("Disputed Neutrality. The Experts' Criticism of Swedish Foreign Policy 1948-1950") Stockholm 1991, where all the relevant references can be found.
7. *Stockholms Tidningen*, 24.4.1948.
8. This critical atmosphere is mirrored in a number of private diaries. Especially rewarding is Sven Grafström: *Anteckningar 1938-1944, 1945-1954*, edited by Stig Ekman, Stockhom 1989. See also Helge Jung's diary in *Helge Jung's Archive*, Krigsarkivet (The Armed Forces Archive), Stockholm; excerpts from Tage Erlander's diary, *Tage Erlander's Archive*, vol. F VIII:1, Arbetarrörelsens Arkiv och Bibliotek (ARAB) (The Labour Movement's Archive and Library) Stockholm; Östen Undén's diary, *Östen Unden's Archive*, Kungliga Biblioteket, (The Royal Library), Stockholm. Undén's diary will be published in 1996.
9. See the newspapers, *Ny Tid*, 12.2.1948; *Göteborgs Handels och Sjöfartstidning*, 12.3.1948, and *Stockholms-Tidningen*, 13.3.1948. Also Alf W. Johansson: *Herbert Tingsten och kalla kriget*, Stockholm 1995, p. 191f.
10. K. Molin (1991): op. cit., pp. 70 ff.
11. Divergences between Undén's policy and Swedish diplomats' arguments were observed and reported by Western diplomats, see for example: memo C.E. Rogers 23.7. 1948, 858.00/7-2348, *National Archives and Record Office*, Washington (D.C.) (NARS). – For an instance of Swedish diplomats' predicting a new foreign policy, see memo C. E. Rogers 17/11 1948, 758.00/11-1748 and also memo by John D. Hickerson 14.2. 1949, 840.20/2-1449, both in NARS. – The conversation between the American Ambassador to Stockholm and the Swedish Supreme Commander is reported in Sth to Secr of State, 8.11. 1948 758.00/11-848; Sth to Secr of State 12.11. 1948, 758.00/11-1248; Sth to Secr of State 8.12. 1948, 758.00/12-848, all in NARS. – The Supreme Commander's version is found in Jung's diary, op. cit., 6.11. 1948 – For further references, see K. Molin (1991): op. cit, chapter 4.
12. Memo by Östen Undén, 2.4. 1948, fasc. XXIII, vol. 982, HP 20 D, *UD's Arkiv*, Riksarkivet (The Foreign Ministry's Archive at the National Archive) Stockholm.
13. References to Undén's memo and to newspaper comments on the Cabinet's foreign policy speeches are found in K. Molin (1991): op. cit., chapter 5.
14. Tage Erlander's diary, op. cit., 9.1.1949.
15. Tage Erlander's diary, op. cit., 4.1. and 9.1. 1949.
16. N. Petersen (1978): op. cit., p. 211
17. Unden's diary: op. cit., vol IV, 10.9.48.
18. I have developed this argument in detail in an unpublished working-paper, see the chapter, "The Scandinavian Defence Union Plans" in Thorsten B. Olesen: *The Lesser Evil. The Danish Social Democratic Party and the Decision to Join the Atlantic Pact 1948-49*, part I, Dept. of History, University of Aarhus, March 1993. See also T. B. Olesen (1994(1)): op. cit., p. 161 and 166 f..
19. The following argument I have developed in T.B. Olesen (1993): op. cit., part III, in the chapters, "The Military-Strategic Dimension" and "The Non-Bloc Perspective". See also T.B. Olesen (1994 (1)): op. cit., p. 160 f.
20. Poul Villaume: *Allieret med forbehold. Danmark, Nato og den kolde krig. En studie i dansk sikkerhedspolitik 1949-1961*, Copenhagen 1995, p. 124 ff.
21. See N.Petersen (1978): op. cit.; and (1991) : op. cit.
22. N.Petersen (1978): op. cit., p. 231.
23. K.Blidberg (1987): op. cit., p. 61 f.
24. The presentation here is based on the chapter, "The Scandinavian Model Priority", in T. B. Olesen (1993), part III. See also T.B. Olesen (1994(1)): op. cit., p.

162, and T. B. Olesen: "Jagten på et sikkerhedspolitisk ståsted. Socialdemokratiets holdninger til sikkerhedspolitikken 1945-1948", in Birgit Nüchel Thomsen (ed.): *Temaer og brændpunkter i dansk politik efter 1945*, Copenhagen 1994, p. 15-54 (T.B. Olesen 1994(2)).
25. *Hans Hedtoft's Archive*, at Arbejderbevægelsens Bibliotek og Arkiv (ABA) (The Labour Movement's Library and Archive) Copenhagen, box. 3, file 14.
26. *Fremtidens Danmark*, (programme of the Danish Social Democratic Party) Copenhagen 1945, p. 4.
27. *Minutes of the Social Democratic Parliamentary Group*, 19.1.1949, at Folketinget's Bibliotek (the Library of the Danish Parliament) Copenhagen.
28. J.O. Krag: "Betragtninger om den atlantiske fredspagt", in *Fremtiden*, no. 4, 1949, p. 4 f.
29. Minutes from the Karlstad meeting, in *Hedtoft's Archive*, box 42, file 1, p. 1. The following presentation is based on the chapter, "The Squeeze of Domestic Politics", in T.B. Olesen (1993): op. cit., part III. See also T.B. Olesen (1994 (1)): op. cit., p. 163 f..
30. See article by F. Just & T. B. Olesen in this book.
31. The most profound treatment of the political economy problems of the Danish Social Democratic Party in the early Post War period is given by Vibeke Sørensen (1987): *Social Democratic Government in Denmark Under the Marshall Plan 1947-1950*, u.publ. PhD thesis, EUI, Firenze. See also Vibeke Sørensen's contribution within this book; Henrik Søborg: *Socialdemokratiet og staten. Socialdemokratiets økonomiske politik 1945-1972*, Copenhagen 1983, and Flemming Just: "Planøkonomi eller liberalisme. Staten og erhvervspolitikken i de første efterkrigsår", in Birgit Nüchel Thomsen (1994): op. cit., p. 55-71.
32. Minutes of the Social Democratic Parliamentary Group: op. cit., 24.2.1949.

The Functioning of the European Payments Union (EPU) 1950-1958[1]

By Monika Dickhaus

The political and economic situation created by World War II made the construction of a new international monetary system necessary. A first step towards this was a UN-conference held in Bretton Woods in 1944 at which it was agreed to establish the International Monetary Fund (IMF). The idea behind this new institution was that following a short transition period the IMF would have to back and monitor a multilateral monetary system based on convertibility and fixed but adjustable exchange rates. It soon became obvious, however, that this goal could not be achieved as easily as had been envisaged. The problems of European reconstruction were too great and the means of the IMF too limited.[2] With the launching of the Marshall Plan scheme in 1947 the USA, therefore, adopted a regional approach. As a consequence US policy now focussed on European reconstruction and European viability based on cooperation, rather than the immediate establishment of a worldwide multilateral system. In the monetary field this lead to the conclusion of several Intra-European Payments Agreements (IEPAs), and in 1950 a European soft currency bloc, the European Payments Union (EPU), was established. This system was in operation until December 1958. Only then – after a transition period of 13 years – was convertibility declared for the major European currencies and the EPU dissolved. Thus, in 1958, the age of Bretton Woods could finally be properly initiated.

This article will deal with European monetary cooperation. It will start by giving a brief sketch of the European payments situation of 1947 and by considering the first efforts to establish a European payments system. Then, it will examine the history of the EPU. Firstly, the importance of the new organisation for European trade and the European economies in general will be highlighted by analysing its performance during the period of the Korean War. Secondly, attention will concentrate on the modifications of the EPU agreed upon in 1954 and 1955. As a consequence of these modifications the European soft currency bloc hardened, and gradually approached the convertibility threshold. Finally, the article will close with an exposé of the limits and shortcomings of the EPU system in its last years of existence.

* * *

The postwar period was characterised by a general dollar scarcity, the so-called "Dollar Gap". War-torn European countries needed capital goods, raw materials and food stuffs for reconstruction purposes. Since neither Germany (previously an exporter of capital goods) nor Eastern Europe (previously a provider of food stuffs) were able to supply these commodities, imports from North America, the Dollar Area, were in high demand. This demand, however, could not be met because of the dollar shortage in Europe: European monetary reserves were run down as a consequence of the war and, in addition, the low level of European competitiveness made it difficult to earn dollars by exporting. Dollars, thus, had to be rationed by applying quantitative trade restrictions as well as foreign exchange controls.

In intra-European trade, quantitative restrictions and foreign exchange controls were also implemented. Since the war a network of bilateral trade and payments agreements, most allowing for a certain level of overdrafts, had been established. These overdrafts had provided greater flexibility in intra-European trade, and had helped to secure trade growth in the wake of the war. By 1947, however, this system was close to collapse. Bilateral credits were exhausted, and the creditors were no longer willing to augment them. It was feared that these credits would never be paid back and, thus, never produce the foreign exchange originally anticipated.[3] As a consequence, even stricter controls on exports and imports were imminent, bringing with them stagnation – if not outright decline – in intra-European trade. Such a development could only boost demand for dollar goods and thereby accentuate the Dollar Gap, which ultimately would be a threat to the whole process of European reconstruction.

The Marshall Plan mitigated this situation. Additional dollars were provided by the USA on the premise that the (West)European countries would cooperate in solving the structural economic problems facing their countries. The view held by the American Administration was that dollar aid could only be effectively dispersed if the Europeans would agree to approach the problems in a united way. In an effort to meet American demands sixteen Western European states participated in the Organisation for European Economic Cooperation (OEEC), set up in the spring of 1948. The task of the organisation was to coordinate allocation of Marshall aid, and also to try to find a remedy to the intra-European payments problems. A first result of the latter endeavour was the conclusion of an Intra-European Payments Agreement (IEPA) for the period 1947/48. Five countries agreed to offset mutual deficits in a 'closed circuit'.[4] But as 'closed circuits' hardly existed in the real world, this agreement proved rather obsolete.[5]

A second IEPA which was concluded for the period 1948/49 also turned out to be problematic. The newly introduced bilateral credit obligations were based on forecasted balances of payments which, of course, had a tendency to be both arbitrary and inaccurate. Furthermore, some complained that the construction of this IEPA was advantageous for debtors and thus provided the 'wrong' incentives: the linking of this IEPA to Marshall aid rewarded a deficit and not an equilibrated balance of payments.[6] Finally, it must be pointed out that this IEPA provided bilateral credit only and was therefore not very flexible. However, when an attempt was made to remedy this defect with a third IEPA (1949/50), fierce opposition surfaced. It was feared that a multilateralisation of this system might lead to a loss of gold or dollars.[7]

In light of the difficulties with the IEPAs, it was obvious by the autumn of 1949 that a new attack on the payments problem was needed. This need became even more urgent as the American Marshall Plan supervisors in the Economic Cooperation Administration (ECA) were pressing strongly for trade liberalisation which would need the backing of a working payments system.[8] Therefore, in December 1949, the ECA proposed an outright payments union between the OEEC countries. After lengthy and complicated negotiations dealing with delicate topics such as the burden-sharing between creditors and debtors, the role of the pound sterling, the amount of credit and the powers of a supervisory board, the European Payments Union (EPU) finally started to operate in the summer of 1950.[9] The successful conclusion of a payments accord spurred the OEEC in August of the same year to approve a trade liberalisation scheme stipulating the removal of quantitative restrictions from 60 per cent of private trade.

The accord on the EPU was a big step forward. Firstly, it introduced a European unit of account (u/a)[10] and by this means full transferability of all European currencies was secured. This full transferability made it futile to discriminate against a specific European partner for monetary reasons. Secondly, credit was made available automatically via the EPU. A creditor to the EPU could not demand gold or dollars for his entire surplus, but had to grant a certain percentage of his surplus as a credit to the EPU. The EPU passed this credit on to the debtor. Of course the credit available was not unlimited, but every country had a quota which was calculated as 15 per cent of its trade turnover. Of this quota the debtor was entitled to draw 60 per cent in credit while being obliged to pay 40 per cent in gold. In turn, the creditor was obliged to give 60 per cent in credit, receiving only 40 per cent in gold. With the intention of encouraging a policy aimed at a correction of balance of payments deficits, an incentive system was built into the EPU: the greater the deficit, the higher the percentage of gold to be paid to the EPU.[11]

The EPU system was directed by a Managing Board comprising seven ordinary members. It had the power to make decisions and recommend policies by majority vote, but only if these were in accordance with the those of the OEEC Council. As decisions by the latter forum required unanimity, the OEEC Council could in fact block Managing Board directives.

Right from the outset, in the summer of 1950, the EPU had the opportunity to prove its usefulness. The outbreak of the Korean War lead to a run on raw materials increasing their prices and altering the overall terms of trade.[12] This caused British and French surpluses, and heavy deficits in the Federal Republic of Germany (FRG), the Netherlands and Denmark. Germany's quota was nearly exhausted by October.[13] If special assistance were not to be provided, Germany would have been compelled to pay its deficits fully in gold, deflate its economy, renounce its recently introduced trade liberalisation or leave the Union. This would have had disastrous effects for the EPU, for the OEEC's trade liberalisation scheme, for the FRG and for other European countries depending on the German market.

The solution of this debtor crisis was largely left to the EPU since the US maintained that the Managing Board should not rely on them to take the lead.[14] The German crisis was discussed at the first meeting of the Managing Board. While several members blamed the German policy as being thoughtless or even reckless, others wanted to allow for special assistance to Germany. Finally, it was decided to send an expert mission to the FRG. On the return from their mission, Per Jacobsson and Alec Cairncross[15] recommended a further credit, conditional on the working out of a concise and acceptable German programme. This condition was accepted by the FRG and a programme was submitted to the EPU at the end of November 1950. It listed the measures the FRG would take to correct the disequilibrium, placing heavy emphasis on credit policy while maintaining its trade liberalisation policy.[16] With the recommendation of the Managing Board this programme was forwarded to the OEEC Council, and in December a credit of 120 million u/a was granted to the FRG.

Upon the receipt of the credit the FRG was to enforce the listed measures. Already in October the discount rate had been raised from 4 to 6 per cent. Furthermore, credit restrictions had been applied and export subsidies were being contemplated. Yet, in January 1951 the situation deteriorated still further, and it became clear that the applied measures had not been strong enough to effect a positive change in the German balance of payments in time.[17] When the special credit was exhausted and fresh credit was not forthcoming, the FRG was forced to de-liberalise. Import planning followed which, together with a return of more stable world market conditions, helped Germany to overcome her balance of payments crisis.[18]

The German balance of payments crisis highlights the significance and importance of European monetary cooperation. First of all, it must be noted that the EPU, via its general credit system as well as its special assistance, had allowed a considerable increase in German imports. Such imports were essential for the rapidly growing German economy. Without them the German export capacity could not have been restored. It was already evident during the crisis that this export capacity was essential for Europe, and it became even clearer with the development of German surpluses after February 1951.

Secondly, the EPU credits prevented the collapse of exports from other European countries to Germany. This was of particular importance to countries like the Netherlands and Denmark. Being debtor nations themselves in the EPU framework, they were particularly keen to export to the FRG. This may also have been the reason why Denmark in the end did not disapprove of the recommendations of the Managing Board in the OEEC Council, despite serious reservations about the principles guiding this policy. The Danish representative stated that "in his opinion, by accepting the principles that Germany should not go back on her liberalisation measures, the Council was endorsing a dangerous concept, namely that the reduction of imports should be brought about by credit restrictions rather than by reimposition of quantitative restrictions. As he had stated before credit restrictions might well lead to unemployment."[19] Whatever moved the Danish representative not to block the OEEC approval, the effects of such a policy are evident. When looking at the Dutch and Danish exports to Germany in the period concerned, it can be seen that these two countries profited considerably from the increase in German imports in the second half of 1950. By contrast, the effects of the German de-liberalisation were felt in the first, and more drastically in the second quarter of 1951. By the third quarter, however, the ebb had been reached since German exports were rising continuously thereby allowing a more generous handling of import planning.[20]

* * *

The EPU was originally intended to operate for a period of only two years, but its term was in fact renewed several times. However, it was precisely these renewals which allowed for alterations and modifications to be made in the operation of the organisation.

The period 1952-1955 witnessed production and productivity increases, European trade expansion, the closing of the Dollar Gap and the growth of foreign currency reserves, all while inflationary pressures were being eliminated. In the summer of 1952 the EPU was prolonged for another year. Its advantages were so obvious that the necessary compromises – be they also after lengthy negotiations – could be obtained.[21] In the summer of 1953 renewal was due again, but this time discussions on convertibility made the outcome more uncertain. The United Kingdom (UK) was contemplating whether or not to introduce convertibility of sterling into dollar which was incompatible with the EPU and which, if pursued, would have necessitated a British withdrawal.[22] Since such a withdrawal would have made the EPU's clearing mechanism less attractive, other members objected. While some preferred maintaining the EPU without any changes, others – mainly the creditors – favoured a gradual hardening of the EPU's payments terms as the way towards convertibility. Such a hardening could take the shape of a general rise in the gold/credit ratio or the introduction of more severe debt repayments conditions. This, however, was not acceptable to the UK and other debtors, and tense discussions ensued. The Scandinavian and British representatives argued that a hardening of conditions would cause a fundamental change in the functioning of the EPU. It would increase possibilities for earning gold or dollars via exports to European countries and thus reduce the incentive to reach equilibrium inside the EPU. They feared that this would prevent the reduction of persistent and extreme surpluses. In 1953 this was already a prominent issue since Belgium, Germany, Switzerland and the Netherlands were exceeding their quotas as creditors. In order to settle their surpluses they had to ask for 'rallonges', that is, a raising of their quota as creditors.

Discussions on this topic lasted for more than a year with no conclusion being reached. Only in the spring of 1954 was the deadlock broken when the UK finally showed itself willing to engage in a debt repayment/consolidation scheme. After lengthy negotiations, several bilateral agreements on debt repayments were then concluded during the summer of 1954. Furthermore, the EPU itself paid the creditors 130 million dollars out of its own assets. Finally, the gold/credit ratio was augmented from 40:60 to 50:50, the EPU's incentive structure was abolished and the quotas were raised in such a way that the changes in the gold/credit ratio did not result in a lowering of the credits made available by the EPU system.

In the summer of 1955 these modifications were carried one step further when negotiations on the EPU's renewal were again due. The hardening of the EPU was continued as it was agreed that the gold/credit ratio should be raised to 75:25. In addition, in the summer of 1955 a new accord, the so-called European Monetary Agreement was negotiated: since the declaration of convertibility and thus the dissolution of the EPU seemed near, a new system of European monetary cooperation, and above all a new credit system, was needed.

The hardening process is often singled out to demonstrate the flexibility of the EPU system and the capacity it provided for compromise. In addition, the continuity in membership and a strong sense of collegiality are also seen to have had a decisive impact on its ability to survive.[23] Although there may be some truth in these assertions, they are on the whole not very convincing. They tend to obscure the basic fact that it was rather the general improvement in economic conditions as well as the European pattern of trade which constituted the reasons for the acceptance of modifications to the EPU system.

As has been mentioned, the economic performance in Europe in the period concerned was satisfactory. An important indication of this performance was the continued increase in monetary reserves.[24] These reserves enlarged to a considerable extent the scope for compromise. This growth in monetary reserves can be attributed to a number of factors. Firstly, sufficient dollars were made available by the United States.[25] Although US military aid and other forms of foreign assistance to Europe were diminishing, dollars were still made available at a sufficient level.[26] Moreover, dollars were by now also distributed to other parts of the world and could thus be made available to Europe through trade with third areas.[27] In this sense, the EPU's capacity for compromise was to a large extent dependent on US foreign economic policy.

A second reason for the growth in foreign currency reserves must be attributed to the European pattern of trade. With the creation of the EPU, intra-OEEC trade was spurred on and with it an opportunity to save dollars was provided. In addition, capacity, productivity and competitiveness had increased inside Europe resulting in a minor need for dollar goods. Instead of dollars other currencies – especially the d-mark – were in rising demand. The EPU's credits, however, were close to exhaustion.[28] Therefore, another method of providing credits had to be found.

In the spring of 1954, at the peak of the debate on transforming the credit system, the FRG pressed for harder conditions. Although consensus on pursuing the break-up of the EPU could not be achieved among German decision makers[29], the FRG tried to convince the outside world of its will to withdraw from the EPU in the event that a hardening of conditions was not accepted.[30] This tactic seemed to work as there were growing concerns in other countries about a unilateral German declaration of convertibility followed by a withdrawal from the EPU. In 1954 a British official stated: "We should, I think, now take serious notice of the publicity activities of Dr. Erhard (the German Minister for Economic Affairs, M.D.) in connection with convertibility."[31]

It seemed clear that something had to be offered to the Germans. With the double aim of securing a German 'good-creditor-policy' as well as providing new credit inside the EPU system, the UK government was willing to accept a debt repayment/consolidation scheme.[32] Other countries, themselves interested in new credit, followed suit.[33] Thus, in the summer of 1954, debts of 858 million dollars were amortised and the creditors accepted new lending obligations of almost 1 billion dollars.[34]

In the spring of 1955 the situation was similar. While negotiations on the future credit system of the European Monetary Agreement were conducted, the creditor nations struck a hard bargain to raise the gold/credit ratio within the EPU to at least 75:25.[35] With Germany being quite de-

The Functioning of the European Payments Union

tached in her sympathies towards the new credit obligations of the European Monetary Agreement, debtors were forced to compromise and the move to 75:25 occurred without major opposition.[36] Although reserves in some countries such as the UK and Denmark were declining rapidly, the European soft currency bloc could be adapted to the new economic circumstances and to the wishes and needs of its creditors.[37] In this way the exhaustion of European credits was avoided.

* * *

In the years 1955-58, the European payments system began to suffer from heavy disequilibria. While Germany continued to accumulate great surpluses, the UK and France were suffering severe balance of payments problems (see graph).

Cumulative position of some EPU members 1950-59 in million units of account (u/a)

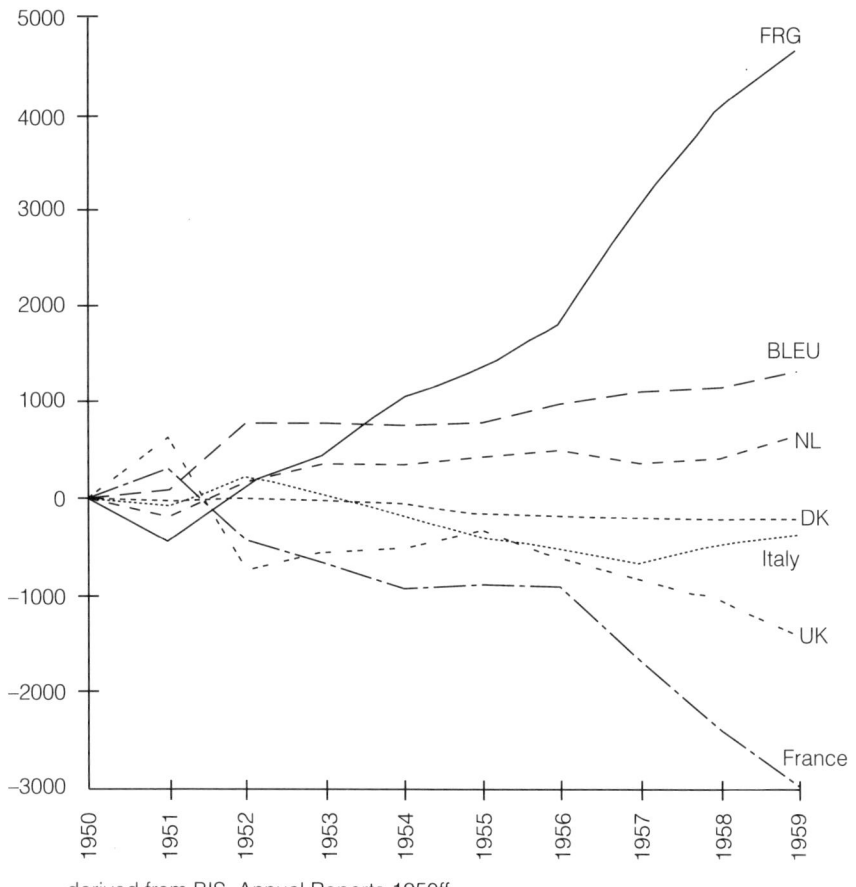

derived from BIS, Annual Reports 1950ff.

Germany had accumulated surpluses in the EPU from 1951 onwards, but in 1955 the situation became more precarious. There were several reasons for this. Firstly, the European framework was quite different from that which existed in 1953/54: the reserves of some countries were constantly falling while the FRG was becoming virtually the only creditor.[38] Secondly, the German Central Bank tried to combat an "overheated" economy with restrictive monetary policies which were bound to aggravate the situation. Thirdly, during the summer of 1956 the air was filled with rumours about devaluations and revaluations, and the consequence was heavy currency speculation. Only in September 1957 were effective steps were taken to remedy this situation. The British and German authorities concerted their bank rate moves and completely rejected the undertaking of any exchange rate adjustment whatsoever. In this way speculation was brought to a halt. However, no remedy for checking the German surpluses was found.

The disequilibria were, of course, discussed by the Managing Board of the EPU. In April 1956 the Board began to question – for the time being 'sympathetically' – the domestic orientation of German monetary policies.[39] Yet, its powers to interfere with German internal affairs were clearly limited: in May 1956 the German Central Bank Council raised the discount rate another point, a move which confirmed that internal stabilisation had top priority for the Central Bank.

It would be reasonable to have expected that these events would have lead to fiercer discussions inside the EPU and that such debates eventually would have influenced the negotiations on the EPU's renewal. This, however, was not the case. Although the Managing Board continued to call the German position into question, the renewal of the EPU accord went through in the summer of 1956 without any changes and, above all, without lowering the gold/credit ratio for extreme creditors.[40] The idea to lower the gold/credit ratio was more thoroughly discussed only after the renewal of the EPU's term, but even then not wholeheartedly. Since the FRG felt "unable to agree to this proposal", it was shelved in September 1956.[41]

Two reasons seem to explain this development. On the one hand, the dependence on German credits together with German readiness to consider "useful palliatives" (as the British called it) such as "a gold loan to the EPU to cover any special credit which EPU might wish to grant to individual countries", was important.[42] On the other hand, it should be noted that convertibility was the underlying aim for all major European currencies, particularly for sterling, but also for the d-mark. Any lowering of the gold/credit ratio was simply seen by all parties as a step away from the path towards convertibility.[43]

In the autumn of 1956, provoked by the Suez crisis, sterling came under severe pressure. The Managing Board continued to debate the German surpluses, but in its special report on the German surpluses it came only to the "hardly earthshaking" recommendations to Germany to export capital and lower the bank rate.[44] This was accepted without any problem by the FRG. The interest rate in fact had been reduced already. Furthermore, German policy makers recognized the British problems and accepted that something had to be done "urgently" to reduce the European tension, to "help" the UK, to diminish the "disturbing" German surpluses and to make some "sacrifices".[45] For this, however, they asked a certain price: British support for retaining the 75 per cent gold ratio.[46]

Thus, while the British as well as the French situation continued to deteriorate at an alarming rate, and while the FRG continued to accumulate great surpluses resulting from trade as well as speculation, the discussions inside EPU continued. But in its report on the EPU's renewal the Managing Board did not recommend any lowering of the gold/credit ratio for extreme creditors. The approval of this recommendation was endangered when Norway blocked it in the OEEC-Council. Later, however, Norway withdrew its reservations when it met "much sympathy for its position but little support given the prevailing instability in the currency markets."[47] Thus, although the tone of discussion, as perceived by German officials, had been "unbearable", nothing was fundamentally changed.[48] The German surpluses persisted, but some relief was obtained with the lowering of the German discount rate and the parallel increase in the British rate in September 1957. The speculation could be halted, but this policy also had serious drawbacks. As was pointed out by the French EPU representative: "the biting restrictive measures by Great Britain made it more difficult for France to bring its own balance of payments in order. In such a way the debtors are passing the buck to each other while the surpluses of the creditors remain untouched."[49]

In the last years of the EPU's operation, it became evident that it did not have the means to correct the evolving disequilibria in European payments. This limitation is attributable to various factors. One was the traditional difficulty in disciplining creditors which became even more acute with the hardening of the EPU credit system. On the other hand, a softening of the system was seen by major members as a step back on the road to convertibility and was therefore rejected. Above all, the FRG fiercely opposed any softening and since the EPU depended on German credits her opposition was decisive. Thus, it can be said that the Europeans were trapped in the concept of convertibility: stepping backward proved to be as impossible as stepping forward as long as the British and French positions remained precarious. Only following the improvement of the British situation after the autumn of 1957 could a move to convertibility be contemplated. Indeed, in the autumn of 1958 the UK took the lead towards convertibility, which was finally declared in December 1958.

* * *

According to the preamble of the EPU agreement, it was the task of the organisation to assist in the non-discriminatory liberalisation of trade and invisible earnings in Europe. Liberalisation was expected to stimulate growth of intra-European trade and close the Dollar Gap while at the same time allowing European reconstruction. Furthermore, the role of the EPU would be to contribute to creating a high level of employment, to secure internal financial stability, and to promote the basis for an increase in productivity and competitiveness. The ensuing result, it was hoped, would be to strengthen foreign currency reserves and thereby allow for a return to full convertibility.[50]

Looking at the development of the European economy in the 1950s, it can be said that the EPU's aims were accomplished. Convertibility had been achieved by December 1958, monetary reserves had grown considerably, the internal financial situation was rather stable. Intra-European trade and European trade with the Dollar Area were liberalised to a high degree, and trade in general had grown considerably. European competitiveness had increased and the Dollar Gap had closed. Furthermore, productivity and GNP had risen "miraculously" for several European countries, and European reconstruction was more or less complete.[51]

All this would surely not have been possible without a regional payments system such as the EPU. The EPU had proved its usefulness already during the Korean Crises. By giving a special credit to the FRG, it helped to postpone German deliberalisation and to keep the German market open. Notwithstanding these successes, however, the EPU system soon came to be questioned. Along with the improvement of the European economic situation came demands for a return to convertibility. The result of the ensuing discussions was the maintenance of a considerably harder EPU. This reflected the interest and strength of the creditors, who had to be persuaded to continue to give credits to the Union and to the debtors. However, in bringing about this compromise the EPU relinquished some of its powers to deal with extreme surpluses. Seeing this weakness and seeing that EPU functions (like transferability and credits) could be provided by convertibility (viz. the European Monetary Agreement), the EPU began to appear dispensable. Thus, the decision to dissolve the EPU and to move towards convertibility seems logical.

Notes

1. I would like to thank Richard T. Griffiths, Lorenza Sebesta and Christoph Thüer for their useful comments on an earlier draft. Furthermore, my thanks go to Sally Dore who provided me with some archival material. When no other reference is given, the present work is based on Monika Dickhaus: *Zwischen Europa und die Welt. Die internationale Währungspolitik der deutschen Zentralbank*, ph.d., European University, Institut, Florence 1995.

2. See Milward, Alan S.: *The Reconstruction of Western Europe 1945-51*, London 1987.
3. See as an example the discussions between Belgium, the Netherlands and Luxembourg as reported in Godts-Peters, Sabine: *La politique européenne du gouvernement belge*, Ph.D., European University Institute (Florence), 1987.
4. For example: if X owes Y one dollar and Y owes Z one dollar and Z owes X two dollars, by closing the circuit – i.e. by cancelling the debts of X to Y (1$), of Y to Z (1 $) and half of the debt of Z to X (1$) – the outstanding balances can be reduced from four dollars to one. For a good technical overview on the functioning of this and the following schemes see Möller, Hans: "Das innereuropäische Verrechnungs- und Zahlungsabkommen", in: *Europa-Archiv*, 4 (1949), pp. 1178 ff.
5. Milwards's figures on intra-European trade clearly show that only limited possibilities for closed circuits existed, see Milward 1987, pp. 228 ff.
6. For example the German Bizone complained about this, see Bundesarchiv (BA) B 146/171: Keiser, Konstruktionsmängel des Marshallplans, 5.11.1949. For an overview of mainly the German case see Abelshauser, Werner: "Der Kleine Marshall-Plan", in: Berding, Helmut (ed.): *Wirtschaftliche und politische Integration in Europa im 19. und 20.Jahrhundert*, Göttingen 1984, pp. 212 ff.
7. See Milward 1987, pp. 272 ff.
8. See the article by Wendy Asbeek-Brusse in this volume.
9. More precise on the negotiations is Milward 1987, pp. 299 ff. and Dickhaus, Monika: "It is only the provisional that lasts: The European Payments Union", in Griffiths, Richard T. (ed.): *Explorations in OEEC History* (forthcoming).
10. One u/a equalled one US dollar.
11. The quota was divided in five tranches. In the first tranche, the debtor received 100 per cent credit. In the second tranche he received 80 per cent credit and had to pay the remaining 20 per cent in gold or dollars. In the third tranche, he received 60 per cent credit and had to pay the remaining 40 per cent in gold or dollars and so on. The overall ratio of gold to credit was 40:60. It has to be noted that on the creditor side this incentive system was much weaker: in the first tranche the creditor had to grant 100 per cent of his surplus as a credit; in the second to fifth tranche he granted 50 per cent as a credit and received for 50 per cent of his surplus gold or dollars.
12. See Bank for International Settlements (BIS): *Annual Report 1951/52*, pp. 4 ff.
13. The German deficit July-September was 173.4 million u/a. The German quota was 320 million u/a, which meant that being almost in the third tranche, the FRG soon had to pay 60 per cent of its further deficits in gold.
14. National Archives (NA), Germany, EPU cables and memos; ECA: Office of the Deputy Director for Operations. Office of European operations, German Division, Subject Files, 1948-1953, Box 10: ECA to Embassy, Paris, 1.11.1950. However, it was accepted that "the European boldness of thinking" had to be stimulated by the US.
15. Financial adviser to the BIS, respectively OEEC.
16. See Ludwig-Erhard-Stiftung (LESt) (ed.): *Die Korea-Krise als ordnungspolitische Herausforderung der deutschen Wirtschaftspolitik. Texte und Dokumente*, Stuttgart 1986, Bundesregierung an den Rat der OEEC, Memorandum, 27.11.1950, pp. 212 ff.
17. It has to be noted that on this aspect different opinions exist. While the central banker, Emminger, stresses in his memoirs the effectiveness of the measures, the historians Geiger/Ross are more critical, see Emminger, Otmar: *D-Mark, Dollar, Währungskrisen*, Stuttgart 1984 and Geiger, Till & Ross, Duncan M.: "Banks, Institutional Constraints and the Limits of Central Banking: Monetary Policy in Britain and West Germany 1950-52", in: *Business History*, 1991, pp. 138 ff.

18. The German imports from EPU countries declined from $224 million (monthly average in the fourth quarter 1950) to $151 million in April 1951 and $132 million in May. The exports rose throughout the crisis, from $130 million (monthly average in the third quarter 1950) to $202 million in April 1951. See Historical Archives of the European Communities, Deposit of the OEEC (HAEC OEEC) 311: CSR 17/1, Special Restricted Committe, Examination of Western Germany, 22.9.1951. For the world economic conditions see BIS: *Annual Report 1951/52*, pp. 4 ff.
19. HAEC OEEC 306: C/M(50)31 (Prov.) Part I, Council, Minutes of the 113th meeting on 14.11.1950, 16.11.1950. However, another motive for the Danish opposition also existed: the liberalisation agreed in OEEC excluded agricultural products. The maintenance of OEEC liberalisation would probably lead to some cut-back in German agricultural imports.
20. See OEEC, "Statistical Bulletins of Foreign Trade", quoted in Milward 1987, p. 433.
21. Compromises were necessary since in 1951/52 the EPU's reserves were running low. In addition Belgium had exceeded its quota as a creditor and was unwilling to extend further credit. It threatened to leave the EPU.
22. See Milward, Alan S.: "Motives for Currency Convertibility: The Pound and the Deutschmark 1950-5", in: Holtfrerich, Carl-Ludwig (ed.): *Interactions in the World Economy*. London 1989, pp. 260 ff.
23. See the semi-official history of the EPU: Kaplan, Jacob J. & Schleiminger, Günther: *The European Payments Union*, Oxford 1989.
24. See OEEC, *Ninth Report*, p. 73: from circa $8.500 million (1952) to $12.500-13.000 million (1954-55). Of course differences between individual countries existed. The UK and Denmark for example lost reserves heavily in 1955.
25. See Block, Fred L.: *The Origins of International Economic Disorder*. Berkeley 1977, pp. 109 ff.
26. Military grants to Europe (without Turkey and Greece) were $2.028 million (1954) and $1.362 million (1955), see *Survey on Current Business* 4/1955, Washington, p. 10 and 4/1956, p. 12. Furthermore, dollar receipts from US troops played an important role, mainly for the FRG but also for other countries like Iceland, see Duke, Simon: *United States Military Forces and Installations in Europe*, Oxford 1989, p. 60. Also off-shore-procurements were important, see Sebesta, Lorenza: *L'Europa indifesa*, Florence 1991, pp. 172 ff.
27. See the overview in Buchheim, Christoph: *Die Wiedereingliederung Westdeutschlands in die Weltwirtschaft 1945-1958*, München 1990, pp. 144 ff.
28. At the end of 1953 the total cumulative accounting surpluses and deficits were higher than the total quotas, cf. BIS: *Annual report 1953/54*, p. 213.
29. For a more detailed account of the German position see Dickhaus, Monika: "German Attitudes Towards Regional Payments Cooperation", in Gillingham, John & Heller, F. (eds.): *The United States and the Integration of Western Europe*, (forthcoming).
30. Even the German Central Bank – usually a stern advocate of the EPU – now urged the display of a harder attitude, see Historisches Archiv der Deutschen Bundesbank (BBK) 1313: Vocke to Blücher, 12.3, 1954.
31. Public Record Office (PRO) T 236/3821: to Playfair, 19.5.1954. In autumn 1953 the UK did not believe the rumours of an Erhard plan to declare convertibility, cf. PRO T 236/3519: to Brittain, 13.10, 1953.
32. See PRO T 232/362: Rowan, note, 27.3.1954. Whether the FRG conducted a good-creditor-policy had been questioned in EPU/OEEC mainly when in 1953/54 discussions regarding the liberalisation of invisibles and the high German interest rates arose.

33. Italy even preceded the UK with a proposal for debt consolidation in January 1954.
34. See EPU, *Fourth Annual Report*.
35. Some preferred even settling the deficits 100 per cent in gold or dollars as for example Switzerland, Belgium and sometimes Germany, all supported by Italy, see PRO T 232/439: UK Delegation to Foreign Office, 22.2, 1955.
36. For the negotiation of the EMA see the minutes of OEEC's Ministerial Examination Group on Convertibility in: BA B 102/12652.
37. In 1955 British gold and dollar holdings declined for $612 million, see BIS, *Annual Report 1955/56*, p. 162.
38. See the instructive graph in BIS, *Annual Report 1956/57*, p. 212.
39. BA B 102/55333: von Mangoldt, Bericht über die 70. Sitzung des EPU-Direktoriums, 17./18.4, 1956.
40. See BBK 1314: von Mangoldt to Emminger, 1.6.1956. To be sure, only after "difficult negotiations".
41. Politisches Archiv des Auswärtigen Amtes (PA AA) Abt.4/Ref.401/94: Macmillan to von Brentano, 19.9, 1956.
42. Bank of England Archives (BoE) OV 46/75: Rowan, Note on talk with von Mangoldt, 17.7, 1956.
43. See Kaplan & Schleiminger 1989, p. 261 who argue that a step back would also have made support for transferable sterling more costly. Apart from this, it must be considered that at the corresponding meeting of the OEEC-Council concern for sterling's exchange rate prevailed. Erhard had proposed to the British Chancellor Macmillan a discussion on the European exchange rate pattern. Disclosing this proposal to the Financial Times in an interview he of course provoked speculation.
44. Kaplan & Schleiminger 1989, p. 259. In autumn 1956, German officials clearly felt that the previous pressure had lessened and the accusations had been overcome, cf. PA AA Abt.4/Ref.401/94: Scherpenberg, Aufzeichnung, 16.11, 1956.
45. BA B 136/2595: Gerbaulet, Vermerk, 24.10, 1956.
46. See BA B 136/2595: Gerbaulet, Vermerk, 24.10, 1956.
47. Kaplan & Schleiminger 1989, p. 239 and see HAEC OEEC 358: TP/M(57)3, Joint Trade and Intra-European Payments Committee, Summary record of 275th meeting, 8.4.1957 and MBC (57)40, EPU, Renewal of the Union, 13.5, 1957.
48. BBK 103: Emminger, Bericht über die Sitzung des Stellvertreterausschusses, 17./18.6, 1957.
49. BBK 1306: Emminger, Bericht von Mangoldt über die EZU-Oktober-Sitzung, 18.10, 1957.
50. See the Agreement on a European Payments Union, published in *Bundesgesetzblatt*, 50/II, pp. 30 ff.
51. See OEEC: *Ninth Annual report*.

European Trade and Commercial Policies. Quotas, Tariffs and the OEEC

By Wendy Asbeek Brusse

Introduction

The decades after the Second World War have witnessed a steady trend towards economic regionalism. Since 1945 discriminatory trading blocs have been founded all over the world, often varying in economic size and functions. Doubtless the most powerful of these blocs is still the EU. In 1991, it signed an agreement with EFTA for the creation of a wider European Economic Area (EEA). Under this agreement, the EFTA members accepted EEC legislation concerning the free movement of goods, services, people and capital and adopted most of the Common Market's economic policies. Sweden, Finland and Austria have since used the EER as a stepping stone towards full EU membership, while Poland, Hungary, the Czech Republic and Slovakia are now considered serious candidates for a further EU enlargement. By the turn of this century, then, the EU might form an economic bloc including 18 nations. It is partly in reaction to this, that the United States, Canada and Mexico have negotiatted a North American Free Trade Area (NAFTA) and that some countries have called for a trading arrangement between the states of the Pacific Basin that would include North America and Japan.[1]

As the world economic system experiences another revival of regionalism, it is easy to forget that nondiscrimination and worldwide multilateralism were once meant to be the cornerstones of the postwar international order.[2] These concepts permeated American thinking about international trade and payments and formed the ground rules for the arrangements known as the Bretton Woods system. They survived in the objectives of the IMF and GATT, yet since the creation of the EEC in 1958 they seldom figure as feasible economic objectives. Admittedly, at least for some time the EEC existed alongside the wider multilateral economic framework of the OECD that brought together all the major industrialised market economies. One could therefore argue that both the Common Market and EFTA complemented rather than substituted the worldwide multilateral trading system.[3] However, after the global recession of the 1970s and the rising trend towards bilateralism and protectionism, both the OECD and the GATT have increasingly lost ground. Again, bilateral relations between the EEC and the other trading blocs dominate the international economic scene. The paradox between the aspirations for multilateralism and the reality of regional economic integration has survived.

This article highlights some origins of postwar economic regionalism in Europe. It discusses the main features of the European trading system and of commercial policies between 1930 and 1958, in particular the policies of the Scandinavian countries and Benelux, which had a long history of trade policy cooperation.[4] In doing so, it stresses the relevance of – what one might call – a less 'Six' oriented approach to the study of European economic integration by focusing on the role of trade cooperation among the sixteen members of the Organisation for European Economic Cooperation (OEEC).

Economic Regionalism since the 1930s

From the mid-19th century until 1928, the worldwide system of multilateral trade can be said to have been supported by five major economic areas, each with widely varying economic structures: the tropics; Canada, Oceania and South-Africa; Continental Europe; the non-Continental European countries (i.e., the United Kingdom, Iceland and Ireland) and, lastly, the United States.[5] This trading network was multilateral in that some areas consistently imported more from other regions than they exported to them. They ran trade surpluses with third areas which they then used to settle net-deficits with the other regions. The multilateral character of trade was further strengthened by several multilateral trading arrangements within the different areas. As a result, some 25 per cent of total world trade was conducted along multilateral lines.[6]

The economic depression of the 1930s ended the effective working of the system, although its gradual undermining had begun much earlier.[7] After 1918, the direct trade controls and customs duties that had fostered domestic industries and that had provided governments with revenue still lingered on. Most countries in Central and Eastern Europe had maintained their protectionist policy instruments. America had drastically increased levels of tariff protection, thus blocking further bilateral tariff negotiations while also provoking retaliatory tariff rises among its competitors. In 1927, the League of Nations summed up the impact of such acts of economic warfare,

> 'Europe remains today with its tariff higher and more complicated, less stable and more numerous than in 1913. Moreover, Europe has failed to restore its former system of commercial treaties, and the habit has developed of putting tariffs designed for purposes of negotiating into force before those negotiations take place. (...) the obstruction remains higher than before.'[8]

At the World Economic Conference in the same year, several governments tried to reverse this trend. They called for drastic tariff cuts and the removal of quantitative impediments to trade. They also pleaded for the unconditional application of the most-favoured-nation clause and urged the conclusion of long-term treaties to promote tariff stability. However, the outbreak of the worldwide depression in 1929 crushed any remaining hopes for freer trade. As prices dropped, foreign direct investment collapsed and industrial output fell, governments tried to avoid mass unemployment by creating yet another layer of tariffs, quotas and export subsidies.[9]

The financial crisis of 1931, culminating in the total breakdown of the world's payments system, provided the final blow to the last remains of the 'normal' trading pattern. It led to a series of competitive devaluations and the introduction of foreign exchange controls. In its wake, four separate currency blocs were to emerge; The Gold Bloc (comprising France, the Netherlands, Switzerland, Italy – until 1934 – and Belgium and Luxembourg – until 1935), the Reichsmark Bloc (Germany, Italy after 1934, parts of Southern and Eastern Europe and Latin America), the Dollar Bloc and the Sterling Area. These blocs tried to expand their internal trade at a high cost to outsiders. The Sterling and Dollar Blocs were to survive the war, while in Europe a new trading bloc emerged among the members of the OEEC.

Britain's retreat into the Sterling Area resulted both in a rise in the ratio of internal trade to total sterling trade and in a growing proportion of Sterling Bloc trade in world trade. The proportion of intra-sterling exports to total sterling exports rose from 40 per cent in 1928 to 47.4 per cent ten years later. Imports increased from 35.1 to 37.5 over the same period. The upward trend in this share would continue until 1954, after which a structural decline set in (see table 1).

The Reichsmark Bloc countries all applied strict trade and exchange controls. They also shared mounting trading difficulties with third countries and steadily growing economic and political dependence on Germany.[10] Due to a strong surge in bilateral trade with Germany, internal trade rose spectacularly; expressed as a proportion of total bloc trade, it more than doubled between 1928 and 1938. Yet the share of Reichsmark imports in intra-European trade declined while that of Reichsmark exports rose by just 1.6 per cent.

The Gold Bloc countries (Belgium, Luxemburg, the Netherlands, France, Italy, Switzerland and Poland) had little more in common than their massive gold holdings and their late time of devaluation.[11]

Within this club, only French trade with Switzerland and Belgium, and Belgian trade with the Netherlands had some importance.[12] Moreover, France, the Netherlands and Belgium concentrated on strengthening ties with their overseas territories.

Another shift in European trading patterns of (future) OEEC members

Table 1. Intra-trade and total area trade of various economic blocs, 1938-1956.

1. Intra-trade as a percentage of world trade*

	Exports							
	1928	1938	1948	1951	1953	1954	1955	1956
Sterling Area	9.8	11.3	14.0	12.6	12.5	12.6	12.1	10.9
Dollar Area	7.6	6.2	13.8	12.5	13.9	13.4	13.4	13.7
Cont. OEEC	14.7	16.3	12.0	16.0	16.3	18.0	19.0	18.8
Reichsmark Bloc	1.1	2.6						
Gold Bloc	2.8	2.7						

	Imports							
	1928	1938	1948	1951	1953	1954	1955	1956
Sterling Area	9.6	11.2	14.0	12.5	12.9	12.7	12.2	10.8
Dollar Area	6.6	5.7	12.8	12.1	14.5	13.9	13.5	13.7
Cont. OEEC	13.8	15.3	12.4	15.0	17.2	18.4	18.8	19.0
Reichsmark Bloc	1.1	2.3						
Gold Bloc	2.4	2.2						

2. Intra-trade as a percentage of total area trade

	Exports							
	1928	1938	1948	1951	1953	1954	1955	1956
Sterling Area	40.0	47.4	51.6	48.1	50.4	51.3	49.3	46.5
Dollar Area	33.4	28.9	38.9	41.7	43.0	43.0	45.6	43.8
Cont. OEEC	48.8	49.7	54.5	52.3	54.7	56.5	57.4	57.8
Reichsmark Bloc	9.6	20.0						
Gold Bloc	21.1	22.1						

	Imports							
	1928	1938	1948	1951	1953	1954	1955	1956
Sterling Area	35.1	37.5	45.0	43.1	49.6	49.3	46.6	44.2
Dollar Area	38.4	40.4	57.8	52.1	56.7	58.3	57.3	56.6
Cont. OEEC	41.6	44.4	38.6	46.2	51.1	51.8	52.1	51.4
Reichsmark Bloc	9.3	19.7						
Gold Bloc	17.0	15.8						

3. Total area trade as a percentage of world trade*

	Exports							
	1928	1938	1948	1951	1953	1954	1955	1956
Sterling Area	22.5	21.3	28.0	26.4	24.9	24.6	24.7	23.5
Dollar Area	22.9	21.3	35.4	30.0	32.4	30.6	29.4	31.2
Cont. OEEC	30.1	32.8	22.1	28.7	29.9	31.8	33.1	32.5
Reichsmark Bloc	11.1	13.2						
Gold Bloc	13.4	12.3						

	Imports							
	1928	1938	1948	1951	1953	1954	1955	1956
Sterling Area	27.3	24.9	31.7	29.2	26.0	25.2	26.2	24.5
Dollar Area	17.3	13.0	22.2	23.2	25.6	23.8	23.6	24.3
Cont. OEEC	33.2	34.5	32.2	32.5	33.6	35.6	36.1	37.1
Reichsmark Bloc	11.9	11.8						
Gold Bloc	14.0	14.1						

* Cont. OEEC stands for continental OEEC Bloc (i.e. excluding United Kingdom, Ireland and Iceland). It includes dependent overseas territories and related areas.
For the post-World War II years, total world trade is exclusive of the Soviet bloc (USSR, Bulgaria, Rumania, Czechoslovakia, Albania, Hungary, East Germany and Mainland China).

Sources: League of Nations: *Direction of world trade*, Appendix I and III, New York, 1942; Thorbecke, *The tendency towards regionalisation*, pp. 96, 132, 171.

concerned the relative decline of trade between Germany and France on the one hand and the group of Scandinavia, Benelux and Switzerland on the other. The share of these seven countries in total OEEC imports remained virtually stable but their share in total continental OEEC exports increased by 4 per cent between 1928 and 1938. This followed to some extent from the protective trading policies of Germany, but also from the defensive economic policies of these smaller economies. They tried to resist the economic penetration of Germany by spreading exports more evenly among them. The Scandinavian states and Benelux, in particular, stepped up efforts to promote mutual trade and economic disarmament. Twice in the interwar period they signed agreements to stabilize tariffs and to remove quota restrictions. Yet both times a competitive scramble for export markets blocked effective cooperation.[13] Intra-Benelux and intra-Scandinavian trade even declined relatively between 1928 and 1938. After 1948, however, this trend reversed. Benelux internal trade as a percentage of total Benelux trade increased from 11.4 per cent in 1938 to 18.3 in 1956 for exports and from 10.4 to 16.2 per cent for imports. The share of intra-Scandinavian trade in the total trade of the three countries rose less sharply in the same period, from 11.0 to 13.2 for exports and from 10.1 to 11.2 for imports. The Scandinavian states also succeeded in improving trading links with the United Kingdom. After leaving the gold standard in October 1931, they stabilized their currencies with depreciated Sterling parities and concluded bilateral preferential trading agreements with Britain for several important export products. It would take until the 1950s before the importance of the British market would steadily decline.

The Dollar Area's internal trade in world trade almost doubled between 1938 and 1948. This was partly as a result of the postwar dollar gap and partly as a result of subsequent attempts by the OEEC-member states to switch to non-dollar imports for basic commodities. As a result, continental OEEC's share in world exports rose from 22 per cent in 1951 to 33 per cent in 1955, while the proportion of its imports increased from 32 to 36 per cent. If the entire OEEC Bloc is considered (i.e. including the United Kingdom, Ireland and Iceland) these shares are higher still. Intra-OEEC exports as a percentage of total OEEC trade continued to rise in the 1950s, reaching a share of more than 52 per cent for imports and 57 per cent for exports in 1955.

A breakdown of the smaller states' main European export markets shows that Britain and West Germany figured most frequently within the top three markets during the 1950s. Together they absorbed some 52 per cent of total Danish exports, 26 per cent of total Dutch exports and 28 per cent of Sweden's total exports in 1952. In Belgium and Switzerland the export pattern was somewhat different although there, too, the share of the West German market in their total exports was expanding quite drastically. The United Kingdom only ranked in fourth position on the list of principal Belgian export markets, after the Netherlands and France. For Switzerland, West Germany occupied the first position but the United Kingdom's role as an export market was far less prominent. Instead, a large part of total Swiss exports went to neighbouring Italy and Austria.

Two main conclusions seem to emerge from the postwar export patterns of these smaller countries. Firstly, West Germany's import policy greatly influenced their economic welfare. If, as happened in the autumn of 1950, Germany imposed import restrictions to reduce its balance of payments deficit, these states were the first to experience drastic drops in their foreign earnings. Conversely, the progressive liberalisation of German imports was likely to boost their exports to the German market and to stimulate economic growth. West Germany became, therefore, an obvious and a prime target in European efforts for market expansion. Secondly, their dependence on the British market declined gradually but was still substantial in the 1950s, especially in the case of the Scandinavian countries. Plans for regional economic cooperation would therefore, at best, try to include the British market or, at least, to minimize the danger to their export trade with Britain.

This brief examination of Europe's trading patterns shows several general trends in the development of European trade before and after 1945. One is the strengthening of trading links between the metropolitan areas and their overseas territories. France offers the clearest example of this, the share of her exports to the dependent territories rising from 27 per cent in 1938 to 38 per cent in 1954. Another is the expansion of trade among the smaller European countries. In the 1930s this was only modest but after 1948 much more rapid mainly because of internal Benelux trade expansion and the growth of internal Scandinavian trade. This, too, caused a further intensification of trade within the OEEC Bloc. Though despite the relative dynamism of their mutual trade, the postwar commercial policies of these smaller states remained preoccupied with the larger British, German and French markets. This will be the theme of the remaining part of this article.

The OEEC's Regional Plans for European Trade Liberalisation

Looking back on the interwar period, many postwar policy-makers concluded that the prevalence of bilateral commercial relations and widespread economic and political instability had been responsible for the disastrous social and economic impact of the Great Depression. The American government translated this belief into a firm commitment to multilateralism and nondiscrimination. These principles should be promoted by worldwide international agencies such as the International Monetary

Fund (IMF) and the International Trade Organisation (ITO). These institutions would start working when production had recovered and governments had removed exchange controls and import quotas. A first attempt in that direction followed in 1947, when the Americans forced the British to abandon their 'transitional' exchange controls and to reintroduce sterling-dollar convertibility. The subsequent events are only too familiar; after a run on the pound sterling the British government suspended convertibility in August 1947. The experiment proved that nondiscrimination would fail if governments refused to adopt 'disciplinary' policies to curb domestic demand and suspend investment programs.

That initial American planning for multilateralism contrasted sharply with reality and expectations that had been apparent in Europe since 1945. European states began by strengthening the quantitative trade restrictions imposed during the war and by maintaining strict controls on prices, consumption and investment. Despite paying lip service to freer trade and payments, they saw quotas as indispensable instruments for maintaining high levels of investment and employment.[14] Moreover, the delayed recovery of trade with Germany and the growing dollar gap seemed to confirm the impossibility of restoring 'normal' external economic relations. As the prospects for currency convertibility appeared more remote than ever, creditor countries refused to extend credits to finance trade with debtors. As a result, a permanent imbalance developed between creditors and debtors that forced trade into inefficient channels and threatened Europe's trade expansion. The exchange of goods became a strictly bilateral affair, based on a network of some 200 agreements.

Against a background of growing economic problems the Americans announced their European Recovery Plan (ERP) for massive dollar aid to Europe. Their immediate aim was to close the widening gap between European imports and exports. This would help to lessen the threat of inflation, to increase production and social stability and to forestall the immediate communist threat in France and Italy. It would eventually have to pave the way for the ultimate political objective in the American State Department's policy: Europe's transformation into an economic and military stronghold of the democratic, free world. A powerful and united economic ally would be a strong military partner and could eventually share in the common defence burden. Moreover, a powerful western European economy would be a precondition for any future move towards a worldwide international economic system. That this also required the continuation of economic discrimination against the Dollar Area was by then seen as an inevitable result of the European dollar deficit.[15]

The OEEC came to play a major role in coordinated European recovery efforts and trade liberalisation. Established in 1948 by the 16 recipients of Marshall aid, it aimed for 'close and lasting cooperation' among participating countries' using 'all methods', including the creation of free trade areas and customs unions. This latter option, though, had already lost attraction in 1947, when a European Customs Union Study Group had failed to agree on the scope for an OEEC-wide customs union. The Group's experiences seemed to prove the impossibility of simultaneously removing quotas and tariffs in times of economic instability and insecurity. The OEEC therefore decided to concentrate on eliminating quantitative restrictions and exchange controls, the main obstacles to freer trade and higher efficiency in Europe. Its members adopted the Trade Liberalisation Programme, a scheme for the gradual removal of quotas on intra-European trade.

The new programme was ready in June 1949. It required members to remove quotas, by mid-December at the latest, on at least 50 per cent of their total imports on private account from other members, in three respective product groups: food and feeding stuffs, raw materials and manufactured goods (see table 2.).[16]

The next step of 60 per cent was fixed for October 1950 and formally laid down in a Code of Liberalisation. Its formulation had been delayed by the protracted negotiations for a European Payments Union (EPU), the payments system sustaining the transition to multilateral trade. The Code urged the OEEC members to remove quotas 'as fully as their economic position would permit', but in exchange for equivalent efforts by their trading partners. Balance of payments deficits or "serious economic disturbances" counted as legitimate reasons for suspending liberalisation measures. The Code further committed states to avoid discrimination in import policies, both for liberalised trade and trade still under quota restrictions.

Table 2. The OEEC's Trade Liberalisation Schedule, 1949-1955.

Council decision of:	Target	Target Date
July 1949	Immediate steps towards progressive elimination of quotas. As complete a liberalisation as possible	1951
November 1949	50 per cent	15-12-1949
January 1950	60 per cent	as soon as EPU established
September 1950 (adoption of Code)	60 per cent 75 per cent and 60	4-10-1950 1-2-1951 in each category
January 1955	90 per cent and 75 in	1-10-1955 each category

In addition, it set a second target for February 1951. By that date, members should have liberalised 75 per cent of their total trade and at least 60 per cent for each of the three product groups.

How successful was the OEEC's program for liberalising intra-European trade? If one approaches this question by examining the Organisation's own targets, the answer would presumably be favourable. Eight of the sixteen OEEC members quickly met (or surpassed) the initial targets of freeing 60 and later 75 per cent of imports in each of the three categories. They brought the general liberalisation percentage to 56. To have reached this within the space of two-and-a-half years was a real achievement. The new target set for October 1955, 90 percent total liberalisation and 75 percent within each category, was met by all but five countries (see table 3.). And by 1959, when GATT took over the task of eliminating the last remaining quota restrictions, the OEEC had reached an average percentage of 90.

On closer examination, however, one could argue that the OEEC's targets were too modest and trade liberalisation achievements unimpressive. It is certainly true that the programme experienced severe setbacks between 1951 and 1954, when Germany, France and the United Kingdom either entirely suspended or considerably reduced liberalisation measures for balance of payments reasons. This severely damaged the liberalisation performances of the other members, who lost free access to major export markets overnight. Furthermore, the official percentages give just one part of the entire picture of European quota liberalisation. The liberalisation measures included in the calculation of a country's performance at a given date were those taken with respect to commodities imported in 1948.[17] This meant that changes in the composition and prices of a country's imports were not reflected in its official liberalisation percentage. Therefore, countries could transfer products imported under quotas from private to government account without officially reducing their liberalisation effort. For agricultural products, which in many states received extensive government protection, this became common practice.

It is safe to assume that this loophole in the calculation method tended to overstate the share of imports really freed from quantitative impediments. To what extent it did so is difficult to assess and differed between countries.[18] The French percentage provides an extreme example of overstated liberalisation achievements. By 1956 France had formally surpassed the 75 percent stage but this concealed almost one quarter of its trade subject to state trade and imported under a quota regime. Similarly, if one included state trading, the British percentage for 1958 would drop from 94 to 85, the Danish from 86,2 to 77 and the Norwegian from 81,4 to a mere 65.[19]

State trading did not form the only obstacle to trade liberalisation. One

Table 3. Percentage liberalisation of intra-European trade on June 30, 1950-1959

	1950	1951	1952	1953	1954	1955	1956	1957	1958	1959
Austria		53	–	–	36	76	82	90	90	90
BLEU	56	75	75	87	87	88	91	96	96	96
Netherlands	55	66	75	92	93	93	91	96	96	96
Denmark		53	50	68	76	76	76	86	86	86
France	58	75	–	–	51	75	82	–	–	91
Germany		47	–	77	90	90	90	92	93	94
Greece	..	..	..	..	..	95	95	95	95	76
Iceland		–	41	41	–	29	29	29	29	29
Ireland		64	75	75	75	77	77	90	90	90
Italy	54	76	100	100	100	99	99	99	98	98
Norway	39	51	75	75	76	75	78	81	81	81
Portugal	53	83	100	93	93	93	94	94	94	94
Sweden	53	75	75	91	91	91	93	93	93	93
Switzerland	81	85	88	92	92	92	92	91	91	91
Turkey	42	63	63	–	–	–	–	–	–	–
United Kingdom	57	90	46	58	80	84	94	94	94	95
OEEC average	56	65	66	71	81	84	89	83	83	90

Source: OEEC, Twelfth annual economic review (Paris, 1961) 185.

other cause for concern was that many governments ignored the initial obligation to remove quotas evenly over broad product categories, once the overall targets were raised. An over-performance in freeing trade in raw materials would, for instance, often compensate for an underachievement in agriculture. This, of course, reduced the degree of reciprocity in liberalisation efforts to the detriment of large agricultural exporters such as Denmark and the Netherlands.

Tariffs proved to be another major problem hampering trade liberalisation. Although it was the OEEC's declared objective to promote a single European market free from quotas *and tariffs*, its members had agreed in 1948 to leave tariff issues to the competencies of GATT. This ad hoc organisation would provide a framework in which the most-favoured-nation clause would pass on the tariff cuts negotiated among the major industrialised nations to all other member states. In practice, however, several major European countries – including France, Italy, West Germany and the United Kingdom – reactivated their previously suspended tariffs to compensate for the loss of quota protection.[20] These policies provoked a series of anti-tariff campaigns from the governments of the trade dependant, low-tariff countries of the Netherlands, Belgium, Luxembourg, Denmark and Sweden, who faced new (tariff) barriers to their own exports and also had to cope with a growing influx of competing industrial imports from their OEEC partners. A closer look at table 4 serves to illustrate the extent of their 'tariff disparity' problem.

The table compares the tariffs levied by the low-tariff states (except Switzerland) (group I) and tariffs in their main European export markets, West Germany, the United Kingdom, France and Italy (group II). It gives a breakdown of all those export products (subdivided up to 5 SITC-digits) each of which accounted for more than 1.5 per cent of the total export of one or more of the low-tariff countries. What is immediately striking is the disparity in tariff levels in agriculture (SITC 0), where Denmark, Sweden and, to a lesser extent the Benelux countries, levied tariffs that were far below those imposed in France, West Germany and Italy. Norway breaks the pattern of the small, low tariff countries with one very high tariff (of 53 per cent) on cream and another of almost 22 per cent on fresh vegetables. Britain is the exception in group II; its agricultural tariffs were clearly below the average in that group and even below those levied by Benelux. Not surprisingly, Danish exports were likely to suffer most from these high tariff levels for agriculture. Almost 70 per cent of total Danish exports in 1952 were concentrated in section 0, and of that more than 52 per cent was taken up by meat, dairy products and eggs (sections 01-02). In West Germany, in particular, where quotas on several of these products had been removed, Danish exports were still severely restricted by high levels of tariff protection. The Netherlands, with more than 30 per cent of total exports in agricultural products, faced similar although less acute problems for its exports of dairy products, meat and fresh vegetables. Furthermore, Norwegian exports of fish and fish meal (SITC 03), which comprised some 18 per cent of total Norwegian exports, were hampered by tariffs of between 9 and 34 per cent.

Although the export interests of the low-tariff countries in chemicals (section 5) were not particularly large if measured as a percentage of their total exports, the existing tariff disparity within this dynamic and fast-growing sector aroused much concern.[21] The Netherlands and Denmark, in particular, were in the process of expanding their relatively young chemical and pharmaceutical industries. They insisted on maintaining quota protection to prevent France, Italy, the United Kingdom and especially West Germany from dumping cheap chemicals while protecting their domestic industries behind high tariff walls.

Like the agricultural sector, the sector of manufacturing goods classified by materials (section 6) contained many separate product groups for which the tariff disparity between group I and II was clearly visible. Again, however, it should be noted that the Norwegian tariffs formed the exception, because these were comparatively high in textiles. Benelux also had some fairly high tariffs within this sector. One may assume that Sweden and Norway would gain substantially from a reduction in tariffs for paper,

Table 4. Tariffs on main export items of low-tariff countries, 1951*

SITC no	Ben	Group I Den	Nor	Swe	Fra	Group II FRG	Ita	UK
0 Food and foodstuffs								
012-01	12.0	0.0 –	3.0	37.0	26.0	33.0	5.0	
013-02	28.0	7.0	3.0	6.0	30.0	23.0	25.0	9.0
022-01	17.0	–	–	3.0	15.0	33.0	19.0	7.0
022-02	17.0	–	53.0	1.0	19.0	20.0	19.0	9.0
023	15.0	–	–	–	25.0	25.0	30.0	5.0
025-01	3.0	0.0	4.0	1.0	18.0	15.0	11.0	7.0
025-02	3.0	0.0	6.0	–	18.0	7.0	8.0	10.0
031	3.0	1.3	–	2.7	19.0	13.0	16.7	9.3
032	24.0	3.5	10.5	8.5	25.5	28.5	34.0	9.3
054	6.0	1.3	21.7	8.8	17.8	14.8	11.0	9.0
061-02	22.0	9.0	18.0	8.0	110.0	45.0	5.0	–
2 Crude materials								
251	0.0	0.0	–	0.0	16.4	5.4	4.8	4.0
262	0.2	0.0	2.8	0.0	0.5	0.6	2.1	4.4
265-01	0.0	0.0	–	0.0	0.0	0.0	9.0	5.0
272	2.5	0.2	0.0	0.0	4.5	2.3	2.2	7.8
281-01	0.0	0.0	0.0	0.0	0.0	0.0	0.0	0.0
292-06	0.0	10.0	9.0	7.0	23.0	17.0	11.0	22.0
3 Minerals, fuels, lubricants								
311-01	0.0	0.0	–	0.0	2.0	5.0	0.0	10.0
313-03	0.0	0.0	–	0.0	3.0	–	5.0	–
5 Chemicals								
541	6.4	0.0	0.6	1.6	17.2	17.6	22.6	20.4
561	0.0	0.0	–	0.8	4.3	15.5	8.0	12.3
6 Manufactures articles mainly by material								
641	13.8	4.2	5.7	3.7	22.0	17.5	26.3	18.3
651	6.3	2.5	7.0	4.5	17.1	11.5	21.9	15.3
652	15.0	4.5	16.0	5.0	22.0	19.5	21.5	21.0
657	23.0	10.0	33.7	8.9	35.0	26.5	31.3	19.0
661-02	3.0	0.0	31.0	4.0	10.0	5.0	25.0	8.0
664	10.2	4.8	20.1	9.6	20.1	20.3	32.2	15.6
664-03	8.0	6.0	23.0	19.0	20.0	25.0	32.0	15.0
672-02	0.0	25.0	0.0	0.0	14.0	2.0	4.0	0.0
681	4.2	0.8	3.4	3.8	16.5	16.2	22.7	21.2
681-04	3.0	0.0	–	5.0	17.0	16.0	24.0	27.0
681-05	4.0	0.0	–	6.0	17.0	21.0	23.0	29.0
682	3.0	0.5	1.0	2.0	8.0	6.0	10.5	10.0
687-01	3.0	0.0	–	0.0	0.0	0.0	2.0	10.0
699	12.3	2.8	9.4	5.4	21.1	14.3	29.4	20.7
699-12	5.0	1.0	19.0	4.0	18.0	15.0	26.0	16.0
7 Machinery and transport equipment								
716	8.1	3.9	15.4	9.5	18.1	11.4	27.8	20.2
716-14	6.0	1.0	20.0	10.0	27.0	20.0	27.0	20.0
721	11.7	6.2	12.7	7.8	20.8	12.1	31.1	17.8
731	11.6	4.6	22.0	9.5	16.9	13.9	22.9	29.6
735	1.7	0.0	7.0	3.0	5.0	0.5	10.7	10.0
735-02	0.0	0.0	–	0.0	0.0	0.0	11.0	10.0
8 Miscellaneous manufactures								
841	22.3	10.8	18.8	9.1	24.0	23.1	25.5	23.2
842	13.0	3.0	7.5	10.5	19.3	18.3	23.7	16.3
9								
921	5.0	0.0	15.0	4.5	15.0	5.0	7.5	2.5

* the figures for Germany date from 1952.

Ben=Benelux states, Den=Denmark, Nor=Norway, Swe=Sweden, Fra=France, FRG=West Germany, Ita=Italy.

Source: PRO,BT 11/4901 Weighted incidences of customs tariffs by sectors, dd.14-7-1953.

paper board and newsprint (SITC 641), in which more than 8 and 10 per cent of their respective exports were concentrated. The Norwegians could also expect large benefits from tariff cuts in ferro-alloys and aluminium, which contributed to more than 10 per cent of their total exports and which met tariffs of between 12.5 and 36 per cent.

Within section 7 (machinery and transport equipment), the Netherlands, Sweden, Denmark and the BLEU had substantial export interests in electrical machinery and appliances (SITC 721), a fast growing sector which Italy, the United Kingdom and France protected by tariffs in the range of 17 to 31 per cent. Norway, however, whose export interests within section 7 were heavily concentrated in ships and boats (SITC 735), seems better placed within the group of 'high tariff' countries. Its tariffs of between 7 and 22 per cent served to protect Norwegian machinery industries from their main competitors in Sweden and West Germany. The group of machinery n.e.s. (SITC 716), a major export sector in Sweden and Denmark, shows a large difference in the tariffs imposed by the Benelux countries, Sweden and Denmark on the one hand and France, Italy and the United Kingdom on the other.

The last group of major export products worth examining in some detail is that of miscellaneous commodities (section 8). Here a division between high and low-tariff states is clearly not applicable since all countries except Sweden levied high tariffs. For Benelux, in particular, tariff protection in textiles represented a blemish on their carefully cultivated free trade image. It served mainly to shelter Belgian industries, which contributed to more than 4 per cent of total Belgian exports. Danish textile producers, a small but politically vocal pressure group, also received tariff protection above standard levels in Denmark.

This breakdown of the main export items of the low-tariff states and their tariff barriers confirms once more that some sectors, and therefore some economies, were more likely to be damaged by high tariffs than others. It also shows that the professed low-tariff countries often used high tariffs to protect some specific domestic industries. As a rule, however, these small states were too dependent on cheap imports to use tariff barriers on a large scale. To them, there seemed only two tactics available; the first, to introduce plans to cut high tariffs and the second, to maintain (retaliatory and protective) quotas. They would apply both approaches simultaneously.

The first strategy in their attack on tariffs, that of launching tariff reduction plans, sparked off a wide variety of proposals. Some aimed at a sectoral removal of tariffs and quotas, others at tariff inquiries by the OEEC's Steering Board for Trade and linear reductions within GATT, and still others at cutting tariffs on so-called 'commodity lists'. There are two reasons for examining this latter commodity approach somewhat closer. Firstly, it dominated most tariff discussions within the OEEC and the GATT during the 1950s. Secondly, it represented an attempt at tackling not just the tariff problem, but also that other major dilemma of the OEEC's Programme that we identified earlier, namely the lack of reciprocity among individual countries' liberalisation efforts.

The commodity list approach to tariff cuts was to work as follows. Members were to draw up a list of 'European' commodities of which at least, say, 80 per cent originated from member states. They could then cut tariffs on these goods in conformity with GATT rules on an unpreferential, most-favoured-nation basis, yet without losing much bargaining power to non-European competitors such as the United States or Canada. These competitors might even be tempted to join in the tariff reductions, if they so wished. If successful, the approach might even be introduced in the process of quota removal, to promote a larger degree of reciprocity among countries with widely varying trade structures.

No matter how ingenious in theory, the commodity lists had considerable practical drawbacks. For instance, they gave rise to endless discussions on the precise selection criteria and classification system for collecting 'European' commodities. It also proved impossible to agree upon the final list if no prior agreement existed on the depth and method of the tariff cuts. Furthermore, there were always some countries complaining that the list failed to provide a balanced picture of the export interests among the OEEC countries. It is doubtful whether that was possible, especially since some export products that proved vital to some economies did not meet the criteria of representing 60 per cent or more of intra-European imports. Yet the main political reason why tariff reductions in the short term did not stand a chance was British opposition. The original British motives for joining the OEEC's exercises in 1952 had been to ease fears among the European countries that Britain's planned move towards convertibility might signal an upward revision of her tariffs. When these efforts threatened to turn into fullblown plans for European tariff reductions, British delegates would usually demand uncommitting studies of some lists with high tariffs that would ultimately end up in some bottom drawer. In the course of the 1950s, however, when the dismantling of quotas increasingly revealed the impact of tariff protection, low-tariff states also turned to their other means of protest; maintaining quotas and blocking the Trade Liberalisation Programme. It was then that Britain began to realise the danger of the tariff issue.

By the end of 1954, Denmark took the lead by threatening to veto the OEEC's move towards 90 percent quota liberalisation if it refused to impose binding measures against high tariffs and state trading.[22] The Danish government had clearly not forgotten the painful experience of liberalising up to 75 per cent, a step that had been taken at a large cost to domestic spending and employment. Further liberalisation would expose its infant industries to – mostly German – competitors who would undercut domestic prices, take over parts of the Danish market, cause unemployment and damage industrialisation efforts. Therefore, it wished to stall the new 90-percent commitment and demanded guarantees for increased export opportunities.

Some safeguards were eventually given. In January 1955, the Council adopted the 90 percent stage for a trial period of 18 months, but tariffs and state trade that were found to be restrictive could no longer be excluded from the national quota lists. Any member suffering from a rise in tariff disparities could withdraw liberalisation measures beyond 75 per cent to compensate for the damage caused to its exports.[23] After these 18 months the Council consolidated the 90 percent stage, and when France eventually attained this in December 1958, private trading within Europe had, to all intents and purposes, been purged of quantitative restrictions. State trading in agriculture remained, however, as did residual quota restrictions against the Dollar Area. It was left to the competencies of GATT to attack these 'hard core' problems.

The Danish case hinted that the Trade Liberalisation Programme had reached its limits. Ultimately, after the termination of the EPU agreement, GATT would have to take over responsibility for removing all trade barriers simultaneously: quotas, tariffs, state trading and subsidies. Yet the problem remained that several European countries held grave doubts about GATT's competencies, if only because the organisation's adequate functioning depended so heavily on the economic policies of its two major sponsors, the United States and Britain. The Benelux states had even concluded that effective, long-term commercial and economic arrangements could only be found in smaller, supranational frameworks of a more binding nature. When, one year later, they relaunched the plan for an economic community of the Six, the British were finally forced to embrace a new European policy. Tariffs, they now argued, could provide the key to the problem posed by a future economic bloc in Europe. Commodity lists, (partial) free trade areas and mutual preference systems suddenly all received serious Cabinet scrutiny. As is discussed elsewhere in this book, the eventual outcome of Britain's u-turn was Plan G, a proposal for an industrial free trade area in OEEC Europe.

Concluding Remarks

This article has tried to deal with the origins and nature of various initiatives for the mutual reduction or removal of barriers to intra-European trade that were launched within the OEEC. All these initiatives form part of a wider set of foreign commercial policy responses to common national or international imperatives, even if these were ultimately experienced in different ways by the various countries. To focus solely on those involving the Six eventual founding members of the EEC, as is still common practice in the literature of economic integration, would therefore be to ignore the contribution of the OEEC to fostering cooperation among its member states.

As we have seen, the OEEC formed a provisional regional economic bloc within western Europe, originally created to strengthen economic and political ties among its sixteen member states and to facilitate the eventual return to a worldwide system of multilateral trade and payments. For more than a decade the Trade Liberalisation Programme and the European Payments Union indeed provided the main instruments for liberalising intra-European trade. By 1958 Western Europe had achieved internal currency convertibility and a liberalised system of internal trade. Moreover, the volume of trade within the OEEC Bloc more than doubled between 1950 and 1960. Its principal objectives had thus been realised.

This certainly does not mean that one should explain western Europe's spectacular record in trade and economic growth in the 1950s by the miraculous workings of the OEEC. Nor should one approach the OEEC-states as a single, regional bloc operating as a unity in the world trading system. The economic (and political) interests and experiences of the individual member states are simply too diverse to allow for such a simplification of the historical record. While in absolute terms all members experienced an increase in the value of volume of their trade, some gained more than others. Export expansion in several of the 'peripherals' such as Norway, Iceland and Portugal clearly stayed behind that of West Germany, the Netherlands, Denmark and Italy. Furthermore, some countries intensified their trading links with member states while others remained largely oriented towards outsiders. France, for instance, had sent one-third of its total exports in 1950 to OEEC-members, compared to 46 per cent ten years later. British interests in Europe remained limited to 30 per cent of its total exports, while Dutch, Belgian, Danish, Swedish and Norwegian shares were all 68 per cent or higher.

Perhaps paradoxically, the widely diverging record of western European countries points at yet another reason for acknowledging the relevance of an 'OEEC-wide' approach for historical interpretation. Only by examining the experiences of the sixteen member states can one trace the causes of the ultimate split of Europe into two separate trading blocs, the EEC and EFTA. The Treaty of Rome, as we have seen, was more than the product of aspirations for a federal Europe or the inevitable outcome of successful earlier economic and political cooperation between the Six. It also reflected the wish, among countries such as Germany and the Benelux states, to complete the OEEC's partial attack on European trade barriers and to have guarantees that such barriers would not re-emerge in the event of a subsequent recession. They felt that this required a more sophisticated institutional structure than intergovernmental organisations such as the OEEC or GATT. Moreover, only a more complicated arrangement could offer the trade-off of industrial for agricultural market access between France and Germany.

One final aspect should be mentioned in a discussion of the OEEC's regional cooperation: the impact of institutionalised discrimination against dollar imports. This system, while initially supported by the USA as a temporary but inevitable evil, gradually promoted more permanent forms of discrimination against American imports. It is beyond doubt that European attempts since the late 1940s to stimulate and foster new, dollar-saving industries (either with Marshall aid or national government funding) created vested interests in keeping out competitive American exports. Discriminatory practices thus played an important role in domestic welfare policies. They seemed the tangible result of effective government intervention aimed at economic modernisation, full employment and economic welfare. The Trade Liberalisation Programme continued to favour the expansion of such dollar-competing industries on the European market, thereby only augmenting their economic importance. When the Americans began pressing for a relaxation in import restrictions towards the Dollar Area, most European countries therefore feared for their weaker economic sectors. Replacing dollar restrictions with the high external tariffs of the Common Market offered some industries a welcome barrier to limit keen American competition. Hence, regionalism in Europe received an extra impulse from dollar discrimination.

Notes

1. J.M. Lutz: "GATT reform or regime maintenance: differing solutions to world trade problems", *Journal of World Trade*, vol.25, no.2 (1991), p. 111.
2. This 'revival of regionalism' has resulted in a renewed discussion on the impact of trading blocs. Recent publications are: J. Bhagwati: "Regionalism versus multilateralism", *The World Economy*, vol.15 (1992), p. 535-555; A. de la Torre & M.R. Kelly: "Regional trade arrangements", in *International Monetary Fund occasional paper*, no.93 (Washington, 1992).
3. See for instance: D. Lorenz: "Trends towards regionalism in the world economy. A contribution to a new international economic order?", *Intereconomics*, vol.24 (1989), p. 67, and E. van Lennep: *In de wereldeconomie. Herinneringen van een internationale Nederlander* (Leiden, 1991) 323.
4. See for an account of their trade cooperation in the interwar period, H. van Roon: *Kleine landen in crisistijd. Van Oslostaten tot Benelux, 1930-1940* (Amsterdam/Brussels, 1985).
5. League of Nations: *The network of world trade* (Geneva, 1942), p. 78.
6. E. Thorbecke: *The tendency towards regionalisation in international trade 1928-1956* (The Hague, 1960), p. 72.
7. R.T. Griffiths: "The economic disintegration of Europe. Trade and protection in the 1930s" in: idem (ed.), *Monetary and economic unions of the past. From Continental System to Common Market* (London/New York) forthcoming.

8. Quoted in League of Nations: *Commercial policy in the inter-war period* (Geneva, 1942), p. 37.
9. W. Asbeek Brusse: *West European tariffs, 1947-1957. From Study Group to Common Market* (Ph.D., European University Institute (Florence), 1991).
10. These countries could only spend their Reichsmark balances on the German market.
11. R.L. Hogg: "Belgium, France and Switzerland and the end of the Gold Standard", in R.T. Griffiths (ed.): *The Netherlands and the Gold Standard, 1931-1936. A study in policy formation and policy* (Amsterdam, 1987), p. 193.
12. R.T. Griffiths: "Economic disintegration .... op. cit".
13. Idem.
14. The exceptions to this were Switzerland, Belgium, Italy and Portugal, which adopted deflationary policies to promote domestic stability and to normalise external economic relations.
15. O. Hieronymi: *Economic discrimination against the United States in Western Europe (1945-1958)* (Geneva/Paris, 1973), p. 89.
16. F. Boyer & J.P. Sallé: "The liberalization of intra-European trade in the framework of the OEEC", in *International Monetary Fund Staff Papers*, vol.4 (1955), p. 183.
17. For West Germany and Austria the base years were 1951 and 1952 respectively.
18. The OEEC itself had made some provisional calculations which indicated that for the majority of members a change in the reference year from 1948 to 1952 would not substantially affect their liberalisation percentages. It argued that although important changes in the commodity composition occurred in that period, the quota free portion of commodities entering intra-European trade since 1948 increased at least as much as the portion still subject to quotas (Boyer & Sallé: op. cit., p. 197.
19. G. Curzon: *Multilateral Commercial Diplomacy* (London, 1965), p. 161-162.
20. W. Asbeek Brusse, op. cit., p. 80-87.
21. The share of chemicals in the total exports of these countries were: Sweden, 1.8, Denmark 2.4, BLEU 6.7, Norway 8.1, the Netherlands 7.5, and Switzerland 16.4.
22. A brief look at the liberalisation percentages reached in 1954 in the different categories of products shows that the BLEU countries and Switzerland had virtually completed the removal of quota restrictions on raw materials and endproducts, but that they fell far behind in food and feeding stuffs (see table below).

Liberalisation percentages of low-tariff countries, April 1954 and November 1955

	April 1954 Overall	I	November 1955 II	III	Overall
BLEU	87.2	61.3	100.0	92.0	87.7
Netherlands	92.6	85.6	99.5	89.2	92.5
Denmark	76.0	79.6	96.2	60.0	75.9
Sweden	91.2	75.7	88.4	70.1	75.0
Norway	75.5	77.5	88.4	70.1	75.0
Switzerland	91.6	62.2	100.0	97.2	91.6

I = food and feeding stuffs, II = raw materials, III = manufactures.

Source: W. Asbeek Brusse: op. cit., p. 208.

The Belgians tried to cover up their chronic problems in agriculture by insisting on a change in the reference year used for calculating the percentages. This could help them in meeting the 75 percent stage, but the remaining quotas would certainly stand out as 'hard cores' of protectionism. The Dutch position was fairly comfortable in all three sectors, although a further increase in the percentage for endproducts would eventually mean giving up protection for a few infant industries. Norway and Denmark had much larger sectors of 'weak' and infant industries for which the removal of quotas would be problematic. In Norway, the larger part of this hard core protected employment in shipbuilding, whereas in Denmark it sheltered sectors such as textiles, leatherware and chemicals.
23. This was formulated in the Council decision C(55)291 of 14-1-1955.

Denmark and the European Coal and Steel Community, 1950-1953

By Hans Branner

Introduction

The creation of the European Coal and Steel Community (ECSC) in the summer of 1952 is generally regarded as a landmark in the history of European integration. This may be seen in three main contexts: (1) *Ideologically* it represents the first successful attempt to establish a supranational international organization and thus marks the beginning of a long, not yet terminated integration process in Western Europe; (2) From a general *foreign policy point of view* the ECSC first of all symbolizes a major shift in the French attitude towards Germany, which has made a subsequent stable French-German partnership possible; (3) Finally the ECSC has been important in the *foreign economic field* by laying the foundation for the community of "the Six", which gave rise to the well-known market-split in Western Europe between the two trading blocs, the EEC and EFTA.

The following analysis of Denmark's relations with the ECSC in the years around its creation must be seen against this background. The analysis will, necessarily, have to touch upon some fundamental questions regarding the conditions in which Danish foreign policy was formulated in the early post-war period. Was Denmark willing to participate in a closely integrated Western Europe thereby ceding formal sovereignty to a supranational authority? With the creation of the ECSC a process began which eventually placed Denmark's two main trading partners, Great Britain and West Germany, in different market blocs. This raised the question of reconsidering Danish relations – both politically and economically – with these two countries, which traditionally had been the principal Great Power actors in the Danish enviroment. Politically the inclination was to go with Great Britain, but economically Denmark was increasingly dependant on the southern market, not least in respect to necessary imports of raw materials for the continued industrialization of the country. Immanent in this situation was a question of priority between political and economic interests; at the same time these interests were far from unambiguous.

The analysis will focus on these fundamental questions. However, its conclusions should be regarded as tentative due to the quality of the material on which they are based. The material is mainly drawn from the archives of the Danish Foreign Ministry. In this material one very seldom finds statements of principle, which forces the historian to draw conclusions in a more indirect way and/or to employ a great variety of different source material. Another reason is a pronounced tendency among Danish decision-makers to postpone important decisions in an attempt to keep all options open as long as possible. In the end Denmark never managed to reach a final decision regarding membership or non-membership in the ECSC. All the way through Denmark kept open the option of applying for membership on short notice.[1]

1950-52: *Denmark as an Interested Observer*

Upon launching the Schuman Plan in May 1950, France invited Great Britain to join. The subsequent Anglo-French talks were, however, already abandoned a month later. In Britain the opposition to such a strong commitment to western European integration was too fundamental. The British 'no' was thus limiting discussions to the six continental countries, which eventually signed the Paris Treaty on the European Coal and Steel Community in April 1951. Denmark had not been invited to participate, and no official interest in joining the negotiations concerning the future community can be seen. The question did not come up in the first instance because Denmark was a steel consumer, not a steel producer, and therefore had little direct stake in the main issues covered by the treaty.

On the other hand, this conclusion does not mean that the Schuman Plan was looked upon with indifference in Denmark. The potential economic consequences of a producer cartel being formed was realized, and the Foreign Ministry also seems to have been fully aware of the far-reaching political implications of the plan, and that its realization would create new conditions affecting Denmark's position in Europe.[2] In May and June 1950 the main newspapers covered the issue in several front page articles and editorials, and it was greatly deplored that negotiations with Great Britain had failed. In general the plan was seen as a positive step towards securing peace and greater European cooperation.[3]

Not taking part in the negotiations, Danish authorities were not forced to make up their minds concerning the supranational aspects of the French proposal. But the initial Danish reaction to this part of the Schuman Plan may be discerned indirectly from the minutes of a UNISCAN meeting in November 1950. UNISCAN was a loose and informal economic cooperation between Great Britain, Norway, Sweden and Denmark, created by a British initiative in January 1950. Financial questions were in the forefront of the deliberations, but discussions in this forum also give an insight into official attitudes towards the principal questions of European integration among the UNISCAN countries.

Already in the autumn of 1950 the implications of the Schuman Plan seem to have given rise to a certain anxiety in Norway. At the above-mentioned meeting, held in Oslo, Arne Skaug, the Norwegian delegate, drew up the fundamental dividing line between the attitude of the UNISCAN countries and the continental countries, stating that the first group tended to favour supranational institutions, whereas the second group preferred intergovernmental cooperation. Answering a direct question from Arne Skaug, the British delegate confirmed the well-known British position. But Dag Hammarskjöld, the Swedish delegate, as well as E. Wærum from Denmark took a somewhat different stand. They were not willing to accept the Norwegian categorization without reservations, stating that their positions would be less doctrinaire; to them the continental approach looked advantageous in some respects.[4]

The discussion showed that the British-Scandinavian 'rejection-front' towards the integration process on the continent was not quite as closely knit as is often supposed. And later on Denmark continued to enunciate a separate position at the UNISCAN meetings – both in regard to general questions of European integration and in regard to the specific issues of the Schuman Plan.

After the ECSC Treaty had been signed in April 1951, Danish authorities began investigations into the future economic impact on Denmark of the new organization. Such investigations seem first to have been undertaken by the Ministry of Trade and Industry in consultation with private industry.[5] The Foreign Ministry, however, did not seriously discuss the Schuman Plan until well into the autumn of the same year. It was characteristic of the Danish approach that the question of possible Danish membership in the ECSC – at least during this period – was almost exclusively dealt with in the Foreign Ministry's economic department.

A couple of reports were prepared in November 1951 spelling out the economic advantages and disadvantages of Danish membership. These reports served as background material for a UNISCAN meeting in London the following month. They contained no clear policy recommendation, however, concluding that Danish policy for the present should be guided by a wait-and-see attitude.[6]

Examining the various arguments, the main report first of all stressed Danish dependency on import of raw materials from the six Schuman countries, especially in respect to iron and steel. The report laid bare how this dependency had increased compared to the pre-war period, whereas imports of the same goods from Great Britain were declining. By becoming a member, Denmark's supply of steel would be better secured, the system of double-prizing could be avoided, and the Danish bargaining position would be strengthened. The tendency in the report was rather in favour of membership from an economic point of view, but it was also stressed that the future trading policy of the member countries could not be foreseen, which made it difficult to reach a final judgement.

Backed by this report, Hjalmar Collin, the leader of the Foreign Ministry's economic department, took part in the December meeting of the UNISCAN in London. Just before he left, the Ministry had received a dispatch from the Embassy in London telling that Great Britain maintained its refusal to participate in any kind of supranational cooperation. According to Lord Hood, the leader of the "Western Organizations Department", "the British Government was prepared to be represented in organizations like the OEEC, whose competence did not encroach upon the autonomy of member countries, but it was firmly committed not to accept a supranational European authority."[7]

But for Denmark, economic considerations carried a heavy weight. During the discussions of the ECSC issue at the UNISCAN meeting Collin was the only delegate willing to consider membership in the planned new organization. He stressed the specific position of Denmark and added,

> "Denmarks depends very much on the import of coal and steel from the Schuman countries. As a consequence of the many uncertain factors attached to the plan, e.g. the trade policy the organization will pursue when dealing with non-member countries and the conditions of entry, it was still not possible to make a final decision as to whether to join or not. By avoiding double pricing and by securing more stable supplies and perhaps lower prices through lower production costs, Denmark wanted to consider carefully the advantages membership might bring for Danish industry on competitive lines."[8]

As can be seen, a purely pragmatic attitude lay behind this mode of argument; an attitude which was an echo of the position defended by Collin earlier during the meeting when more general principles were being debated. Here the first item on the agenda concerned current tendencies and problems in European cooperation. The three other delegates all started out by discarding the supranational approach; as an alternative they came out in favour of what, respectively, was labelled an intergovernmental, a functional and a multilateral approach. To begin with Collin did not at all enter this discussion. Instead he stressed three main points of a more concrete nature, guiding Danish policy-making in international economic cooperation: (1) the economic problems of Europe cannot be solved without cooperation with the United States and Canada; (2) the participation of Sweden and Switzerland should be ensured (in order to prevent economic questions from being entrusted to NATO); (3) overlapping of functions between different organizations should be prevented (taking account of the limited resources of small countries). Only towards the end of this discussion of principles he made a short – not very precise – contribution by stating: "concerning the federalist approach Denmark had not yet made a final decision regarding the ECSC."[9]

It may, of course, be questioned how much importance can be ascribed to loose Danish statements at UNISCAN meetings as regards the Danish position in the political-ideological discussion on integration. Nevertheless, it is remarkable that Danish top officials seem to have had fixed political guidelines in entering these discussions to a lesser degree than their British, Norwegian and Swedish colleagues. Also, UNISCAN meetings were the forum where Britain had the most direct opportunity to be informed about the attitudes of what were considered her closest partners on the question of integration. Finally, Danish statements at these meeting were parallel to the ones that were voiced regarding the role of the parliamentary assembly of the European Council.[10]

The most obvious explanation for this Danish middle-course is the fact that Denmark had an overriding interest in preventing further 'bloc-building' in Europe. From the beginning of the 1950's it was a recurrent nightmare scenario of the various Danish governments to see Britain and West Germany, the country's two main trading partners, being placed within two different economic camps. With the date of the establishment of the Coal and Steel Community approaching, this scenario gained its first real bit of substance, which may contribute to explaining the less rigorous Danish opposition to the principle of integration.

To this argument must be added the fact that, very early, Ole Bjørn Kraft, the Danish Foreign Minister 1950-53, had been an ardent supporter of the European idea. During the debate on the ratification of the Statute of the Council of Europe in 1949 he spoke out in favour of a closely knit European Union;[11] and he regarded the gradual giving up of sovereignty on the part of the nation states as both a necessary and feasible road towards the creation of a United States of Europe.[12] When Foreign Minister he was less outspoken in his statements on future European development, but one can find indications of his sympathy for the integration initiatives taken by the continental states.[13]

What has been said so far makes it hardly surprising that the perception was spread among "the Six" that Denmark might be willing to participate in the supranational community of the Schuman countries. This seems to have coincided with a wish on the part of some of these countries to have Denmark as a member.

1952-53: Denmark Considers Membership

In the spring of 1952 endeavours to reach a decision on Danish relations with the now almost established ECSC organization were intensified. In a new Foreign Ministry report of April 22 it was recommended that as a first step towards possible membership, Denmark should approach the French government confidentially in order to be informed on conditions of admittance. In the report some of the main articles of the treaty were examined. It was especially emphasized that, according to art.59, a system of allocation between member countries could be established in periods of shortage, and as a consequence restrictions in exports to third countries could be introduced.[14]

Apparently, the report was approved by the director as well as the minister, but the suggested step of approaching the French government does not seem to have been taken. One reason was probably the information Denmark received a few days later during the visit by D.V. Spierenburg to Copenhagen.

Spierenburg was head of the division for foreign economic relations in the Dutch Ministry of Economy and was to become the Dutch member of The High Authority. At a meeting in the Danish Foreign Ministry on April 25, Spierenburg indirectly offered Denmark the still vacant 9th seat in The High Authority, stressing that a quick decision had to be made. A candidate would soon be nominated, and then it would be extremely difficult for Denmark to obtain a seat, since it would require a new ratification process in the member states. Spierenburg also held out the advantages of membership, seen from not only a Danish but also from a European point of view. The ECSC would block any future German plan of expansion, and would thus be of great foreign policy importance to all Germany's neighbouring countries.[15]

It is hardly surprising that contacts between the Netherlands and Denmark were established at this stage. Both countries had a vital interest in the ongoing discussions of a supranational Green Pool, and this issue was also taken up during Spierenburg's visit to Copenhagen. Moreover the Netherlands was the most west-orientated of the six Schuman countries and was quite uneasy about its position in a club dominated by France and Germany. This fact appears in communications from the Danish Embassy in Hague.[16]

Later on in the same year Eivind Bartels, the Danish ambassador to France, who was to became the first head of the Danish representation to the ECSC, could likewise report that political rather than economic calculations determined a favourable attitude towards Danish membership among members of the High Authority. Again Spierenburg was the main source,[17] but Jean Monnet also belonged to this group. After an official visit to Luxembourg in November Bartels could report to the Foreign Ministry:

> "Furthermore, it was obvious, especially from M. Monnet's comments, that the organization would be favourably disposed towards Danish membership. The interest of the organization in such membership does not depend on economic conditions directly related to the coal and steel problems, but on the fact that it would be desir-

able for the organization to have a *Scandinavian* member country with considerable *consumer interests*. Besides it was fully in accordance with M. Monnet's line that the Schuman Organization marks the beginning of more intensive cooperation in Europe."[18]

On the basis of his talks in Luxembourg Bartels concluded, that "it may be said with rather great certainty, that Danish membership would be welcomed."

Although external conditions for a Danish application for membership in the ECSC seemed favourable, Danish authorities – while keeping the option of membership open – had no haste in taking decisive action. At the UNISCAN meeting in June Collin went a little further than previously, stating "that Denmark may find it desirable or even necessary to join the Community".[19] But neither the desirability nor the necessity of Danish membership was evident in 1952.

Below, we shall return to the internal political discussions among the Danish parties. For the moment it must suffice to say that the Danish position in 1952 was still very unclear and undecided. But so was the European development. That year saw the further development of supranational plans on the part of the Six. The Green Pool and the EDC negotiations were progressing; and from September an inquiry was started – under the auspices of the ECSC Parliamentary Assembly – into the possibility of creating a federalist-inspired political community among the Six (EPC). At the same time developments on the steel market meant that the "necessity" Collin had talked about at the UNISCAN meeting in June had not yet materialized. In spite of the ongoing rearmament speed-up after the outbreak of the Korean War in 1950, there was a surplus of steel on the world market and prices were falling. The Danish hesitation to make a final commitment regarding ECSC membership must be seen against this background.

Nevertheless, in January 1953 the issue was brought up for political decision in Denmark. But, perhaps characteristically, no definite conclusion was reached. At a meeting of the Government's Economic Committee on Jan. 7th it was decided that Denmark should not take steps to become a member, but for the time being appoint the Danish representative at the OEEC (Bartels) as an observer, assisted by a representative from the Ministry of Trade and Industry stationed at Luxembourg.[20] However, the subsequent instruction to Bartels indicates that the decision should be regarded as only a temporary one and that all options should still be kept open.[21]

The available sources for this analysis do not disclose to what extent considerations of a political rather than economic nature played a role for the decision-makers. Earlier indications from inside the Foreign Ministry will be discussed in the next section in an attempt to throw light on this question.

Was Denmark Rready to Join "The Six"?

Several aspects are involved when trying to assess the Danish willingness to join the community of the Six at this early stage. The first to be discussed here is the ideological one concerning the general Danish attitude towards the transfer of sovereignty to supranational institutions.[22]

In the preceding sections it has already been demonstrated how Danish delegates at UNISCAN meetings argued for a pragmatic and non-doctrinaire approach to the integration question; this was done somewhat at odds with the other delegates, except perhaps for the Swedish one. As already mentioned, a similar Danish approach can be found on other European issues. This is especially true of the Danish position in the discussions on the future political structure of the European Council. Thus, in an internal Foreign Ministry note of March 1952 you read:

> ".... the Danish position is that we view favourably the establishment of specialized agencies that exercise supranational authority within limited fields. The functional integration of Europe in an ever increasing number of fields seems a much firmer basis for the final unification of Europe than a once and for all federation with competence in just about every field; a federation whose consequences cannot be predicted in advance and without a basis of experience on which to build."[23]

This statement comes close to an endorsement of the so-called neo-functionalist approach to integration. In the material of the Foreign Ministry it is possible to find further documentation of this line of thought although the question never seems to be have been treated at length or at higher levels in the Ministry. On the basis of this material it is not possible to refute the general conception of a certain Danish hesitation regarding supranationalism; the material basically documents the prevailing attitude among certain officials in the Ministry and refers to a situation, when the question had not yet become deeply politicised. Nevertheless, it seems safe to conclude that the supranational character of the ECSC was not in itself an argument against closer Danish ties to the community of the Six, at least not in so far as the issue was considered inside the Foreign Ministry.[24] Beside the ideological aspect, Danish relations with the two great powers in the area with whom Denmark had the closest trade links, e.g. Great Britain and Germany, are important to examine.

The Foreign Ministry material clearly documents that the fears of Germany as a potential threat to Danish independence were still vivid. In Autumn 1952 in correspondence with Eivind Bartels in Paris on Danish relations with the ECSC, Erling Kristiansen, the deputy head, later head of the economic department, pointed to the danger of German dominance in Europe. He considered it possible that the ECSC would provide Germany with a short cut to a "Viertes Reich" by creating a West European "Grossraum" directed by West Germany. Kristiansen, thus, expressed an opinion at variance with the intentions which induced France and other members of the Six to establish closer ties with West Germany after the War. Bartels opposed this view, pointing to the French motives behind the ECSC, and Danish interest in participating in the organs where the European development was being shaped.[25]

The 'classic' Danish fear of succumbing to German influence or even dominance obviously still permeated large sections of the decision-making environment. The delicate relationship with the big neighbour to the south probably played a prominent role in shaping general attitudes to European integration; attitudes which, contrary to the European integration approach, favoured other solutions, for instance intensified Nordic cooperation.[26] But more research into the role of Germany in the formulation of Danish post-war foreign policy is definitely needed to clarify this matter in full detail.[27] Here we shall finally touch upon certain aspects of Danish-British relations relevant for understanding the Danish attitude towards the ECSC in 1952-53.

A certain ambiguity characterized Danish-British relations in the post-war period. On the one hand, Britain was regarded as the great liberator from the Second World War, and she remained by far the main Danish trading partner. Of total exports appr. 40% went to the British market in 1950.[28] And at meetings of the UNISCAN, Danish representatives never hesitated to stress how important the British attitude was for Danish positions on questions of European cooperation. Thus, when during the meeting in June 1952 Collin aired the possibility of Denmark joining the ECSC, he ended up by stating that "Denmark's attitude will be influenced decisively by the stand taken by Great Britain and our Scandinavian neighbours."[29]

On the other hand, in the beginning of the 1950's there was a growing realization that the British market would become less important in the future, whereas the opposite would be the case for the continental market, especially the German one. Moreover, since the end of the war Danish-British trade relations had not been all that harmonious. From 1945 to 1950 Britain had been very reluctant to let Denmark import scarce commodities such as coal and steel and had always demanded at least world market prices for these products, whereas her willingness to pay the same prices for her agricultural imports from Denmark had been proportionally low. It is this policy which prompted the Swedish scholar Bengt Nilsson to conclude that "the British Labour government pursued an aggressive trade policy towards Denmark and sought in the years before its fall in 1951 to treat Denmark as an economic satellite of Britain and her Commonwealth".[30]

123

From the UNISCAN meetings Britain was well aware of the Danish wish to eventually join the ECSC, and it seems that the Foreign Office was quite worried about Denmark taking such a step.[31] Shortly before the Danish "decision" of Jan. 7th 1953, Her Majesty's Ambassador in Copenhagen, Bertoud, received a cable saying that the Foreign Office "would regard such a development as unfortunate, and should do what we can to prevent it, both for political and for economic reasons."[32] Later on in January during a lunch with Erling Kristiansen in the British Embassy, Bordet – "off the record" – expressed concern over Denmark's "flirt" with the Schuman Plan. To this Kristiansen replied, according to his own account, "I confirmed the importance of the supply question and added that also a political aspect was involved. I firmly believed that in certain circles of the population there was a growing interest in the basic idea on which the special efforts to cooperate are founded: the world situation requires such intensification of Western European cooperation that new ways must be found, e.g. economic, military and political integration. The possibility that the realization of these plans might influence Denmark's relations with her partners could hardly be rejected."[33]

This way Kristiansen did nothing to overcome the British concern. On the contrary, he did not hesitate to include political-ideological considerations in explaining the Danish openness towards ECSC membership – considerations that did not fit well into official British policy.

Danish willingness to depart from a British-led course in its policy towards European integration may be further substantiated from the sources relating to a subsequent meeting between the Foreign Minister Ole Bjørn Kraft and his British colleague, Anthony Eden. On that occasion, according to the speech notes prepared by the Foreign Ministry, Kraft told Eden:

> "In our opinion ... the Schuman Plan is logically only a first instalment of integration, to be followed if possible by similar results in other economic fields as well as in the military and ultimately in the political field. Therefore, we are inclined to adopt what I may call the global approach. That is to say that, from the political point of view, it would be preferable not to reach any final decision on the question of our relations with the ECSC until it is clear what becomes of the other integration initiatives so that, on the basis of that knowledge, it will be possible for Denmark to make a general decision with regard to our future relations with Continental Europe. ... I think I should add that it is my impression that among the Danish people there is a growing instinctive interest in an intensification of cooperation in some form or other in Western Europe, and that, in the absence of better plans, this interest might be focused on the idea of a "Little Europe."[34]

Also on this level the Foreign Ministry regarded it as appropriate to convey to the British government the impression that Denmark might follow more independent ways in her European policy. Undoubtedly, there was an element of tactics in the Danish behaviour towards Britain on this point. Politically, there was at this stage, like later on, not much support for a close alignment with the continental powers at the expense of Great Britain. But new developments on the Western European scene were under way. And the prospect of a change in attitude in the population and in the political parties may not have been considered unrealistic or even undesirable by the officials in the Ministry and by the Minister himself.

If we return to the meeting of the Government's Economic Committee on Jan. 7th, it seems most obvious to conclude that the situation was not yet sufficiently clarified to warrant a final decision on Denmark's relations with the ECSC – neither from an economic nor from a political point of view. Considerations regarding the specific British reaction do not seem to have played any substantial role in explaining the Danish prudence. At a more general level the source material even seems to indicate that at least some of the high-ranking decision-makers in principle were quite open towards joining a more binding kind of cooperation together with the Six. Still, the conditions for such a substantial change in the country's foreign policy were not yet at hand. One reason must be sought in the internal political situation in the country, while another related to Denmark's position within the general European framework.

Obviously, in the beginning of 1953 the Danish Government had great difficulties in mapping out the political coordinates of the future European development. A Foreign Ministry memorandum of May 1953 analyzing Danish relations with the Six, reads:

> "Participation in the endeavours to bring about economic, political and military integration within this group requires an over-all analysis of the various problems of primary importance for the foreign policy of the country, among other things an appraisal of the expected development of world politics with special reference to the German question plus a judgment of the effects of such a change in foreign policy on Denmark's relations with the other Nordic countries and Great Britain."[35]

Such an overall analysis seems never to have been undertaken. European developments still did not compel the Danish government to make a definite choice. But as a conclusion it may be noted that several years before the creation of the EEC the prospect of a unilateral entry (i.e. among the UNISCAN countries) into the community of the Six was already part of the deliberations of the Danish Foreign Ministry. It seems also safe to conclude that, regarding the more narrow question of Danish membership in the European Coal and Steel Community, economic considerations rather than those based on ideological or general foreign policy preferences were decisive in establishing the Danish position – or lack of position.

Concluding Remarks

After the spring of 1953 the question of a possible Danish membership in the ECSC was no longer on the agenda; at least not until the beginning of 1955. At this point Danish relations with the ECSC had become somewhat strained because of several Danish complaints regarding the price policy of the organization. Inside the ECSC the issue was referred to as "la quèstion danoise".[36] According to a statement in January 1955, Monnet was of the opinion that the easiest solution to this question would be Danish membership;[37] but not until the autumn of 1955 was the character of Denmark's relations with the ECSC again to be discussed internally in the country. During a further visit to Copenhagen, Spierenburg proposed what amounted to partial Danish membership (concerning coke and coal). This was followed by lengthy deliberations by Danish authorities; but once again no final decision was reached.[38] One of the reasons was that in 1956 the issue was overshadowed by other developments, first of all by the British-inspired plan for a Wider Free Trade Area in Western Europe and by intensified negotiations on a Nordic Customs Union.

As regards the entire period 1950-57 one may conclude that Denmark followed the integration process on the continent with an open mind, but abstained from making any final commitment either one way or the other. It is difficult to talk about a deliberate Danish integration strategy, but the Foreign Ministry source material from the period suggests that a kind of pragmatic middle-of-the-road course was followed, leaving all options open. But as long as the general European development was still so much in a state of flux, Denmark seems to have preferred to sit on the fence watching developments rather than influencing them or committing herself irrevocably to any definite solution. This was fully in accordance with modern Denmark's basic foreign policy tradition.

Notes

1. This article is the result of my participation in a Danish research project on Danish European policy 1945-55 carried out under the auspices of the Research Council Initiative "Dansk Politik Under Forandring 1945-1985 ("Danish Politics in Transition 1945-1985"). A more profound treatment of the questions raised in this article will result when my research project has been completed. At this stage a general reference may be given to Vibeke Sørensen: "How to Be-

Denmark and The European Coal and Steel Community, 1950-1953

come a Member of a Club Without Joining. Danish Policy with Respect to European Integration Schemes, 1950-1957", in *Scandinavian Journal of History*, 1991(2). Here a first account is made of Danish relations to the ECSC based on primary sources with an emphasis on foreign economic relations. See also her treatment of the issue in Vibeke Sørensen 1993: "Between Independence and Integration: Denmark's Shifting Strategies", in Alan S. Milward (ed.): *The Frontier of National Sovereignty*. History and Theory 1945-1992, London 1993, pp. 96-98 and pp. 103-05. A more general presentation in Danish may be found in Vibeke Sørensen: "Fra Marshall-plan til de store markedsdannelser, 1945-1959", in Tom Swienty (ed.): *Danmark i Europa 1945-1993*, Copenhagen 1994, pp. 9-91.

2. The political implications of the plan were extensively covered in dispatches from the Embassies in Paris and London. June 22nd. the Ambassador in London reports a confidential statement by Schuman saying that he regarded a realization of his plan as a first step towards the rearmament of Germany (*Danish Foreign Ministry Archives* (= UM) at Rigsarkivet (The National Archives), 74 B 8a, file no. 1).
3. In a dispatch from Copenhagen dated June 8th. the French Ambassador gave a detailed overview of Danish press reactions. *ECSC archives*, AE 3/13 (Ministère des Affaires Etrangères 1948-1960. Communauté Européenne du Charbon et de l'Acier (1950-1960), file no. 558).
4. Minutes from the second UNISCAN meeting in Oslo, Nov. 23-25, 1950, in UM 73 C 37a, file no.2.
5. Account of a meeting in the Foreign Ministry June 12th. 1951 preparing a UNISCAN meeting in Stockholm June 18-19th., in Ibid.
6. The reports were dated Nov. 22nd., Nov. 27th. and Dec. 4th. 1951, Ibid, file no.3.
7. Dispatch of Dec. 1st. 1951, UM 74 B 8a, file no.2.
8. Summary of proceedings at the fourth meeting of UNISCAN, London Dec. 12-13th. 1951, in UM 73C 37a, file no.3 (translated from Danish).
9. Ibid.
10. Hans Branner: "På vagt eller på spring. Danmark og den europæiske integration 1948-1953", in Birgit Nüchel Thomsen (ed.): *The Odd Man Out. Danmark og den europæiske integration 1948-1992*, Odense 1993, pp.33-42.
11. For the Danish parliamentary debates, see *Rigsdagstidende, Folketingets Forhandlinger* (Parliamentary Records) 1948-49, col. 5208-10.
12. Cf. Ole Bjørn Kraft's memoirs: *Danmark skifter kurs. En konservativ politikers erindringer 1947-1950* Copenhagen 1975, p.65.
13. See below pp.13-14. When the so-called Eden plan was discussed in the Committee of Ministers of the European Council in March 1952, Kraft said: "It was now necessary to establish the links which should exist between the more limited group resolved to form a supranational authority with limited functions and the other countries which remained outside, *though perhaps only for the time being*" (my italics, HB). Minutes of meeting March 19-20, in UM 74 B 8a, file no.3.
14. Report by the economic department, section 4 (ØP IV). UM 74 C 13f, file no.1.
15. UM 74 B 8a, file no.3. Spierenburg was invited to Copenhagen by the Danish minister of Finance, Thorkil Kristensen.
16. E.g. a letter from Ambassador F. Lund to C.A.C. Brun, the Foreign Ministry, May 15, 1952. Ibid.
17. Letter from Bartels to Collin, the Foreign Ministry, Oct.2., UM 74 C 13f, file no.1.
18. Report on an officiel visit to Luxembourg Nov.24-26, 15 p. Ibid.
19. UM 74 B 8a, file no.3.

20. The wording of the decision can be be found in a Foreign Ministry memo of May 13th. 1953, UM 74 C 13f, file no.2.
21. Ibid., file no.1.
22. Only a short presentation of this issue can be given here. For a more extensive treatment, see Hans Branner: "Danish European Policy since 1945. The Question of Sovereignty", in Morten Kelstrup (ed.): *European Integration and Denmark's Participation*, Copenhagen 1992.
23. Working paper prepared for a meeting March 19-20th. 1952 of the Council of Ministers of the European Council to discuss the so-called Eden plan, UM 5 E 34 b/1, file no.7.
24. Cf. a draft-letter written by the Foreign Ministry in June 1952 for Hans Hedtoft, the former Social Democratic Prime Minister, who had been asked by a Dutch party colleague what the Danish attitude towards the Schuman Plan was. In the draft it is stated that questions of principle are not important to explain Danish hesitation about participation in the plan. What matters the most is concern about becoming dependent on producer and export countries of protectionist inclinations; but also the attitude of the other Scandinavian countries and the U.K. is important to Denmark (UM 74 B 8a, file no.3.).
25. Letters of Oct. 11th. (Kristiansen) and Dec. 1st. 1952 (Bartels), UM 74 C 13f, file no.1.
26. Although also very important, relations with the other Scandinavian countries will be omitted from this presentation. These relations had a less pronounced influence in the years 1950-53 with a Liberal-Conservative government, compared to periods before and after when the Social Democrats were in power. On this point, see also the articles by Molin & Olesen and Laursen & Malmborg in this volume.
27. According to a later statement by Erling Kristiansen there was a marked change in the Danish perception of the German "threat" before and after 1955. That year a Danish-German protocol was signed regulating the minority questions on both sides of the border. *Interview* made Sept. 19th, 1992.
28. See article by F. Just & T.B. Olesen in this book.
29. Cf. note 19.
30. Cf. Bengt Nilsson: "Butter, Bacon and Coal. Anglo-Danish Commercial Relations, 1947-1951", in *Scandinavian Journal of History*, 1988 (2/3), p. 277.
31. Dispatch by C.Weir, Luxembourg to Foreign Office, Nov.26, 1952, in *Documents on British Policies Overseas*, Series II, vol.I, London, p.996.
32. Ibid.
33. UM 74 C 13f, file no.1.
34. Ibid. The speech notes are undated, but probably stem from the end of Jan. 1953. Records of the conversation have not yet been found.
35. Ibid, file no.2.
36. *ECSC archives* (Florence), especially CEAB (= Commission des Communautés Européennes) 4/186, 5/349 and CM 1/1954/217, 1/1955/9, 1/1955/16, 1/1955/315.
37. Ibid. CM 1/1955/9.
38. UM 74 C 13f, file no.3

Danish Agriculture and the European Market Schism, 1945-1960

By Flemming Just & Thorsten B. Olesen

The Forgotten Decade

In many ways the 1950s is a forgotten decade, at least in Danish historiography. Nothing in particular happened it seems. The overall performance of the Danish economy was rather disappointing, with low growth rates, relatively high unemployment rates and chronic balance of payments problems. These problems reflected the structural imbalances of the early Danish post-war economy. On the other hand, one should not overemphasize the stalemate situation of the Danish economy. After all, structural adjustment took place in the 1950s laying the foundation for a process of sustained economic growth from the end of the decade onwards and for completing the transformation of the Danish economy from a predominantly agriculturally based economy to an industrial economy.[1]

The lack of research into the 1950s is also revealed in the field of agricultural history.[2] The following analysis will attempt to fill a bit of this particular gap. It will focus on the period 1945-1960, analyzing economic and trade developments in relation to the Danish agricultural sector. Before entering into this analysis a short introductory section will present the basic features of the evolution of a modern capitalist economy in Denmark with particular focus on the role of agriculture in that process.

The period under scrutiny, 1945-1960, started with great expectations of a revival of international markets, but ended in disillusionment for Danish agriculture. World markets did revive again, but trade liberalisation was much quicker for industry than for agriculture. In fact, trade in agricultural products experienced growing levels of protectionism and subsidization during the 1950s. The present article will explore this process in more detail. It will discuss how post-war international trade cooperation and organization affected the Danish economy in general and the agricultural sector in particular. At the same time it will analyze how this development influenced the political balance between agricultural and industrial interests and between liberal free trade policies and Social Democratic state intervention. Within this context the article will finally discuss how agriculture's attitudes to the various European market schemes, from the OEEC trade liberalisation plans of 1949/50 over the Green Pool negotiations to the creation of the EEC and EFTA, were shaped.

Flemming Just & Thorsten B. Olesen

The British Larder

Until the last third of the 19th century grain and livestock were the main Danish export articles. But animal production came to the forefront as the growing industrialised markets in Great Britain and Germany demanded butter and pork. This development was furthered by decreasing grain prices and by the creation in the 1880s of a very viable co-operative food processing industry. The limited requirements of the home market coupled with the high productivity of the farming sector meant that two-thirds of the production could be sent abroad.

As a consequence Danish agriculture acquired the role of larder of the industrialised British economy, a situation which still persisted fifty years later. During the interwar period 70-75% of agriculture's total export value derived from Great Britain and 20-25% from Germany. Only 5% was accounted for by other countries.[3] The extraordinary market conditions after World War II forced agriculture to find new markets. But in 1950 Great Britain still represented 54% of the compound agricultural export share, followed by Germany with about 20%.[4]

For these reasons the Danish economy could be claimed to be linked to the British economy in a manner resembling a typical colonial dependency. In 1950 about 70% of the entire value of Danish exports consisted of agricultural products, mainly staples such as butter, bacon and eggs, being sailed over the North Sea.[5] The other Scandinavian countries, Norway and Sweden, found themselves in much the same dependent position vis-a-vis Great Britain and Germany with exports based on a few specialised (processed) goods such as timber, paper, iron, steel, and fish. On the other hand, this dependent position constituted the framework for the particular Scandinavian road to economic modernization. The export of the above-mentioned products was the result of natural comparative advantages in the international division of labour. The Scandinavian supplies of raw materials and food stuffs were exchanged for processed industrial goods, thus forming part of a complementary trade.[6]

The close links between agriculture and Great Britain was one of the most important structural features of the Danish economy. Another feature was the lack of natural resources. Agriculture had to import feeding stuffs, grain and fertilisers, while the nascent industry was completely dependent on imports of raw materials and semi-manufactured articles. The need for open markets for exports and imports explains why Denmark was traditionally one of the most free market orientated countries in Europe. Together with the Netherlands she maintained the lowest tariff rates which, however, were compensated through quantitative import restrictions.

The free trade orientation was a consequence of the political strength of Agriculture, both at the organisational level and the parliamentarian level. The agricultural and co-operative organisations were the strongest interest organisations in the country whereas the political backing stemmed from the influential Liberal (Venstre) and Social Liberal (Det radikale Venstre) parties, supporters of the farmers and the small-holders respectively.[7] In the period after 1929 the Social Democratic Party was in power most of the time, but although ties to rural areas were weak, the party had to pay serious attention to the interests of Agriculture. The reason was both economic and political. Economically the Social Democrats were dependent on the foreign currency earning capacity of Agriculture both in order to secure employment in the food processing industry itself, but also to pay for the fundamental imports needed to stimulate an overall process of industrialization in Denmark. On the political side the Social Democratic Party, unlike its Norwegian and Swedish sister parties, never achieved a parliamentary majority. The Party, thus, had to look for coalition partners which usually turned out to be the small-holders party, Det radikale Venstre.

The power of the agricultural interest groups is demonstrated by the fact that most parties accepted that the agricultural organisations exerted strong influence on the running of the Ministry of Agriculture. Broadly speaking, the civil servants of the Ministry were only fully charged with matters of a legal, veterinary and controlling character whereas Agriculture had a virtual monopoly on agronomic expertise, production, sales etc.. For that reason powers were often delegated from the Ministry to the agricultural organisations, for instance when long term trade contracts were negotiated with other countries.

All in all agricultural policy in Denmark was characterized by a high degree of segmentation in the sense that it excluded most other interests from the formulation of agricultural policies other than those originating within the sector itself. Nevertheless, agriculture's political leverage had its limits. In 1929 industry and the crafts in fact employed a larger proportion of the workforce than agriculture (32% vs. 29%) ensuring that attention was also paid to their sectoral interests, which were less free trade orientated than those of agriculture.

However, the worst blow dealt to the free market economy was delivered by events in the international system, by the world depression and subsequently by World War II. During the 1930s and 1940s the Danish economy became strongly regulated. Imports were controlled, consumer prices fixed and even agriculture had to rely on various measures of state intervention to overcome the worst period during the depression.[8] During the German occupation of Denmark 1940-1945 Agriculture regained economic strength and as a consequence returned to its dogma of an unregulated economy. Thus, the immediate post-war period witnessed a major political clash between Agriculture's and Venstre's free market orientated attitudes, on the one hand, and Social Democratic visions of a planned road to industrialization on the other.[9]

Post-War Production

After the war the attempts by the Liberal government (1945-1947) to effect a quick abolition of import restrictions and economic regulations proved disastrous. The Danish balance of payments deficit soared to unparalleled heights in 1946 and in the face of such a development the government had to put a brake to its liberalization schemes. Like other countries Denmark had serious foreign currency problems and had to reserve her limited currency resources for imports of feeding stuff and corn. These items were essential for expanding butter and bacon production and, thus, essential for the Danish foreign currency earnings. This link was also recognised by Social Democrats who saw no short-run alternative to boosting agricultural exports as a means to secure the necessary imports of industrial raw materials and consumer goods. In fact the Social Democratic minority government which replaced the Venstre-government in 1947 was willing to employ stricter regulations on trade and domestic prices to secure this goal.[10]

Therefore, when the prospect of Marshall aid was introduced in 1947, it seemed god-sent. Still, political attitudes to the plan varied considerably. The original emphasis of the programme, on planning, productivity improvement and growth appealed to Social Democrats who even hoped that the plan would provide the crucial margin for an industrial take-off. Agriculture and Venstre (and Industry and the Conservative Party), on the other hand, also realized the advantages of the dollar influx, but were sceptical of the planning aspects, especially the requirement of operating a long-term programme setting targets for investments, productivity and production. By and by, however, attitudes were reversed. When the American Marshall aid administration (the ECA) from 1949 onwards began to give higher priority to balanced state budgets, monetary discipline and the dismantling of trade barriers, the scepticism of Agriculture and the Liberals gave way, whereas the Social Democratic government could only observe that the political scope for its industrial development strategy was constantly shrinking. This tendency was reinforced by strong political pressure on the domestic scene. The government's attempts to control imports and to stimulate the export quota by limiting the supply of pork and butter on the home market was not popular. In the face of growing problems in accessing foreign markets Agriculture joined the chorus of those demanding a stop to the regulated economy – an issue which played an important role in the Social Democratic minority government's fall from power in October 1950.[11]

Thus, one can argue that the ECA policy politically benefitted the Liberal forces and, amongst them, Danish Agriculture in their opposition to Social Democratic plan economy experiments. But Agriculture's benefits from the Marshall Plan were also more direct in character. One of the most obvious advantages of the Plan, not only in Denmark but in most of Western Europe, was the transfer of technology built into the programme. Despite its competitiveness Danish agriculture needed such a technological injection. Mechanisation, for instance, had been slow to pick up due to the lack of foreign currency and the abundance of cheap labour during the recession of the 1930s. Even in 1948 less than 3% of the 200.000 Danish farms were equipped with a tractor. In 1960 more than half of the farms had one or more tractors.[12] During the same period one-third of all hired workers in agriculture left the land and migrated into Copenhagen and the major provincial towns attracted by higher wages and more leisure time. Nonetheless, agriculture was able to double its value of production from 3.67 billion DKK. in 1948 to 7.62 billion in 1960.[13]

These figures testify to a considerable increase in productivity, and must – everything being equal – be termed a success for the initial strategy of boosting agricultural production as a means to improve foreign currency earnings. But everything did not prove to be equal. From the late 1940s Danish agriculture experienced growing difficulties on the export markets, not because of lack of competitiveness, but because of protectionism. This problem, of course, might have been alleviated by increasing reliance on the home market. However, Danish home market consumption was already among the highest in Europe, and even Danes had limits to the amount of pork they could consume.

Danish Exports in the Immediate Post-War Years

Immediately after World War II food supplies in Europe were generally scarce and distribution chaotic. In order to secure a fair distribution of not only scarce food products, but also of feeding stuffs, industrial raw materials and ship tonnage, the allied authorities set up so-called Combined Boards. No country could, for instance, buy provisions in Denmark without an allocation authorization from the Combined Food Board and the connected Combined Executive Food Surplus Committee.

In Denmark the latter committee held a meeting every week, during which the distribution of surplus production was allotted. Prices and terms of trade were settled in negotiations between the British Ministry of Food and the Danish government which in fact meant the Danish agricultural organisations whose representatives dominated the State export boards.[14]

After one and a half years the committee was abolished and the export boards were entrusted with full responsibility for the fulfilment and administration of the many bilateral trade agreements. The boards, however, also took an active part in the negotiation of new agreements. They gathered information on production volume, stock in trade, and prospects for exports in different markets. The trade delegations were headed by a civil servant from the Ministry of Foreign Affairs, but the real bargaining in the agricultural area was left to the leaders and experts from the agricultural organisations and export boards. Civil servants from the Ministry of Agriculture also participated, but they seldom voiced serious disagreement with Agriculture's conduct of the negotiations. In 1950 the State export boards were abolished. They were replaced by new boards, also directed by the agricultural organisations, but with a private legal status. However, this did not change trade negotiations. As long as most trade was arranged through bilateral agreements state representatives and representatives of the private agricultural organisations were sitting close together in trade delegations.[15]

In the first years after World War II the international economy was a seller's market. For that reason in the autumn of 1947 Danish agriculture did not hesitate to reject a new trade agreement with the United Kingdom, and in the following months the total export was sold in other markets at more profitable prices.[16] In 1948, however, the agricultural market pendulum swung to a buyer's market. In such a situation Danish agriculture once again found it wiser to enter into long-term contracts with the United Kingdom although prices here were lower than world market prices. Decisive for the decision was the fact that export quantities were fixed and guaranteed for the next six years. Until the mid-50s Great Britain agreed to import 75% of the Danish butter export, 90% of bacon and pork, and 85% of the egg export. From a British point of view such an agreement also seemed advantageous. The three products constituted between 40% and 60% of total British imports in these product categories securing the British market a stable and cheap import flow.[17]

Stable prices often have a strong attraction. In a world of bilateral trade agreements, however, it is difficult to see the overall Danish advantages of such an arrangement (if Sterling surpluses cannot be converted into dollars or gold). Even taking account of the fact that negotiations were left in the hands of the representatives of Agriculture themselves, such dependency is best explained with reference to international developments restricting the free flow of agricultural products.

International Attempts to Regulate Agricultural Trade

When from the end of the 1930s food-importing countries had been faced with major financial difficulties, tariff barriers had been erected and domestic production increased in response. The result had been a collapse in trade resulting in great production surpluses in the traditional exporting countries. Meanwhile, the pioneering studies by John Boyd Orr had demonstrated how widespread a phenomenon malnutrition was even in the most advanced economies. In Great Britain one-third of the population was malnourished, mainly due to poverty.[18]

The creation of the United Nations' Food and Agriculture Organization (FAO) in 1945 was directly aimed at bridging the gap between surplus production on the one side and the existence of malnutrition and hunger on the other, by securing a better distribution of food. One of the means to achieve that goal was enunciated in the first FAO resolution, which stated that the aim was "to reduce barriers of every kind to international trade and to eliminate all forms of discriminatory restrictions thereon".[19]

In 1946, as a consequence, a FAO-initiative was responsible for setting up the World Food Board. Through a series of specialized committees working to establish maximum and minimum prices for the most important commodities, the Board sought to reduce the imbalances in world trade. Price stability was to be ensured by building up sufficiently large world food reserves or buffer stocks to cope with crop failure in any region. Later the proposal was moderated to create a simpler commodity clearing house.

The FAO-plan was idealistic, but unfortunately rather unrealistic and failed to pass at the FAO conference of November 1949. According to Martin Peterson's work on international interest organisations the project stumbled on the British Labour government's unwillingness to squeeze British consumers' purchasing power.[20] However, Britain was not alone in adopting this stance. In fact, most states were reluctant to sacrifice independence on the alter of binding multilateral arrangements as they wanted to preserve the maximum freedom of action. Such attitudes are also mirrored in the simultaneous efforts to form an international trade organisation, ITO, which finally were given up in 1950 when the American government realized that it could not persuade Congress to ratify the Havana-charter. Henceforth attempts to establish an international free trade regime centred on the much looser "General Agreement on Tariffs and Trade" (GATT) signed in 1947.[21]

Denmark became a member of GATT in 1949, but benefits were small. In GATT negotiations were carried out bilaterally. It was a principle that every tariff concession yielded by the one part should be compensated by a similar concession from the other part. As a low-tariff country Denmark did not possess much bargaining clout, and high-tariff countries were generally not willing to expose their own agricultural and industrial sectors to foreign competition. In Danish eyes, therefore, the only organisation of an overall international character left with some credibility as an agent of reconstruction and free trade was the OEEC. As the European organizer of Marshall aid one of its principal, formal tasks was to foster removal of all impediments to private commerce.[22]

Flemming Just & Thorsten B. Olesen

The OEEC-Liberalisation Proposal 1949

In October the legendary British Chancellor of the Exchequer, Sir Stafford Cripps, proposed that before December 15th 1949 the OEEC-countries should remove on average 50% of their quantitative import restrictions on private import. Before the end of 1950 an additional 25% were to be liberalised and by the end of 1951 total quota liberalization was to be a fact. In the end the plan was modified when the OEEC in the summer of 1950 agreed upon a 75%-rate of liberalisation from August 1951 and an easing of inter-European trade through the establishment of a European Payments Union.[23]

The British initiative was by no means a tribute to the idea of European integration. On the contrary, Cripps and the Labour government were very sceptical towards all plans of European unification. But quota liberalisation held conspicuous advantages for Great Britian. The 50% liberalisation was not a problem to Britain. Almost 40% of her imports were directed through the State, and state trade was exempted from the liberalisation scheme. Non-OEEC imports were also exempted, and in the British case only 14% of total imports actually derived from the OEEC countries. Consequently Britain would only have had to transfer 3-4% of her imports to the so-called free list.

Denmark, on the other hand, was severely hit by the OEEC liberalisation scheme. First through the exemption of state trade, because most agricultural commodities were comprised by state regulation. Second, because the OEEC decision did not forbid the raising of tariffs. In fact it became the norm among many countries that every gain in the liberalisation of quotas was neutralised through higher custom duties.[24] In relation to Danish-West German trade the liberalisation scheme had direct harmful consequences for Danish agriculture. Since the autumn of 1949 a quasi free-trade regime in agricultural products had been reached between the two countries, but the OEEC decision from the summer of 1950 had as a direct consequence that such liberalisation achievements had to be rolled back. The argument ran that the Danish-German trade rested on a one-sided bilateral agreement discriminating against other countries, and for that reason the German liberalisation quota for agricultural products had to be lowered to 60%. To make matters even worse for Denmark, West Germany reintroduced high tariffs as well.[25]

Denmark, however, remained a low-tariff country due to Agriculture's opposition to higher import prices. So, although Denmark and the Netherlands obtained a few concessions on the liberalisation requirements, they could not prevent increasing deficits on their balance of payments from materializing. These difficulties were reinforced by another external event which occured only a few weeks earlier in September 1949. The British economy and the pound sterling were under severe strain which forced

Britain to devaluate the pound by more than 30%. With Danish exports so closely tied to the sterling market, Denmark had no choice but to follow in the footsteps of Great Britain. As a result import prices from the dollar area rose by around 40% This was a major problem because Danish agricultural production and exports were dependent on the vital imports of feeding stuff from the dollar area. Thus, the devaluation was not able to prevent Danish agricultural exports generally from becoming more expensive.

These developments in the second half of 1949 crushed the growing optimism of Danish agriculture which lately had been stimulated by a steadily expanding production, the long-term contracts with Britain, and the recovery of Germany. In total the terms of trade fell from +23 in August 1949 to -26 in January 1950 and -40 in April the same year.[26]

The Green Pool

Seen from a purely agricultural point of view the OEEC plan was a complete disaster. Meanwhile, however, other initiatives were taken with the aim of regulating European production and exports of basic farm products. Several plans were promulgated by the Dutch and French governments, resulting in the Green Pool negotiations of 1950-54.[27]

The Green Pool plans may be seen as the first step to create an EEC-type common European agricultural policy. The driving force behind the plans was to avoid general overproduction once again threatening farm incomes as in the 1930s, but also to promote free trade as a means to increase productivity, raise incomes and secure employment in anticipation of the termination of Marshall aid in 1952. Thus, in 1950 both the Dutch Foreign Minister, Dirk Stikker, and the Dutch Minister of Agriculture, Sicco Mansholt, produced plans with the aim of coordinating and integrating agricultural production in Western Europe. In 1951 the French Minister of Agriculture, Pflimlin, took the initiative to call for a European conference the following year.

Pflimlin's 'Plan vert' had much in common with the Dutch plans, which in turn were inspired by Schuman's plan for the European Coal and Steel Community (ECSC). Like the latter 'Black Pool', the idea was that Western European agriculture should form a Green Pool through which the member states would construct a joint export pool of agricultural products. Free trade was seen as an ultimate goal, but owing to the very different economic and agricultural structures and conditions in the European countries, a regime of production and price regulation had to be installed as a temporary means of achieving this goal. Efforts should be concentrated on directing production to areas where maximum efficiency would be guaranteed in order to spark rationalisation, boost agricultural incomes and offer consumers cheaper food products. These ambitious goals required a strong supra-national body equipped with powers to regulate prices, to buy and store production surpluses, and to regulate imports from, and exports to, non-members. The French government was well aware of the difficulties in realizing the plan. Therefore, it proposed to restrict negotiations to wheat, dairy products, sugar and wine (coincidentally all categories where France produced surpluses).

From the outset the Danish government and Danish Agriculture met the French plan with much scepticism. However, the agricultural organisations recommended that the government participate in all conferences and negotiations to avoid being left out in the cold if the French efforts, contrary to expectations, proved successful. Negotiations took place in Paris from 1952 to 1954. Throughout this period Danish negotiators kept a very low profile. For both political (supra-national solutions never acquired many followers in Denmark) and economic reasons (Danish dependency on the British market) it was considered wiser to operate in the shadows of the British position. The traditional British attitude fostering development through general liberalisation schemes and international commodity agreements enjoyed much more support in Denmark than the French integration approach.[28]

Nonetheless, during these years Danish Agriculture's scepticism towards accepting supra-national institutions actually became less pronounced. The reason for this new flexibility is simple. In 1953 when the Dutch delegation launched a proposal to create a Green Pool of the six ECSC countries, the threat that Denmark might be left out in the cold suddenly acquired a real dimension. In the eyes of Danish Agriculture the Dutch initiative, therefore, demanded increased flexibility on the Danish side.[29]

The point stressed in Richard Griffiths' work on the Green Pool is that strong national agricultural pressure groups hindered any progress.[30] In so far as negotiations were sector divided Griffiths' observation is probably correct. Not surprisingly, agricultural organisations have always had overwhelming influence as long as policy-making has been kept inside the agricultural segment. But judging from the Danish experience the Green Pool negotiations did not founder only on opposition from the strong agricultural pressure groups. As demonstrated by Vibeke Sørensen the Danish agricultural organisations did take a more positive position regarding the Green Pool plans than did the Danish government which was always inclined to view the negotiations in a broader perspective, anxious to ensure that Denmark was not seperated from her traditional partners, the UK and the other Nordic countries.[31] This Danish experience may have been unique, but according to the laconic assessment made in 1953 by the Danish Agricultural Council, one gets the impression that the experience was more general in nature:

"As a whole the Council took a wait-and-see attitude, conscious of the lack of interest by the other participating countries in a real integration of European agriculture through effective means such as the liberalisation of trade in agricultural products."[32]

Danish Agriculture in Nowhere Land

From the mid-1950s the economic climate worsened for Danish agriculture. Owing to the diffusion of growing subsidies and protectionist measures agricultural production was increasing on a world scale, while at the same time exports were falling for a number of products.

Table 1. Development in agricultural production and export in the ten largest producing and exporting countries 1950-57 (%)

	Production	Export
Butter	+ 28,6	– 9,3
Meat and bacon	+ 156,0	– 35,0

Source: F. Just: *Axelborg og Christiansborg. Landbruget i dansk politik 1960-90*, (forthcoming).

More problems arose from the fact that the British long-term contracts were not renewed. Instead imports were deregulated and a 10% duty was imposed on bacon i 1956.[33] Furthermore foreign products were met with growing competition from British products due to a substantial increase in subsidies. The consequence was a decline in the traditional agricultural export to UK.

Table 2. Distribution of Danish agricultural export (in million DKK and %)

	The Six DKK	%	UK DKK	%	Others DKK	%	Total DKK	%
1954	976	25	2098	53	872	22	3946	100
1955	1355	33	2046	49	734	18	4135	100
1956	1513	37	1926	47	835	16	4074	100
1957	1584	39	1713	43	727	18	4024	100

Source: "Danmarks vareindførsel og -udførsel", in *Statistisk Tabelværk*, 5. række, litra D, no. 76, tabel VIII, 1955; and no. 78 tabel VIII, 1957.

However, even more ominous were the dark clouds gathering in the horizon. Having witnessed the collapse of a great many integration initiatives, including the Green Pool, in the mid 1950s, the Six now launched a new and very ambitious initiative, the creation of a Common Market. The first step was taken at the Messina conference in June 1955 and a real breakthrough secured by the adoption of the Spaak-report in the spring of 1956. On March 27, 1957 the European Economic Community became a reality through the signing of the Rome Treaties. Agriculture was to play a prominent part in the development of this community, and the overall scheme was so ambitious it was foreseeable that the sector interests of Agriculture would be more easily subordinated to the general foreign and economic policy interests inherent in the scheme. This was not another Green Pool round, and that worried Danish Agriculture.

Therefore, from the outset Danish Agriculture did not conceal its agenda: it wanted to join the Six. The development in exports was one reason. Another, the forecasts in European demography indicating a stronger growth in both population and income within the Common Market than elsewhere in Western Europe. During the process a third reason gained in importance. When it was proposed that the agricultural price system inside the future EEC should be based on high and secured minimum prices, the attraction of the whole scheme became nearly irresistible to Danish Agriculture. Such a system, if joined by Denmark, promised to relieve the sector from the growing strain of declining world market prices and surplus production. These prospects looked so lucrative that Agriculture was willing to sacrifice her dominant position on the British market in exchange for membership in the EEC.[34]

However, Agriculture's ambitions met strong opposition from other pressure groups, not least Danish Industry, and a majority of political parties. A variety of different economic and political considerations fuelled this opposition. The dominant economic fear was that Danish industry would be exposed to overwhelming competition within the EEC. Denmark was slowly moving towards a sustained industrial build-up, and this process risked being halted by premature membership. Second, in contrast to the priorities of Danish Agriculture, it was often stressed that Great Britain still constituted the greatest market for both agricultural and industrial products. Going solo, without Britain, would be hazardous. To the Social Democrats (who held government responsibility as a minority government from 1953-1957, and as the dominant part in a coalition government from 1957-1960) membership in the EEC, although not completely unattractive, posed too many risks. Future prosperity and growth in Denmark had to be based on increased industrialisation, and the EEC looked more promising from the point of view of agriculture rather than industry.[35]

Also political tradition and sentiment worked against linking with

Christian Democrat and Catholic Central Europe. The consequence of joining the EEC would be to give up aspirations of Nordic cooperation which most politicians and the broad population were not (yet) ready to accept. Therefore the primary Danish priority was to hope for a Wider Free Trade Area in Western Europe as suggested by the British, in which the EEC, Britain and its Commonwealth preferences and a Nordic customs union could coexist. In the end this project also failed, leaving Denmark the option of joining the European Free Trade Area (EFTA) in 1960. She did so with no enthusiasm. Joining EFTA meant that she had nearly the worst of all worlds. She joined a market arrangement which did not include agricultural products and which forced her to let go of her potentially most interesting market, West Germany.[36]

As hitherto, bilateral agreements were the only way out of this predicament. Until 1966 this policy functioned rather successfully (see table 3), but from then on the implementation of the Common Agricultural Policy made exports to the EEC countries much more difficult.

Table 3. Index for the distribution of the Danish agricultural export

	EEC	EFTA	Others	Total
1960	100	100	100	100
1965	110	133	151	129
1968	94	134	175	129
1971	95	137	217	139

Source: Anita Dethlefsen: *På vej mod EF. Landbruget og de europæiske markedsplaner 1957-72*, 1988, p. 140.

The relative importance of the British and German markets was almost halved between 1950 and 1970 receiving respectively 39% and 10% of the total agricultural export on the eve of Danish EEC-membership in 1973. The only remedy was to compensate in third markets. This latter remedy could not cover all losses, however. As many markets dried up and farmers in other countries received substantial subsidies, Danish farmers also required and received increased financial support from the state.[37]

The entrance into the Common Market in 1973 solved almost all the problems Danish agriculture of the post war period had encountered with international markets. The British and German markets were now merged into the same bloc, and it was even possible to receive substantial restitutions for exports to third markets outside the EEC. What proved to be an increasing dilemma to EEC-budgets was the delight of Danish farmers.

Flemming Just & Thorsten B. Olesen

The Political Economy of Danish Market Policy

Throughout this century the economic importance and the political power of Danish Agriculture has been substantial. Denmark was a slow industrializer, but even as the relative importance of Agriculture's contribution to the Danish GDP was diminishing the sector was able to maintain a very high degree of political influence. Political tradition was one reason among many, but agriculture's continued importance as a foreign currency earner was fundamental. Not until the beginning of the 1960s did the overall export value of industry surpass that of agriculture.

Although during the inter-war period Social Democracy established itself as the dominant political force in Denmark, the party's political leverage had its limits. The party never acquired a parliamentary majority and also had to accommodate itself to the basic production and foreign economy structures of the Danish economy. This limited the scope for Social Democratic policy-making. A fundamental clash occured around attitudes to free market and free trade economic policies. Agriculture and the liberal parties, Venstre and Det radikale Venstre, were advocates of such policies, but on questions like social distribution, defence and culture the Social Democratic Party and Det radikale Venstre held compatible views. This explains why the small social-liberal party normally functioned as coalition partner for the Social Democrats.

The economic and political structures combined to limit the extent to which market regulation and state intervention could be applied by Social Democratic government. But international developments also influenced this balance, and the world depression of the 1930s tipped the balance in favour of increased state intervention. The creation of new regulatory state institutions and the proliferation of corporatist practices, both born out of the attempt to fight recession, were important steps in this direction, as was the subsequent experience with managing the economy during the occupation years, 1940-1945.[38] Bolstered by the additional influence of the worldwide spread of Keynesianism and American Productivitism, the Social Democrats entered the post-war period with strong beliefs in the feasibility of transforming Denmark into an industrial economy by means of state intervention and plan economy experiments. These beliefs, on the other hand, produced a strong political-ideological reaction from the Liberal forces, including Agriculture, which had regained strength during the war. In their view the primary objective of Danish economic policy should consist of de-regulating the domestic as well as international markets as quickly as possible. Danish Agriculture held great expectations for the demand for agricultural products in the post-war period and regarded a traditional free market approach as the better instrument to exploit such a situation.

By 1949-1950 it was evident that the liberal approach had won the day.

Danish Agriculture and The European Market Schism, 1945-1960

The Marshall Plan administration's stronger emphasis on balanced budgets and monetary discipline, the British devaluation and the OEEC trade liberalizing schemes, combined with a growing dissatisfaction with economic restrictions among Danish citizens, worked to undermine the credibility of the Social Democratic approach. For Agriculture, however, triumph proved to be shortlived. The ambition to turn the effective Danish agricultural producers loose on the West European markets was never fulfilled as trade liberalization of the 1950s did not embrace agricultural products. Despite technological innovation and strong productivity gains Agriculture, as demonstrated, was not able to draw the dividends of the victory of their free market strategy. On the contrary, the sector suffered from dropping world market prices, difficulties in penetrating increasingly protected export markets and the effects of competing with state-subsidized farmers in these markets.

This development helps to explain why Agriculture and the Liberal Party, Venstre, were the first in Denmark to fly the European flag of supranationality. By the mid 1950s its was acknowledged that heavy dependency on the British market produced meagre results and promised to produce even less in the future. According to Liberal expectations, the prospect of expansion lay in merging with the Six. This development is not without historical irony. The Liberal forces were among the first in Denmark to support a European solution which entailed clear protectionist features and which foresaw the creation of a system of 'artificial' income support through centrally regulated prices.

But times were changing in other respects, too. The process of industrialization in Denmark had finally acquired momentum. Even from a foreign economy point of view, it was no longer self-evident that primary attention should be paid to the interests of Danish Agriculture.[39] This realization was one of the main reasons why Denmark ended up in EFTA instead. EFTA, however, was not a lucky marriage either – rather the lesser evil compared to being left out of both West European market arrangements. EFTA did not include trade in agricultural products and it did not comprise the West German market. If the OEEC-liberalization schemes of the early 1950s represented the first serious blow to Denmark in the postwar struggle to organize the West European markets, the EEC/EFTA divide must be considered the second.

This gap was not bridged until the EEC enlargement of 1973. However, when it did occur, it represented a real novelty. For the first time during the post-war period a major European market construction had sufficient appeal to be attractive to both Agriculture and Industry. In this respect at least, Denmark ceased to be Europe's odd man out.

Notes

1. For a general introduction to the so-called "stop-go" economic period 1950-1957, see Svend Åge Hansen: *Økonomisk vækst i Danmark*, Vol II 1914-1970, Copenhagen 1974, p. 125-154. For the comparative view, see Angus Maddison: *Economic Growth in the West*, New York 1964, p. 213.
2. See for instance the new four volume work on Danish agricultural history, in which the problems of the 1950s are dealt with very briefly. Claus Bjørn (ed.): *Det danske landbrugs historie*. Bd. 1-4. Copenhagen 1988.
3. Flemming Just: *Landbruget, staten og eksporten 1930-1950*, Esbjerg 1992, p. 129.
4. *Landbrugsraadets virksomhed*, 1951, p. 76.
5. Hans Chr. Johansen: "Dansk økonomisk statistik 1814-1980", in *Gyldendals Danmarkshistorie*, vol. 9, 1985, table 4.1b, p. 193.
6. Vibeke Sørensen: "Den skandinaviske model og Europa-dilemmaer i dansk arbejderbevægelses holdning til europæisk integration 1950-1980", in *Årbog for Arbejderbevægelsens Historie*, 1991, p. 13-48.
7. Flemming Just: "Butter, Bacon and Organisational Power in Danish Agriculture", in Flemming Just (ed.): *Co-operatives and Farmers' Unions in Western Europe. Collaboration and Tensions*, Esbjerg 1990, p. 137-156.
8. Flemming Just: "Agriculture and Controls in Denmark 1930-1950", in *Scandinavian Economic History Review*, vol. XLI, no. 3, 1993, p. 269-285.
9. In an extensive study Leon Dalgas Jensen has demonstrated that at the level of concrete policy-making the disparity between Liberal and Social Democratic behaviour was not all that evident. The international political and economic framework and tactical political considerations were much more important in shaping the economic policy behaviour of the two blocs. Leon Dalgas Jensen's point is well taken although he goes too far in harmonizing the contents of Social Democratic and Liberal attitudes to economic policy-making (Leon Dalgas Jensen: *Politisk kamp om Danmarks importpolitik 1945-1948*, Copenhagen 1993, p. 389-400).

    The real contention was, maybe, not regulation or planning itself, but how it was used. To achieve the long term goal of Social Democracy in Denmark, i.e. full industrialization, selective but extended levels of planning and market regulation was considered essential. Not least in a period characterized by a scarcity of basic resources. This was a fundamental Social Democratic view in the period 1945-1950, even though the party's plan economy rhetoric largely faded away after the 1945 electoral defeat. Not surprisingly, the Liberals, on the other hand, did not see any necessary link between their long-term interests and state intervention policies (which did not rule out that they would use them if basic economic requirements demanded it). For a fine analysis of the Social Democratic plan economy debate of the early post war period, see Niels Wium Olesen: *I en verden der lægger planer. Det danske Socialdemokratis politiske linie fra 1945-1947*, Unpubl. MA thesis, Dept. of History, Aarhus University, 1995.
10. See Leon Dalgas Jensen (1993): op. cit., p. 364.
11. The most comprehensive analysis of the political economy implications of Marshall aid in Denmark is made by Vibeke Sørensen in: *Social Democratic Government in Denmark and the Marshall Plan 1947-1950*, un. publ. ph.d., European University Institute, Florence, 1987. See also Flemming Just: "Planøkonomi eller liberalisme. Staten og erhvervspolitikken i de første efterkrigsår", in Birgit Nüchel Thomsen (ed.): *Temaer og brændpunkter i dansk politik efter 1945*, Odense 1994, p. 55-71; and Dan Larsen: "Smørstormen 1950. Et socialdemokratisk sammenbrud", in ibid., p. 73-99.

    It should be stressed, that Agriculture's opposition to the elements of the regulated economy was not equally pronounced in all respects. Agriculture did not sanction government attempts to decide investment levels or production targets. Neither did it accept import control and rationing of butter or pork as a means to stimulate the export quota. However, opposition to the import/export control was not an opposition of principles. For instance, when import control was applied to secure feeding stuff from the dollar area, Agriculture could support the policy. Not surprisingly, on the other hand, when it was employed to cut down feeding stuff imports in order to employ the scarce amount of dollars to import basic raw materials for Industry, Agriculture objected. The centrally controlled export trade system was another typical feature of the regulated economy. Again this system was not criticised by Agriculture as long as the agricultural organisations themselves were controlling and directing the export committees (Flemming Just (1992): op. cit., p. 484-489).

12. Jens Skriver: "Traktordriftens gennembrud i Danmark 1945-65", in *Bol og by. Landbohistorisk tidsskrift*, 1991, no. 1, p. 133-178.
13. Hans Chr. Johansen (1985): op. cit., table 2.7., p. 142, and table 2.11, p. 152-156.
14. Since 1932-33 state export boards for nine agricultural products had been both regulating the export and collecting fees on the export in order to equalize prices. Formally they were state boards, but they consisted almost entirely of representatives from the agricultural organisations, the co-operative sales organisations and, to a lesser extent, private exporters. Gradually the boards were delegated more authority, and by the outbreak of war in 1939 they exercised a monopoly on all agricultural exports.
15. F. Just (1992): op.cit., pp. 236ff.
16. Bengt Nilson: "Butter, Bacon and Coal: Anglo-Danish Commercial Relations, 1947-51", in *Scandinavian Journal of History*, 1988, vol. 13, no. 2/3, p. 257-277.
17. *Landbrugsraadets virksomhed*, 1950, pp. 124ff.
18. FAO (ed.): *FAO – the first 40 years*. Rome 1985, p. 6.
19. Ibid. p. 10.
20. Martin Peterson: *International Interest Organisations and the Transmutation of Postwar Society*. Stockholm 1979.
21. Leon Dalgas Jensen: "Danmark og Den internationale Handelsorganisation (ITO) 1945-1950", in *Konflikt og samarbejde. Festskrift til Carl-Axel Gemzell* (edited by Carsten Due-Nielsen et al.), Copenhagen 1993, p. 243 ff.
22. The defeat of the World Food Board plan meant from the end of the 1940s that FAO concentrated its efforts on the development of agriculture in Third World countries.
23. Alan Milward: *The Reconstruction of Western Europe 1945-51*, London 1984, p. 303.
24. Martin Peterson: "Sweden and the Green Pool: 1950-1955", *EUI Colloquium Papers*, DOC. IUE 310/90 (Col 44), 1991, p. 4f.
25. *Landbrugsraadets virksomhed*, 1950, pp. 46 and 76-80.
26. F. Just: op.cit., 1992, p. 380.
27. The Green Pool was the object of a special colloquium at the European University Institute, Florence, in 1990. See especially the contributions by Thierry Mommens: "The Stichting voor de landbouw and the Green Pool Negotiations"; by R.T. Griffiths: "The Green Pool Negotiations"; by Werner Bührer: "Agricultural Pressure Groups and International Politics. The German Example"; and by Gilbert Noël: "Les groupes de pression francais et le projet d'organisation de l'Europe agricole entre 1950 et 1954". All papers are printed in *EUI Colloquium Papers*, DOC.IUE, 308/90 (col. 42), 313/90 (col. 47), 314/90 (col. 48) and 315/90 (col. 49). These papers and several more are all going to be printed in

Brian Girvin (ed.): *The Green Pool and the Origins of the Common Agricultural Policy*, (forthcoming 1995).
28. *Landbrugsraadets virksomhed*, 1950, pp. 48-55; 1951, pp. 678-683.
29. Vibeke Sørensen: "How to become a member of a club without joining. Danish policy with respect to European sector integration schemes, 1950-1957", in *Scandinavian Journal of History*, 1991, 16, pp. 105-124; Michael Tracy: *Government and Agriculture in Western Europe 1880-1988*, Third Edition. New York 1989, pp. 246-248; *Landbrugsraadets virksomhed*, 1953, pp. 65-70.
30. R.T. Griffiths (1991): op. cit., p. 45 f.
31. V. Sørensen: ""Free Trade" Versus Regulated Markets: Danish Agricultural Organisations and the Green Pool, 1950-54", 1994 p. 27, to be published in B. Girvin (1995): op. cit.
32. *Landbrugsraadets virksomhed*, 1953, p. 70.
33. E. Helmer Pedersen et al.: *De første hundrede år. Danske Slagterier 1887-1987*, Copenhagen 1987, p. 126.
34. *Dansk Landbrug og de europæiske markedsplaner*, published by De Samvirkende Danske Landboforeninger, Aarhus 1957; and Flemming Just: *Axelborg og Christiansborg. Landbruget i dansk politik 1960-90* (forthcoming).
35. Johnny Laursen: "Mellem fællesmarkedet og frihandelszonen. Dansk markedspolitik 1956-1958", in B. Nüchel Thomsen: *The Odd Man Out. Danmark og den europæiske integration 1948-1992*, Odense 1993, p. 73 ff.
36. Vibeke Sørensen: "Fra Marshall-plan til de store markedsdannelser, 1945-1959", in Tom Swienty (ed.): *Danmark i Europa 1945-1993*, Copenhagen 1994, p. 87 ff.
37. From the second half of the 1960s subsidies constituted one-third of agriculture's overall income.
38. Flemming Just: "Agricultural and corporatism in Scandinavia", in: *Critical Perspectives on Rural Change*, vol. V (ed. by Philip Lowe and Terry Marsden), London 1994, pp. 31-52.
39. In 1963 the total value of industrial exports for the first time surpassed that of agricultural exports, see table 4.1b in Hans Chr. Johansen (1985): op. cit., p. 193 (canned food products are counted as agricultural exports).

Political and Economic Foundations of the European Economic Community

By Thomas Rhenisch

The creation of the European Economic Community (EEC) in 1957 was a milestone in the history of (West)European integration. Following the trend of recent research into the process of European integration this article will identify integration as a specific political answer or instrument developed in the post-war period to deal with Western Europe's recovery and reconstruction problems. However, in this interpretation the individual nation states are seen as the central units of organisation. European integration did not serve to overcome the concept of the nation state; rather it was a means to stabilise and strengthen them.[1]

Such an interpretation, obviously, stresses a different aspect of the integration process than many of the prevailing interpretations of European integration which, for a long time, were strongly influenced by the views of European federalists and by politicians active in the process.[2] These interpretations have tended to overemphasize the importance of European idealism and the political action of a few politicians and high ranking bureaucrats. With the opening of state archives and those of the European Economic Community, this image is gradually giving way to less idealistic and more detailed and comprehensive historical analyses of the foundation of the Common Market.[3] The central question to be examined in an analysis of the creation of the EEC, therefore, can be summarised as follows: What was every individual member country's specific interest in a customs union covering the free trade of all commodities as well as the free movement of capital and labour? In this article great importance will be attributed to the fact that the "Relaunching of Europe" took place in the economic sphere. Thus, the customs union of the Six will be interpreted not as a means to political ends, but as an end in its own right. The analysis of economic needs and expectations as well as possible trade-offs between different sectors of the economy will play a predominant role in this approach.[4] Appropriate consideration will, nevertheless, be given to the sometimes crucial influence of political aspirations and ideologies, especially related to the so-called German problem.

A key-notion in the analysis will be "national interests". The process of integration may be seen as a compromise between or a harmonisation of different national interests. On the other hand, the specific policy of each individual nation state may also be regarded as a compromise between different economic and social interests represented within the single nation state itself. From a methodological point of view one should therefore be rather careful when employing the term. However, it is not the aim of this short article to reveal how national interests found expression within the nation states and how they were translated into concrete politics. The aim is to analyze how the pursuit of national interests worked to promote an integrationist solution such as the Common Market. Such an approach also entails the risk of excluding the international political prerequisites for political decision-making. World political events such as the Suez crisis or the uprising in Hungary, to name but a few, may not be given due attention by the "national interests" approach. There is a danger, therefore, that the following analysis will underrate the impact of such events. However, it is crucial to stress that an integral component of the "national interest approach" is to view European integration against the specific historical environment of the post-war period: the choice of integration can never be fully explained unless it is related to the pressure exerted by the Cold War, by America's positive attitude to Western European integration and by the need to find a lasting solution to the German problem. The hypothesis on the pursuit of national interests as the real engine of European integration is only valid within this framework.

A further clarification is required. This article focuses on only three countries: France, the Federal Republic of Germany and the Netherlands. Although this is a reductionist approach, there is hardly any doubt that these three countries were the core countries during the negotiating period from the Messina Conference to the drafting of the Rome Treaties. This limitation, however, should not invalidate the overall project of demonstrating how national interests were at work in the creation of the Common Market. A few introductory words on the policies of Italy, Belgium and Luxembourg, thus, must suffice.

Closer European cooperation or integration has been one of the persistent and constant aims of Italian foreign policy in the post-war era. It is one of the particularities of Italian politics that despite the regularly changing governments, (until the 1990s, at least) the same group of politicians have remained in power. Italian foreign policy, as a consequence, had a strong element of continuity. It aimed at the full integration of Italy into almost any kind of European communitarian framework. This attitude had a political and an economic aspect. The political drive behind Italy's pro-European attitude was rooted in the need to regain international recognition after having fought most of World War II on 'the wrong side' and in fears of political exclusion from bilateral French-German cooperation. On the economic side, Italy was highly dependent on access to foreign raw materials and capital, and, on the other hand, on having an outlet for her huge labour surplus. If these prerequisites were met,

Italy was normally willing to compromise on almost any other issue.[5] Combining political and economic aspects one should perhaps also add that for the governing Christian Democrats close links with 'rich' Central Europe looked very tempting as a way of promoting economic growth and thereby excluding the radical Italian 'Left' from political power in the country.

Although Belgium is often mentioned together with the Netherlands and although it drafted the Benelux memorandum with the latter, the policies of these two countries towards European market integration have differed more than just in details. The Belgian attitudes towards trade liberalisation seem to be often inconsistent and sometimes difficult to explain.[6] Nevertheless, Belgium had a general interest in trade liberalisation in Western Europe although Foreign Minister, Spaak, especially, would have preferred a vertical integration of economic key sectors along the lines of the European Coal and Steel Community rather than the horizontal integration method of the Common Market. This situation also helps to explain the somewhat hybrid character of the Benelux memorandum of spring 1955.

Luxembourg did not have the political and economic weight to do anything without its Benelux partners and thus had no option but to join the Common Market.[7]

France

It is said that the key to understanding the character and achievements of European integration in the post-war period, lies in France.[8] Not only was France the initiator of several of the european projects, but these projects themselves also reflect almost exactly the political and economic circumstances and problems which France was facing during that period.

This is not the place to analyze socio-economic and political developments in France after the war, nor to go into detail about the history of all the European initiatives leading eventually to the Messina Conference and the EEC. To understand why France could engage in negotiations on creating a European Common Market less than a year after the failure of the European Defence Community in 1954, it is, nevertheless, necessary to briefly outline the post-war history of economic integration in Europe as well as political and economic developments in France.

The most important stimulus towards economic integration after 1945 arose from the economic situation in France. In particular, the technocrats in the French economic planning staff linked French reconstruction goals with the creation of common economic structures in Europe, without, however, specifying these structures in any detail. Consequently, French reconstruction and modernisation plans aimed at preparing the French economy for European competition through high investment rates in key sectors. In this sense the productivity and integration aspects of the Marshall Plan tailored nicely with French modernization ambitions. Yet, these visions encountered resistance from within France herself. The prospect of European integration also evoked fears of social decline, and strong political objections and resentments which seemed to be impossible to overcome for a long time.[9]

Also, the fact that it was impossible to reach agreement with the U.K on a common policy towards Germany blocked the integration strategy. Christian Democrats as well as Communists still insisted on the separation of the Ruhr and the Rhineland as a "sine qua non" for accepting a solution on the future of Germany.[10] Such a separation would have shifted the European industrial centre to France and therefore met resistance from the U.K.. Even more limiting, however, was the fact that the very idea of closer European integration did not seem to appeal to the British government at all. British cooperation was needed if the French plans were to materialize. Being the only greater power to balance the influence of Germany within a future European construction was not a French favourite dream, at least not in the late 1940s. Thus, during this period French European policy was caught in a dead end from which there was no escape for a long time.

This impasse is confirmed when one takes a look at the European economic cooperation initiatives involving France in the late 1940s.[11] French participation in the Benelux customs union failed because France refused even to consider German membership, which was a prerequisite for the Netherlands. The work of the "European Custom's Union Study Group" (ECUSG), introduced within the framework of the Marshall Plan negotiations, also suffered from this fundamental difference of opinion between France and the Netherlands. However, an agreement about a customs union was in fact achieved with Italy in March 1949, although it was never ratified because of the negative vote by the French "Conseil Economique". A further regional economic integration plan initiated by France was the attempt to solve the French balance of payments problems with Belgium through a "mini payments union"[12] which eventually led to the Fritalux negotiations. But again, as soon as the Dutch participated in the negotiations, they confronted their partners with the demand that Germany should be included, too.[13] The negotiations came to a halt when the establishment of the European Payments Union (EPU) rendered the project irrelevant.

By the beginning of the 1950s the French had abandoned their former policy on Germany. They accepted that the Ruhr and the Rhine could not be separated and gradually realized that the best way to contain Germany was to integrate her into a binding European structure, even if the U.K did not participate.[14] The obvious example of this change is the Schuman Plan and the subsequent creation of the European Coal and Steel Community (ECSC) in which France, Italy, Germany and the Benelux participated. Part of the rationale of the ECSC was a French attempt to control the industrial heart of the West German economy, i.e. the Ruhr, after the separation approach had proved in vain.[15] Equally important, however, was the desire to secure the German economic potential for the Western block in the face of the escalating East-West conflict. But the rationale behind the creation of the ECSC was not only political. There was a strong economic impetus as well. For the French the Coal and Steel Community was a means of preserving the German steel market for French producers and a way of supplying French consumers with cheap German coal.[16] Decisive groups within the French economy, however, were still not prepared to extend ECSC-style cooperation to other sectors of the economy. A clear indication of this is the hostility with which these groups met the plans for a general customs union set up within the framework of the European Defense Community (EDC).

The French experience so far tells us that France could accept a limited sectoral integration approach as epitomized by the ECSC. The story also reveals that France had come to terms with the idea that it was better to integrate Germany into a mutually binding European structure – that it was better to let her in than to leave her out. The escalation of the Cold War was probably instrumental in making French politicians realize this, and the creation of NATO in 1949 was decisive in bringing about the security platform on which France considered it safe enough to embark on such a policy. As demonstrated above, however, France of the mid-1950s was still in many ways a reluctant European. France harboured strong reservations about European integration both in its widening and deepening aspects. Thus, strong sections of the French economy were very sceptical about extending the supranational ECSC-type of cooperation to other sectors of the economy, and the French political system found it extremely difficult to come to terms with integration projects such as the EDC which entailed a substantial element of transfer of sovereignty. Still, by 1957 France had both signed and ratified the Treaties of Rome; treaties which both sanctioned a widening and a deepening of European co-operation. What were the events and developments which made the French adjust their European policy once more? Why did France embark on negotiations with the aim of creating a general Common Market of the six Schuman Plan countries when less than one year before she had turned down the custom union idea within the EDC framework.

An important, but not new French impulse behind the drive for a Western European customs union came from the French farmers' interests in a protected agricultural market, which would provide an outlet for French surplus production of cereals and beets at prices well above the level of the world market and at the same time protect French farmers against competition from overseas producers.[17] Germany and Belgium were targeted as importers. It was certainly no coincidence that especially producers of cereals and beets were the most ardent supporters of the EEC in France.[18] As P. Guillen has put it: "Thus, the Common Market appeared to be a unique chance for French agriculture."[19] Only the extreme political Left and Right feared negative consequences for small and medium size producers.

All previous attempts to find a solution to the problems of West European agriculture during the so-called Green Pool Negotiations between 1950 and 1955 had failed, mainly because of the unwillingness or the inability of the negotiating Ministers of Agriculture to override the specific interests of the national producers. In most countries national farmers' associations were very influential and often exercised strong formal power through a delegation of authority from the Ministries of Agriculture.[20] Without the consent of the national farmer's lobbies the Green Pool negotiations were unlikely to succeed. However, by inserting agriculture into the broader framework of the Common Market negotiations, trade-offs between different economic sectors could be obtained. Thus, compromises were reached, which also held an appeal for Agriculture. Since French support for the EEC depended largely on whether or not a solution to Agriculture's problems could be found, the inclusion of agriculture in the Common Market negotiations was crucial in order to secure a sufficient majority for the scheme within the French National Assembly. The trade-off between French access to the German market for agricultural products and German access to the French industrial market can indeed be identified as one of the fundamental keys to the creation of the EEC.[21]

However, the EEC treaty's clauses on agriculture were not much more than a general agreement of intent. They did not specify what the common agricultural policy should look like. The detailed formulation of that task was reserved for the future Community.[22] Yet, the method worked. By avoiding controversial discussions on detailed problems during the treaty negotiations and by transferring them instead to the future institutions of the Community, a new approach was developed which paved the way for a European solution to the problems of agriculture.

Also within French Industry attitudes towards European economic cooperation were changing. There was a growing realization that the structural problems of French industry could only be solved within a European framework. In the wake of the economic modernisation process of the late 1940s and early 1950s characterized by high rates of state investments in key sectors, industrial production showed its first signs of substantial growth in 1952. As a consequence, the most dynamic parts of French industry, such as the automobile and electrical industry, began to divert their interest from the domestic market to foreign markets. Market expansion was regarded as a necessary prerequisite to sustained growth.[23] The tight French capital market was a further limiting factor to industrial growth which increased the attraction of European integration. Yet, due to the uneven distribution of growth rates within French industry which limited dynamic growth to a few sectors, the central industrial association, the "Conseil National du Patronat Francais" (C.N.P.F.), still displayed much scepticism towards the EEC project. Tactics also played their part, and paid off handsomely as the C.N.P.F.'s negotiating position vis-a-vis the government was clearly improved. Only after having obtained substantial concessions on social harmonisation, the common external tariff and French export subsidies, would the C.N.P.F. agree to the creation of a European customs union. Most of these demands were indeed pursued by the French delegation in Brussels and many of them found their way into the Rome Treaties.[24]

The new self-confidence of the dynamic sectors of French Industry played a crucial role in increasing the attraction of binding European cooperation. By the mid-1950s the escalating French balance of payments crisis, which threatened to undermine the achievements of the modernisation programme, was equally important. A growing number of businessmen, civil servants and politicians were convinced that only an increase in exports could remedy this danger, caused by high military and colonial expenses and high labour costs. A protected European market seemed to allow for export expansion without exposing the French economy to devastating competition, especially from the Dollar Area. The Euratom Treaty within the Rome Treaties offered similar advantages as it was hoped that the functioning of the Euratom would result in lower levels of imports of fossil fuels and thereby contribute to a reduction of the balance of payments deficit.[25]

But the EEC-construction had more features to recommend it. By demanding that the French overseas territories be integrated into the Common Market, the French introduced a new concept of burden-sharing into the negotiations. The proposal was an overt attempt to make the other member states contribute to financing the immense costs of running the French colonial empire. Again, this had been an essential demand by French Industry before it was adopted by the Economic Council and the French government.[26] By the mid-fifties the attitude of French Industry towards European economic integration had acquired a more positive (or, at least, less negative) dimension. However, the French participation in the EEC cannot be explained only in economic terms. Political considerations played a crucial role for the French decision-makers, as well.

Only nine years after the end of World War II the French idea of creating a European Defence Community failed – due to French resistance.[27] Difficulty in accepting West Germany as a military partner and reluctance to surrender national sovereignty to a supranational body in a vital area such as defense policy were decisive factors behind the French National Assembly's decision not to ratify the EDC-Treaty. American political, economic and military domination in Western Europe was yet another reason for the negative vote of the French parliament in 1954.[28] In the mid-1950s the French body politic had a rather ambivalent attitude to the American presence in Europe. On the one hand, it recognized that American presence was an essential security guarantee, not only against the Soviet Union, but also against Germany. On the other hand, France was not ready to accept American dominance in Western Europe. To many French politicians the EDC arrangement did not promise to be sufficiently independent of the USA and NATO. Seen from this perspective the rearmament of West Germany was better secured directly within the NATO alliance. In this way Germany became a member of NATO, France ensured that the U.K. took a higher degree of responsibility for the re-militarization of West Germany through the new accord on the Western Union (WEU) and France herself did not have to sacrifice national control over her own armed forces. This settlement was regulated by the Paris Treaties of October 1954.[29]

Seen from an integration perspective the importance of the Paris-Treaties lies in the fact that they secured a firm security policy order in Western Europe. This meant that security policy issues no longer prevented progress in other fields of European cooperation. With the necessary checks and balances on potential German militarism established through the Paris Treaties, French politicians were more willing to engage in a profound and binding type of cooperation with Germany in other policy fields. This willingness was further stimulated by the German-French agreement on the Saarland and the canalization of the Mosel, events which eased the difficult relationship between the two countries and contributed to the French support for the "relaunching of Europe".[30]

Developments in French domestic politics were also crucial. The January 1956 elections brought about a majority for the Socialists (SFIO) and resulted in a pro-European government under the leadership of Guy Mollet. For the French Socialists it was important that the German Socialist Party (SPD) had taken a positive stance on the EEC. The SPD's new attitude could be used by the SFIO as an argument against the classical criticism by the French Left, that European integration would only serve to create a capitalist, clerical, conservative European block. The new SPD attitude helped Mollet to obtain a stable majority in the National Assembly supporting his European policy.[31]

However, not until the end of 1956 when most of the French demands had been met during the negotiations was it certain that France would sign the Rome Treaties. Opposition was still widespread in parliament and in French public opinion. In contrast to disagreements on the EEC Treaty, support for the Euratom Treaty had been strong from the start.[32] Jean Monnet had always favoured this sector approach in the field of atomic energy.[33] In French economic planning nuclear energy played a key role in the modernisation of industry. Technological spin-off effects and a lower degree of dependence on imports of traditional energy resources were the results which France expected to gain from the Euratom project. But two additional aspects were just as important for the pronounced French interest in the project. France wanted desperately to develop an advanced nuclear energy sector. The costs, however, would be staggering. But a joint European project promised to ease the burden on French budgets when all member countries had to contribute their share. If Europe wanted to escape total dependence on the USA in this field, Europe had to develop its own programme. The other great advantage of a supranational sector-approach to this problem was that it offered the member states, and France in particular, a say in the development of a nuclear energy industry in West Germany. Because of its military implications such a control body had a high French priority even though, as a consequence, France herself also had to give up complete national self-determination in the nuclear energy sector. In contrast to the EDC-intermezzo, only a right-wing minority was unwilling to accept this transfer of sovereignty.[34]

During the Brussels-negotiations of 1956 it became clear that the other five negotiating countries were not willing to accept Euratom without the Common Market. In particular, the Netherlands and the Federal Republic insisted on this negotiation package.[35] This position was also strongly endorsed by the president of the negotiations, the Belgian Foreign Minister, Paul-Henri Spaak. In the end, France had to swallow the EEC if it wanted Euratom.

Seen in this light the success of the Messina initiative was less the result of a "relance europeenne", than of a redefinition of the national French interest within a framework of changing political and economical conditions. A further step in the direction of trade liberalisation and economic cooperation in Europe probably would have been impossible without this redefinition.

The Fedral Republic of Germany[36]

The Federal Republic was in many respects the counterpart to France in the European integration process. Yet, at first it seems to be far less profitable to analyze German attitudes towards European integration than the French. From the very start in 1949 the first government of the newly formed Federal Republic took a positive stance on European integration. There seemed to be no realistic alternative to Adenauer's pro-European foreign policy. Despite the rhetoric, it is doubtful whether a Socialist government could have pursued a different foreign and European policy without endangering the political basis of the Federal Republic. In the first decade after the War the ends as well as the means of German foreign policy were determined by the Allies. The prevailing principle was a rigid 'do ut des'. The margin within which Adenauer could manoeuvre was extremely narrow, and the progress that West Germany made towards full sovereignty was only partially to his credit. But for every step Germany took in the direction of integration, she was rewarded with an increase in sovereignty. Consequently, all important European initiatives were backed by the German government, at least in public.[37]

Adenauer's European policy was, nevertheless, based on a broad pro-European movement in Germany as well. Industry as well as trade unions supported European integration, albeit with different expectations. By 1955 even the Social Democratic Party had changed its attitude towards Europe and welcomed the Messina initiative. Until then the SPD had voiced severe scepticism towards an overly committed integration of West Germany into the West, because of its negative repercussions on German unification.[38] By the mid-fifties, however, SPD's alternative policy had been definitely undermined as unification seemed very far away and the pro-West European policy had established itself as an important feature of West German state legitimation.

It can be argued that SPD's policy was much more untenable just before October 1954, when the Paris treaties were signed, than in 1955. The Paris treaties endowed the Federal Republic with almost full sovereignty and she had, thus, also regained her freedom of action in foreign affairs. The foundations of Adenauer's foreign policy, however, remained the same: full integration of the Federal Republic into the West and maintenance of a special relationship with France within a European context.[39] Only a few months after the Paris Treaties had been signed, the Germans made a proposal for further European economic integration. Although the German memorandum was a reaction to the Benelux proposals for the Messina Conference, it shows that the German government had an independent interest in European economic integration and wanted to pursue its previous line of policy, even though Germany had regained a greater degree of freedom in international politics.

A brief look at the statistics on industrial production and foreign trade of the FRG discloses that this European interest was not only politically motivated.[40]

By the mid-fifties the Federal Republic had developed one of the most dynamic economies in Europe. The annual industrial growth rate between 1950 and 1957 amounted to 13%. But due to the loss of traditional markets in Eastern Europe, German industry depended on new outlets for its growing production. Although coal and steel still held the biggest share of industrial production, this unprecedented growth was primarily based on manufacturing industries. Most important were mechanical engineering (9% of total industrial production in 1957), the chemical industry (8%), electrical engineering (6.5%) and car manufacturing (5%). The annual growth rates in these industries varied between 15% (mechanical engineering) and 27% (car manufacturing). Also the export quota of these very dynamic sectors lay well above the industrial average of 15.2%. All in all these industries were responsible for half of West Germany's industrial exports.

On this background it seems safe to conclude that exports were an important factor in the economic performance of the German Wirtschaftswunder. It is also true that these manufacturing industries were seriously interested in easier access to foreign markets, and it was therefore to be expected that these industries would take a positive attitude towards the creation of the Common Market. Yet, the scenario is a bit more complicated. In 1959 only 23% of the compound exports of mechanical engineering, car manufacturing, the chemical industry and electrical engineering were sold in the EEC market. Around 34% went to other OEEC countries and 42% were shipped to the rest of the world. These figures demonstrate why Germany's biggest exporting industries were as much interested in trade liberalisation within the framework of the OEEC as within the Common Market framework of the Six. For these industries European economic integration was only desirable if it did not jeopardize Germany's position on world markets.[41] Also, German dependence on imports of raw materials from outside the EEC pulled in the same direction. A protectionist Common Market would have increased the import prices of raw materials from outside the customs union, thereby increasing production costs in Germany with negative effects for the competitiveness of German industry.

If we bear in mind that we are operating on a very general level, and that German industry also comprised highly protected sectors such as the textile industry which did not always favour the same policies as the above-mentioned industries, we can simplify the analysis by saying that German Industry took exactly the position which one would expect on the EEC. Support for the EEC was always coupled with the demand that the EEC be inserted into the British proposal for a broader market arrangement within the OEEC, the so-called Free Trade Area. It is surprising, however, that even sectors which were barely competitive in export markets, foresaw positive results from West Germany joining the EEC.[42] The main thrust of criticism directed against the Common Market construction centred on the limited geographical size of the Community, the French demands for social harmonisation, tariff harmonization when tariffs were expected to supersede German tariffs, build-up of investment funds, and the inclusion of the French overseas territories.

More important, however, was the opposition of German Industry to Euratom.[43] In the end the Atomic Community was only accepted because it was linked to the Common Market in a package deal. The Association of Chemical Industries (VCI) was especially opposed to Euratom. The president of the Federal Association of German Industry's (BDI) Committee for Atomic Energy, Alexander Menne (himself a representative of the VCI) expressed his opposition in several meetings with the German negotiators in Brussels.[44] The formal reason for this negative attitude was the limitations of private property rights in nuclear fuels and nuclear technology inherent in the Euratom treaty. Menne argued these restrictions would weaken entrepreneurial initiative and be a threat to the liberal market economy. Further concerns were hidden behind this rhetoric. Thus, it was simply believed that German industry was strong enough to profit more from straight, bilateral cooperation with the USA than from the regulated and formalised type of cooperation within the Euratom. Therefore, German Industry only submitted to the inevitable when the Americans had made it clear that if Euratom failed because of German obstruction there would be no bilateral deal with the Americans either.[45]

Moving the search light from German Industry to German Agriculture we discover that attitudes here were generally more hostile to the EEC.[46] In general German agricultural producers preferred that the EEC not include agricultural products. They feared superior competition from abroad and demanded efficient protectionist measures be introduced. Liberal free trade arguments did not count for much in the face of hard commercial facts, especially when these were coupled with a political preference for national self-sufficiency. Germany was by no means an exception in this respect. In most European countries the agricultural economy was subordinated to state and/or corporate controls with monopolistic sales and purchasing agencies. Since German agricultural productivity was low, German farmers were not looking for expansion abroad and rather feared French, Dutch and Italian competition in the German market. And as in most other countries at that time, German agricultural associations, with the Deutsche Bauernbund in front, had strong political leverage. Consequently the Deutsche Bauernbund together with the Ministry for Agriculture torpedoed trade liberalisation for agricultural products whenever possible. This is one of the reasons why the Common Agricultural Policy remained a mere sketch in the Rome Treaties.

Moving to the government level a mixed picture emerges. Despite widespread political support for the Messina initiative, different members of the Federal government held almost opposite ideas about the content and meaning of European economic integration. Being the ardent liberal he was, the Minister of Economics, Ludwig Erhard, objected to both the protectionist features and the institutional framework of the Common Market plans of the Six.[47] Erhard always suspected common institutions of being somewhat 'dirigiste'. Constructing a preferential area in Western Europe represented a setback for a return to the multilateral world trading system based on full monetary convertibility which had existed prior to World War I and which Erhard would have liked to see restored. Whereas Erhard's views on European cooperation were motivated by economic considerations, Adenauer's approach was much more political in nature. The integration of West Germany into the Western Alliance and the special relationship with France continued to be his lodestars. This policy had such a high priority that he was determined to overrule the objections of his most important minister.[48]

It may seem surprising that Erhard was not supported by German Industry, at least by those parts of Industry which had worldwide commercial interests. There is one very important explanation for that. In the mid-1950s, the coal and steel industry of the Ruhr area was still the most important industrial sector in the Federal Republic. It was also dominant within the BDI to such a degree that it was almost allowed to monopolize policy formulation for German Industry.[49] And the "Ruhr" was definitely not to be found in the chorus demanding a liberal free trade system in Europe. German heavy industry still clung to its taste for protected markets and international cooperation through cartelization. On several occasions Erhard and the BDI had fought severe battles, especially about competition rules and price policy.[50] As a consequence the relationship between the Ministers of Economics and Industry was rather strained, and it is, therefore, no coincidence that the BDI sided with the European approach of the Adenauer wing within the Federal Cabinet.[51]

The Foreign Ministry, in particular, of the government bodies had supported the Messina initiative from the start.[52] This could be taken as a hint that political rather than economic considerations carried the highest weight within the German government; a view which over the years has been supported by numerous accounts by the decision makers themselves. Nevertheless, to conclude that the EEC was only a means to political ends would be premature. It is true that Adenauer generally paid little attention to economics. But although Adenauer's personal role in bringing about the final decision should not be underrated, the outcome of the German decision-making process cannot be explained by the influence of one or a few prominent politicians. Reality was more complex. The broad pro-European coalition in the Federal Republic was indeed held together by a general economic interest in European trade liberalisation. As this concern could be merged with West Germany's overall political interests as interpreted by the dominant faction within the Christian Democratic Party and the government, a formidable coalition supporting the restricted Europe-approach of the Six was formed. The West German endorsement of the Rome Treaties finds its strongest rationale here.

The Netherlands

Together with France and Germany the Netherlands played a dominant role in the creation of the EEC. The very idea of a Common Market was put back on the European agenda by the Dutch government, and without constant Dutch pressure for more binding economic cooperation, it seems likely that the EEC would not have materialized as quickly as it did.[53]

In 1950 the Dutch Foreign Minister, Dirk Stikker, launched a plan for economic sector integration within the framework of the OEEC. This so-called "Stikker Plan", however, never made it much further than being examined by various working groups within the OEEC. Two years later Stikker's successor in the Dutch Foreign Office, Johan Willem Beyen, proposed the creation of a European customs union within the framework of the European Political Community which was discussed in relation to the European Defence Community.[54] Thus, Beyen's proposal was also buried when the French National Assembly rejected the EDC treaty. On the other hand, the Dutch proposals had not been in vain. They had a considerable impact on the Brussels negotiations leading to the Rome Treaties. And equally important, with the Beyen Plan the Dutch themselves had constructed a policy platform guiding future Dutch participation in the European process. The Dutch knew what they wanted and were not swept away by political initiatives taken by the great powers.[55]

To understand why the Dutch insisted so strongly on a European customs union requires a few words on the economic situation in the Netherlands.[56] First of all, given the country's high dependency on trade and international services, Dutch economic policy was based on a genuine interest in trade liberalisation in Europe. Foreign trade is generally vital for the economic performance of a small but economically highly specialised country like the Netherlands. Trade with the Federal Republic was particularly important to the Dutch economy. West Germany was the primary supplier of manufactured and semi-manufactured goods, and on the export side the German market looked like a golden outlet for the Dutch agricultural surplus production. The basic requirements of the Dutch economy therefore consisted in creating stable trading conditions within a framework that included West Germany. The EEC promised to fulfil both of these goals.[57]

Yet, on the Dutch side the EEC solution also created a set of dilemmas. Dutch trade, thus, was not limited to the Six. Since it was likely that the common external tariff of the EEC would be fixed at a considerably higher level than the existing, relatively low level of the Dutch tariff, the Common Market of the Six would result in increased import prices for commodities from outside the EEC. A further point of criticism against the EEC was that Dutch producers would lose their privileged position in the Benelux trade. The third worry concerned the likelihood that the U.K. would not be included in the EEC. Both from economic and political points of view this probability caused concern within Dutch government circles. Two of these dilemmas indicate that economic integration in a broader framework than that of the EEC would have served the interests of the Netherlands much better. Why did the Dutch then persist so eagerly down the path of the EEC model?

To explain this one must understand that in international politics, as in political decision-making generally, one can rarely choose between two ideal options. More often the choice is between what is considered more or less of an improvement or between what is desirable and what is possible. In the opinion of Dutch decision-makers the EEC type of integration had one great political advantage. Albeit weakly developed, the supranational features inherent in the Rome Treaties seemed to guarantee a more binding and committed type of cooperation than that available in the traditional type of interdependent framework within GATT and the OEEC. By the mid-1950's the Dutch government was convinced that neither GATT nor the OEEC would be able to undertake further decisive steps in the direction of trade liberalisation. And worse still, it had no confidence that the degree of trade liberalisation obtained until then could be maintained in the future. The pre-EEC system lacked the essential stability sought by the Dutch. Despite its imperfection the EEC-system at least seemed to offer a higher degree of stability and irreversibility. Throughout the Brussels negotiations (as in the period after the signing of the Rome Treaties) the Dutch support for the geographically limited and supranationally orientated EEC-model was coupled with a demand for maximum openness towards the outside world.[58]

It would be an exaggeration to claim that the Dutch government had much success in defending this demand during the Brussels negotiations. Agreements concerning such crucial sectors as transport and agriculture were either clearly protectionist or mere declarations leaving the real decision-making to the future institutions of the Community. The Dutch government was also highly dissatisfied with the way the future external tariff would be calculated, the incorporation of the overseas territories, and the French demands for social harmonisation.[59] Dutch Industry was even more outspoken in its opposition recommending the government abstain from ratification if the Netherlands could not obtain some last-minute concessions.[60]

The Dutch finally agreed to the EEC because they were aware that under the circumstances a solution more favourable to the economic needs of the Netherlands was impossible to achieve. Although far from perfect, the EEC foresaw the removal of trade barriers within a community which included three of the Netherlands' most important trading partners.

Conclusions

Looking for the motivations behind the creation of the EEC one has to examine the individual interests of the participating nation states. The overriding interest was the desire to re-establish an international trading system because trade was considered essential for sustained economic growth, and thus for political stability. This primary interest, however, cannot explain the specific shape and character of the EEC established in 1958.

France, in particular, was reluctant to open up its feeble and protected economy to international competition. Although structural economic change took place in France during the 1950s increasing the weight of the international-orientated sectors of French Industry, most French producers were only willing to accept an economic community which would guarantee a high degree of protection of the home market. Such a guarantee, however, would not have been enough to secure French backing if the EEC did not also promise to alleviate the problems of the French farmers. Bringing agriculture into the provisions of the Common Market, thus, became crucial for a successful conclusion of the Messina Initiative. Although the other five future member states went a long way to accommodate these and other French demands (for instance the incorporation of the French overseas territories), the French negotiators continued to prefer the sector-by-sector approach inherent in the Atomic Community scheme, rather than the more general integration approach represented by the EEC proposal. It was only in the face of the other five participants' determined refusal to consider a separation of the two projects that France had to give in and accept the condition that there could be no Atomic Community without a customs union. This acceptance probably represented France's greatest concession during the negotiations.

In contrast, the Federal Republic of Germany was self-confident enough not to fear the stronger competition inside a customs union of the Six. West German industry was very dependent on industrial exports and on cheap imports of raw materials. But from a West German perspective, the European Economic Community also represented only the second-best solution. German negotiators would have preferred trade liberalisation to take place within a broader geographical context and without the supranational elements of the EEC. This would have met the economic requirements of the Federal Republic much better than the restricted customs union of the six ECSC countries. Nevertheless, the German government strongly promoted the EEC solution, firstly because after all it was a step in the right trade liberalising direction and secondly because the Adenauer government recognized the great political importance of the project. As demonstrated Adenauer's foreign policy was based on two guiding principles: full integration of West Germany into a stable Western European framework and the development of a special relationship with France. Only within this framework could the Federal Republic regain political independence and freedom of action. The EEC could be anticipated to work to both these ends. This was an accomplishment not to miss even if there was a d-mark bill to pay to make the Community function.

The Netherlands, finally, were as much dependent on an increase of intra-European trade as West Germany, and would also have preferred the Community to comprise a wider geographical area than actually became the fact. But compared to the OEEC and GATT, the EEC promised more than a mere liberalisation of commodity trade. The liberalisation rules were more radical and binding, more economic sectors were involved, it included the Netherlands' potential most interesting trading partners, first of all West Germany, and it comprised agriculture. Seen in this light the Dutch government could live with the fact that many of its original demands had been discarded during the Brussels-negotiations. The Netherlands accepted the rule, to live is to choose, and she chose.

Notes

1. The main exponent of this interpretation is Alan S. Milward. See A.S. Milward: *The Reconstruction of Western Europe 1945-1951*, London 1984; *The European Rescue of the Nation State*, London 1992; and (ed.): *The Frontier of National Sovereignty. History and Theory 1945-1992*, London 1993.
2. For the influence of European federalists on the Treaties of Rome, see Pistone, S.: "Il movimento federalista europeo e i Trattati di Roma", in Serra, E. (ed.): *Il rilancio dell'Europa e i Trattati di Roma*, Brussels/Milan/Paris/Baden-Baden 1989, pp 629-652.

    A good deal of the literature on the foundation of the EEC has been written by political figures who were themselves involved in the historical process. See for example Albonetti, A.: *Vorgeschichte der Vereinigten Staaten von Europa*, Baden-Baden/Bonn 1961; Groeben, H. von der: *Europa. Plan und Wirklichkeit. Reden, Berichte, Aufsätze zur europäischen Politik*, Baden-Baden 1967; Monnet, J.: *Erinnerungen eines Europärs*, Munich/Vienna 1978; Müller-Armack, A.: *Auf dem Wege nach Europa. Erinnerungen und Ausblicke*, Tübingen/Stuttgart 1971; Müller-Roschach, H.: "Die deutsche Europapolitik 1949-1977. Eine politische Chronik", in: *Europäische Schriften des Instituts für europäische Politik*, Vol.55, Bonn 1980; Spaak, P-H.: *Memoiren eines Europärs*, Hamburg 1969; Uri, P.: "De la Communauté Européenne du Carbon et l'Acier au Marché Commun", in: *Revue du Marché Commun*, vol.10, 1976.
3. Until the beginning of the 1980's little academic research on the history of the EEC had been accomplished. Important titles of this early period include: Bjøl, E.: *La France devant l'Europe et le rapprochement franco-allemand*, Paris 1972; Camps, M.: *Britain and the European Community 1955-1963*, Princeton (New Jersey)/London 1964; Haas, E.B.: *The Uniting of Europe. Political, Social and Economic Forces 1950-1957*, London 1958; Hrbek, R.: *Die SPD – Deutschland und Europa, Die Haltung der Sozialdemokratie zum Verhältnis von Deutschland-Politik und West-Integration (1945-1957)*, Bonn 1972; Kaiser, K.: *EWG und Freihandelszone. England und der Kontinent in der Europäischen Integration*, Leiden 1963; Mahant, E.E.: *French and German Attitudes to the Negotiations about the European Economic Community 1955-1957*, Ph.D. London 1969; Mayne, R.: *The Community of Europe. Past, Present and Future*, London 1962; Willis, F.R.: *France, Germany and the new Europe 1945-1967*, New York 1971.

Archive based research from the last 10-15 years include: Berding, H. (ed.): *Wirtschaftliche und politische Integration in Europa im 19. und 20. Jahrhundert*, Göttingen 1984; Dumoulin, M. (ed.): *La Belgique et les débuts de la construction européenne. De la guerre aux traités de Rome*, Louvain-laNeuve 1987; Gerbet, P.: *La construction de l'Europe*, Paris 1983; Griffiths, R.T. (ed.): *The Netherlands and the Integration of Europe 1945-1957*, Amsterdam 1989; Herbst, L.; Bührer, W.; Sowade, H. (eds.): *Vom Marshallplan zur EWG. Die Eingliederung der Bundesrepublik in die westliche Welt*, Munich 1990; Küsters, H.J.: *Die Gründung der Europäischen Wirtschaftsgemeinschaft*, Baden-Baden 1982; Loth, W.: *Der Weg nach Europa*, Göttingen 1991; di Nolfo, E. (ed.): *Power in Europe*, Vol. 2: Great Britain, France, Germany and Italy and the Origins of the EEC 1952-1957, Berlin, New York 1992; Serra, E. (ed.), op. cit..

4. Although this approach shares some elements with the neo-functionalist theory as it was first formulated by Haas, it differs in many other respects. It is for example rather sceptical about the spill-over effects from integrated sectors of the economy to others as were predicted by the neo-functionalists.
5. Serra, E.: "L'Italia e la Conferenza di Messina", in: Serra, E. (ed.): Il rilancio op. cit., pp 94.
6. See Milward, A.S.: "Belgium and Western European Interdependence in the 1950's: Some Unexplained Problems", in: Dumoulin, M. (ed.): op. cit..
7. For Luxemburg's role in the EEC negotiations see Trausch, G.: "Le Luxembourg face aux Traités de Rome. La stratégie d'un petit Pays", in Serra, E.: Il rilancio op. cit., pp 423.
8. See Loth, W.: "Die europäische Integration nach dem zweiten Weltkrieg aus französischer Perspektive", in: Berding, H. (ed.): op. cit., pp 225.
9. Ibid.
10. For the French policy towards Germany in the late 1940s, see: Loth, W.: "Die Franzosen und die deutsche Frage 1945-1949", in: Scharf, C.; Schröder, H.-J. (eds.): *Die Deutschlandpolitik Frankreichs und die französische Zone, 1945-1949*, Wiesbaden 1983, pp 27.
11. For a short history of the different economic integration attempts after 1945, see Griffiths, R.T. & Barbezat, D.: "The European Integration Experience", *Conference Paper for the Workshop: Promoting Regional Cooperation and Integration in Sub-Saharan Africa*, held in Florence, February 26-28th, 1992.
12. Ibid., p 10.
13. For the course of the Fritalux negotiations, see Griffiths, R.T., and Lynch, F.M.B.: "L'échec de la `Petite Europe'? Les négociations Fritalux/Finebel, 1949-1950", in: *Revue historique* 274 (1985), pp 159.
14. Loth, W.: "Die deutsche Frage in französischer Perspektive", in: Herbst, L.: *Westdeutschland 1945-1955*, München 1986, pp 37.
15. Gillingham, J.: *Coal, Steel and the Rebirth of Europe, 1945-1955. The Germans and French from Ruhr Conflict to Economic Community*, Cambridge, New York, Port Chester, Melbourne, Sidney 1991; and: "Die französische Ruhrpolitik und die Ursprünge des Schuman-Plans", in: *Vierteljahrshefte für Zeitgeschichte* 35, 1 (1987), pp 1-24; Milward, A.S.: *The Reconstruction of Western Europe 1945-1951*, London 1984, pp 126-167.
16. Frances M.B. Lynch: "Resolving the Paradox of the Monnet Plan. National and International Planning in French Reconstruction", in: *The Economic History Review* 37 (1984), pp 229-243, goes as far as to interpret the Schuman plan as a means for the French to gain economic hegemony over Western Europe.
17. Guillen, P.: "Frankreich und der europäische Wiederaufschwung. Vom Scheitern der EVG bis zur Unterzeichnung der Verträge von Rom, in: *Vierteljahrshefte für Zeitgeschichte* 28, 1 (1980) p 14; for European integration of agriculture, see

also Kluge, U.: Wege europäischer Agrarintegration 1950-1957, in: Herbst, L.; Bührer, W.; Sowade, H. (eds.), op. cit., pp 301-311.
18. Willis, F.R.: op. cit..
19. Guillen, P.: op. cit., pp 15.
20. Concerning this argument, see also the article by F.Just & T.B. Olesen in this volume.
21. Statz, A.: "Zur Geschichte der westeuropäischen Integration bis zur Gründung der EWG", in: F. Deppe (ed.), *Europäische Wirtschaftsgemeinschaft (EWG). Zur politischen Ökonomie der westeuropäischen Integration*, Reinbek 1975.
22. Küsters, H.J.: op. cit., pp 356.
23. Willis, F.R.: op. cit., p. 257.
24. Guillen, P.: op. cit., p 17.
25. Guillen, P.: op. cit., p 13.
26. Küsters, H.J.: op. cit., pp 379.
27. Noack, P.: *Das Scheitern der Europäischen Verteidigungsgemeinschaft. Entscheidungsprozesse vor und nach dem 30. August 1954*, Düsseldorf 1977.
28. Guillen, P.: op. cit., pp 3.
29. Küsters, H.J.: op. cit., pp 33.
30. See Willis, F.R.: op. cit..
31. Guillen, P.: op. cit., p 4.
32. For the course of the Euratom negotiations, see Weilemann, P.: *Die Anfänge der Europäischen Nukleargemeinschaft. Zur Gründungsgeschichte von Euratom 1955-1957*, Baden-Baden 1982.
33. Monnet, J.: op. cit.
34. Guillen, P.: op. cit., pp 6.
35. Rhenisch, T.: *Die deutsche Industrie und die Gründung der Europäischen Wirtschaftsgemeinschaft*, PH.D.-thesis, Florence 1994, pp 105.
36. The following chapter on Germany is based on the author's PH.D.-thesis. Ibid.
37. See Herbst, L.: "Stil und Handlungsspielräume westdeutscher Integrationspolitik", in: Herbst, L.; Bührer, W.; Sowade, H. (ed.): op. cit., pp 3-18.
38. Hrbek, R.: op. cit.
39. For Adenauer's European poliy, see Schwarz, H.-P.: *Adenauer. Der Staatsmann 1952-1967*, Stuttgart 1991; Schwarz, H.-P.: "Adenauer und Europa", in: *Vierteljahrshefte für Zeitgeschichte*, 27 (1979), pp 471; Weidenfeld, W.: *Konrad Adenauer und Europa*, Bonn 1976; Schwarz, H.-P.: "Das außenpolitische Konzept Konrad Adenauers", in: Morsey, R.; Repgen, K. (eds.): *Adenauer-Studien I = Veröffentlichungen der Kommission für Zeitgeschichte, Reihe B, Bd.10*, Mainz 1971, pp 71.
40. The statistical material is taken from the *Statistischen Jahrbuch für die Bundesrepublik*, 1960, ed. by the Statistisches Bundesamt, Wiesbaden.
41. See Neebe, R.: *Überseemärkte und Exportstrategien in der westdeutschen Wirtschaft 1945-1966. Aus den Reiseberichten von Dietrich Wilhelm von Menges = Zeitschrift für Unternehmensgeschichte, Beiheft 68*, Stuttgart 1991.
42. Survey on industrial attitudes towards the EEC by the Ministry of Economics in the summer of 1957, *Bundesarchiv Koblenz* (BA), B102/18373.
43. Rhenisch, T.: op. cit., pp 128. For industrial attitudes towards the Euratom, see also Deubner, C.: *Die Atompolitik der westdeutschen Industrie und die Gründung von Euratom*, Frankfurt/M, New York 1977.
44. *Records of the BDI Committee for Nuclear Energy*, in the Haniel-Archiv, Duisburg.
45. *Politisches Archiv des Auswärtigen Amtes in Bonn* (AA), Politische Abteilung 2 AZ 225-20-02 Bd.1. See also Weilemann, P.: *Die Anfänge der Europäischen Atomgemeinschaft*, Baden-Baden 1982, p. 98.
46. Kluge, U.: "Du Pool noir au Pool vert: Wirtschafts- und Sozialprobleme des

'Marché Commun Agricole de l'Europe' 1949-1957 aus deutscher Sicht", in: Serra, E. (ed.): op. cit., pp 239; see also Küsters, H.J.: op. cit., pp 352.
47. Lappenküper, U.: "Ich bin wirklich ein guter Europäer." Ludwig Erhards Europapolitik 1949-1966, in: *Francia* 18, 3 (1991), pp 85.
48. Küsters, H.J.: "Der Streit um Kompetenzen und Konzeptionen deutscher Europapolitik 1949-1958", in: Herbst, L.; Bührer, W.; Sowade, H. (eds.): op. cit., pp 335; see also: Carstens, K.: "Das Eingreifen Adenauers in die Europa-Verhandlungen im November 1956", in: Blumenwitz, D.; Gotto, K.; Maier, H.; Repgen, K.; Schwarz, H.-P. (eds.): *Konrad Adenauer und seine Zeit. Politik und Persönlichkeit des ersten Bundeskanzlers. Beiträge von Weg- und Zeitgenossen*, Stuttgart 1976, pp 591-602.
49. See Berghahn, V.: *Unternehmer und Politik in der Bundesrepublik*, Frankfurt/M 1985, and: "Montanunion und Wettbewerb", in: H. Berding (ed.): op. cit., pp 247.
50. Koerfer, D.: *Kampf ums Kanzleramt. Erhard und Adenauer*, Stuttgart 1987.
51. Rhenisch, T.: op. cit., p 142.
52. Baring, A. (ed.): *Sehr verehrter Herr Bundeskanzler! Heinrich von Brentano im Briefwechsel mit Konrad Adenauer 1949-1964*, Hamburg 1974.
53. Griffiths, R.T.: "The Common Market" p. 204, in: Griffiths, R.T. (ed.), op. cit., pp 183-204. For the Dutch policy towards the Common Market see also Harryvan, A.G. & Kersten, A.E.: "The Netherlands, Benelux and the Rélance Européenne 1954-1955", in: Serra, E. (ed.): op. cit., pp 125-157, and Mannig, A.: "Die Niederlande von 1945 bis zu Beginn der fünfziger Jahre", in: *Vierteljahrshefte für Zeitgeschichte* 29 (1981), pp 1-20.
54. Beyen, J.W.: *Het spel en de knikkers: Een kroniek van 50 jaren*, Rotterdam 1968. For the history of the Beyen-plan, see also Griffiths, R.T.: "The Beyen Plan", in: Griffiths, R.T. (ed.): *The Netherlands and the Integration of Europe 1945-1957*, Amsterdam, 1990, pp 165-182, and: Griffiths, R.T.; Milward, A.S.: "The Beyen Plan and the European Political Community", in: Maihofer, W. (ed.): *Noi si mura. Selected Working Papers of the European University Institute*, EUI, Florence 1986, pp 595-621.
55. Milward, A.S.: "Nationale Wirtschaftsinteressen ..." op. cit., p 102.
56. See Griffiths, R.T. (ed.): *The Economy and Politics of the Netherlands*, The Hague 1980.
57. Griffiths, R.T.: "The Common Market", op. cit..
58. See Griffiths, R.T.: "The Common Market", op. cit..
59. Küsters, H.J.: op. cit., pp 427.
60. *Bundesarchiv Koblenz*, "Reports of the Ministry of Economics on the reactions to the Rome Treaties in the member states".

The United Kingdom and the Free Trade Area: A Post Mortem

By Richard T. Griffiths

When the negotiations that were eventually to result in the Rome Treaties began in the early summer of 1955, there were not six countries represented but seven. Also present was a delegation from the United Kingdom. Partly because of an antipathy towards federalist ventures and partly reflecting the lack of orientation of the UK's trade towards Europe, in November 1955, the British cabinet decided against joining the Common Market. Since, at the time, the Foreign Office was cultivating the view that the most likely outcome of the talks was failure, the cabinet ignored the warning that should the Six succeed, Britain's position outside the group could be painful. Therefore, when the Common Market negotiations singularly failed to collapse, the need for an alternative strategy began to penetrate some sections of the government.[1]

The driving force behind the new approach was Peter Thorneycroft, president of the Board of Trade. He was firmly supported by Harold Macmillan who had recently been transferred from the Foreign Office to the Treasury. Their concern was to channel the efforts of the Six in directions that could contain British interests. As Thorneycroft warned the Prime Minister in January 1956:

> "No fine words would disguise the reality of a discriminatory bloc, in the heart of industrial Europe, promoting its own internal trade at the expense of trade with other countries in the free world."[2]

A restricted meeting of ministers decided in May 1956 to focus the study for an alternative policy on the possibility of creating a partial free trade area in Europe.[3] Properly conceived, it seemed big enough to be attractive to Europeans, whilst leaving open the possibility for keeping privileged access to Commonwealth imports.[4] At the end of July the plan was ready for consideration by cabinet. It would apply to all OEEC countries, but only to industrial products. By excluding agriculture, policy-makers hoped to be able to keep preferences on most goods bought from the Commonwealth (and thus the reciprocal preferences enjoyed by UK manufacturing exports) and to keep tariff protection for British horticulture. Largely because European trade gains no longer had to be set against Commonwealth losses, the balance of official reaction was more positive than it had been on the Messina initiative.[5] However, it was not until November, after consultations with the Commonwealth and the Federation of British Industries, that the cabinet finally approved the scheme.[6] A week later it passed through Parliament without a vote. Closing the debate, Thorneycroft expressed the challenge in the following terms:

> "Here, in Europe, we have the cultural centre of the free world. We should not leave it Balkanised, divided and weak, but growing closer together, stronger, more compact and linked through us with a great Commonwealth and Empire. Here is a chance of achieving something which matches the scale of present events."[7]

Instead of launching a great crusade, the formal announcement of the UK's free trade area initiative marked the start of two year's frustrating and increasingly acrimonious negotiations. In February 1957 the plan was presented to the OEEC Council which decided to create three working parties (to investigate industrial trade, agriculture and the problem of Europe's less developed economies) under Thorneycroft's chairmanship. These duly submitted their reports just before the summer and in October the OEEC authorised the start of formal intergovernmental negotiations under the chairmanship of the UK Paymaster-General, Reginald Maudling.

British policy was directed at securing an agreement before 1 January 1959 when the first mutual tariff cuts within the EEC would take effect. Although allowed under GATT rules, this would mark the start of tariff discrimination against non-members. Nonetheless, events moved at an excruciatingly slow pace. Early on the French made clear their reluctance to accept the British proposals but took their time presenting their own. Once they arrived, they went first to the Six who were attempting to co-ordinate their approach throughout the conference. And then, in April/May, with still no concrete counter-proposal on the table, everything was delayed as France tottered on the brink of civil war. For France the crisis was resolved by the accession to power of General de Gaulle, but this did little to speed up progress on the FTA. When the considered reactions of the Six finally appeared in September 1958, their contents were unacceptable. Time was running out, the sides were still poles apart and there was little evidence of a genuine willingness to compromise. This painful situation was abruptly terminated in November 1958 when the French Minister of Information announced the impossibility of continuing any longer along the lines wanted by the British. The same day, de Gaulle, in a private letter to Macmillan, repeated the message. Conservative politicians and the press boiled with righteous indignation and hurled angry recriminations across the Channel but to no avail; the pan-European free trade area was dead.

The story of these negotiations has been told and analysed in several

The United Kingdom and the Free Trade Area: A Post Mortem

contemporaneous histories[8], in subsequent political memoirs[9] and two interesting 'eyewitness' collections[10]. Each of these has its drawbacks: the contemporary analysts, however assiduous, are short of 'insider' information; the politicians' memoirs, however objective, are invariably shaped by subsequent selectivity of memory. What, we ask ourselves, did they really think at the time? Just occasionally, we get an answer.

In 1959 a number of British civil servants and a junior minister exchanged notes, in the form of a post mortem on the events spanning these two years. The initiative was taken by Sir Frank Figgures, a leading Treasury civil servant and destined to become the first chairman of EFTA. It was adopted and further coordinated by Otto Clarke, also from the Treasury, who chaired the interdepartmental committee that coordinated UK policy planning throughout the negotiations. Among the other participants were Dennis Wright, the senior Foreign Office official directing policy on the subject; John Coulson, Reginald Maudling's senior assistant and Figgures' successor as chairman of EFTA; Paul Gore-Booth, a junior Foreign Office minister who steered UK policy towards France through the aftermath of the November 1958 veto; and Russell Bretherton, the senior Board of Trade official involved in the negotiations and the man who had led the UK delegation at the 'Messina' talks in 1955. Their analysis and the archival record of UK policy-making in this period form the basis of this article. Before starting, however, it is interesting to note that they never once questioned whether a free trade area was a sound or an appropriate policy in its own right. Instead they preferred an organisational paradigm for the analysis of foreign policy problems.

* * *

1. The first error that Figgures identified was that "we assumed we were wanted". Whilst conceding that most governments wanted closer UK involvement with the Continent, he considered that as early as 1949 influential federalists "had hesitation about us being full members, lest we hold up the march to federation". This tendency had only been strengthened by the vacillation on troop commitment during the European Defence Community debacle of 1953-54. Clarke, at least, recognised that there might be some reality behind the 'Europeans" view. The UK, he suggested, underestimated the political value the Six attached to the EEC; the stress on economics was therefore bound to slow things down.[11]

There is a remarkable disingenuity about this analysis, with its pathetic plea that the genuine motives had been misunderstood. It totally ignores the ways in which British tactics contributed to poisoning the atmosphere. The UK withdrawal from the Common Market negotiations was a case in point. Instead of a polite recognition of differences in aspirations, Sir Ellis-Rees (head of the OEEC delegation) openly denounced the actions of the Six as divisive to the cause of European solidarity.[12] Similarly, Macmillan's request that the Six delay their own work on the customs union so that provisions common to it and the FTA could be drafted together, was seen as an attempt to sabotage the Rome Treaties.[13] This could be interpreted as an unfortunate misinterpretation, were it not for the fact that British policy was indeed to derail progress on the Rome Treaties and hold them hostage.

After the failure to delay the conclusion of the Treaty of Rome, officials in Whitehall considered reestablishing the link with the FTA by trying to delay the EEC's ratification in one or more member states. Alternatively, they kept open the option of encouraging opposition within GATT against the waiver that the EEC required. The problem with this tactic was that it could also work in reverse. The French especially, refused to begin work on a FTA until the Treaty of Rome was 'safe'.[14] They argued that they could scarcely accept a less attractive deal within the OEEC than they had already secured in the Treaty of Rome.[15] However, if the French refused to start serious bargaining, then the rest of the Six could not start either, since the Treaty of Rome had bound them to a common commercial policy. Then, nothing would happen. And for the first three or four months nothing is precisely what occurred. In the end the British decided to abandon this tactic. Approaches were made to France and West Germany to obtain 'binding commitments of support' for the FTA once national parliaments had approved the Treaty of Rome.[16] In effect this meant that from then on the British colluded with the Six in emptying the preliminary discussions of any meaningful content.

It was not as though the bad atmosphere generated by these manoeuverings was quickly dispelled. For example, three weeks after bludgeoning the French to provide statements of good faith, the President of the Board of Trade, David Eccles, addressed an audience of Commonwealth and Empire businessmen. Twice in a lifetime, he reminded them, they had joined wars to oppose the formation of "a hostile bloc across the channel". Now, although not military or hostile in intent, "six countries in Europe have signed a Treaty to do exactly what, for hundreds of years, we have always said we could not see with the safety of our own country".[17] Equally, in June 1958, immediately after his accession to power, Macmillan virtually threatened de Gaulle with the withdrawal of UK troops from Europe if the FTA failed.[18]

2. A second policy error identified was that "almost insensibly, and without considering the consequences, we became committed to negotiating a 17-country Free Trade Area." Figgures thought that the UK should have approached the Six directly in Autumn 1956. The only other person to address this issue, Wright, mentioned that the OEEC link also increased the apprehension of Europeans who, like Marjolin, had already aban-

doned it as a vehicle for greater unity.[19] The consequence was that the UK became saddled with the Organisation's requirements for unanimity and therefore, with having to secure the acquiescence of Greece, Iceland, Ireland and Turkey that were unlikely to join the FTA anyway.

In retrospect there is no reason to disagree with the opinion that the OEEC proved an inappropriate forum. However, it is difficult to see how an early bilateral approach could have been made since the UK's first preference was for the common market to collapse and the second was to get it into a framework where it could be contained. The OEEC, with 17-country unanimity rules, was the perfect vehicle for the second option. Indeed, when Ellis-Rees suggested that the initial UK response to the Messina invitation should be to steer it into the OEEC, he slavered at the prospect of adding to the impressive list of initiatives he had already smothered there.[20] The move was so transparent that the Six wasted little time in even considering it and, theoretically, the UK's options were still open. They closed irrevocably a year later.

Since the OEEC had started its scheme for removing import quotas on intra-European trade, the smaller European countries had complained bitterly that it was inherently unfair since abnormally high tariffs could neutralise its impact. The UK had continuously denied this. As a result of the subsequent discontent, the decision in 1955 to move from 75 to 90 per cent quota removal had been made provisionally for 18 months, conditional upon appropriate action being taken on tariffs. The intervening months had passed without anything happening so that, by July 1956, the UK faced the prospect of losing trade concessions if nothing were done. The Benelux countries, Scandinavia and Switzerland arrived at the OEEC meeting with a new tariff reduction scheme.[21] The British cabinet wanted to reject this too, even though it realised, that "there may well be complete deadlock" and that this "might leave the Messina group as a focus of further activity in Europe."[22] The solution was sought in the tried and tested method of yet another study group. The costs of this victory were high. The Six felt that the British were trying to "sideline Messina and smother it" and the sponsors of the new plan were incensed that it would not even be discussed.[23] Nonetheless, in June 1956 the OEEC created Working Party No 17 to study future relations between the Six and the rest of Europe. It was here that the free trade option was initially discussed. Although its creation had been designed to solve a completely different problem, politically the linkage was then established. It was impossible thereafter to propose the FTA plan elsewhere, far less to discuss it bilaterally with the Six – always assuming that they were prepared to listen.

3. As Chairman of the OEEC at the time of the FTA launch, the UK also exercised the option of chairing the negotiations. Figgures admitted that this had given great advantages but it had also created the impression that

the FTA was largely a UK interest. Although another chairman would have led to greater embarrassment for the UK position, it might also have built up more pressure on the French. Coulson, anxious to defend his minister, thought that the UK decision to chair was understandable since it would allow the country to force the pace at a time it was considered its bargaining position was at its strongest. Once progress had been registered, he contended, Maudling would have handed over the chair and concentrated on his function as a negotiator. Gore-Booth could not see the fuss. Had things gone better, having Maudling in the chair would have been viewed in the same (positive) light as Spaak being in the chair in the final stages of the EEC negotiations.[24] It is difficult to refute the argument that chairing negotiations in which one is a major protagonist is going to create the illusion of partiality. Yet historical explanations focussing on negotiating methods always seem to end with a collation of successful method and successful outcome. There was no lack of advice of how to improve matters: a neutral OEEC chairman, the creation of more small specialist committees, a stronger role for the Commission in coordinating the policy of the Six. However, it is hard to avoid Gore-Booth's conclusion that had the parties not been allowed to drift so far apart, the chairmanship issue would have made no difference.

While one line of criticism lay in the function of the chairmanship, another questioned the way it was fulfilled. This took two forms. Gore-Booth, for example, thought that if someone was in the chair, he should have 'lived on the job' rather more. In order to mute the personal criticism implicit in the remark, he asked whether this was compatible with the task of a cabinet minister?[25] If this line of attack was valid, it was only when applied to Thorneycroft, who chaired the Conference while holding the office of Chancellor of the Exchequer in its study group phase between February and July 1957. It was true that he was not an ever-present driving force in these months and that unfavourable parallels were drawn with Spaak; not least by Spaak himself.[26] This analysis ignores the curious circumstances surrounding the start of the FTA's career: the need for a second study round, the stalling of the Six and, after May, the collusion of the UK in this tactic. What difference, under these circumstances, could a minister's vigilance have achieved? Like the growing pile of paper, Thorneycroft's more visible presence would only have represented the illusion of progress.

A more serious charge was that of a lack of political leadership. The cabinet seemed content to shove the project onto the portfolio of a couple of ministers and forget about it; parliament was not really mobilised to add political weight. As a result there was no "large and vocal political interest to override sectional opposition" and observers drew their own conclusion on British commitment to the project.[27]

The explanation lay in the considerable reserve within the cabinet towards the FTA. The then Prime Minister, Anthony Eden stated that he would have preferred a Commonwealth initiative. He warned that the Conservative Party would not take happily to abandoning "traditional policies based on maintaining the solidarity of the English speaking peoples in favour of closer union with European nations".[28] Rab Butler, who became Macmillan's Home Secretary, feared that the FTA would inhibit the government's ability to pursue full employment policies, would damage industry and would weaken Sterling. He, too, warned that a poor treatment of agriculture would damage the Conservative vote in the shires.[29] Lord Home, first Commonwealth secretary and later Lord President, yearned for a "return to our old Conservative Policy goal of United Kingdom producer first, Commonwealth producer second, and foreigner last".[30] The Colonial Secretary felt that colonial development plans would be destroyed as their products were ousted from British markets by European competition.[31] Finally, James Stuart, of the Scottish Office, voiced what was probably really behind these attitudes:

> "Any idea that we were departing from these principles (the unity of the English speaking peoples -RTG) in favour of a mixed collection of Europeans, who have not all been our friends in the past, would have disastrous repercussions within and beyond the Party."[32]

Notwithstanding the almost messianic fervour with which Macmillan and Thorneycroft supported the scheme, cabinet and party support for the FTA was decidedly thin. In fact, it probably only secured acceptance because the party needed some new initiative to deflect attention from the Suez fiasco, and because its main proponent looked increasingly likely to become the next Prime Minister. Having steered it through cabinet and parliament once, Macmillan was obviously reluctant to risk attracting too much attention to such an obviously divisive issue. But this meant that the public crusade began and ended in the House of Commons in November 1956.

4. This squeamishness before domestic interest groups was also reflected in the FTA proposals themselves. In particular, the omission of agriculture was universally recognised as a mistake; the only question was, how large a one. Opinion ranged from "a major error" (Figgures) to "an irretrievable blunder" (Gore-Booth). Still, as Figgures suggested, the error appeared unavoidable because without Commonwealth agreement it would have been politically impossible to secure domestic acceptance in the first place. Probably worse, in his eyes, was the continuous reassurances about agriculture to the Commonwealth and to domestic interests. Clarke saw these pledges as reducing negotiating room until the position became frozen into "complete immobility". The overall result was to antagonise not only

opponents but also the friends that the UK needed (the Netherlands, Denmark) as well as the peripherals that had to be kept out of the way.[33]

The exclusion of agriculture from the FTA had been designed partly to pacify the domestic agricultural lobby. It also served to maintain Commonwealth preferential access to UK markets, upon which reciprocal British industrial preferences depended. Both were thoroughly British interests. Yet for agricultural exporters on the Continent this appeared like wanting to have one's cake and eat it: to gain access to their industrial markets without purchasing their foodstuffs in return. Although the riposte, that arrangements within the EEC did not envisage agricultural free trade either, was inherently correct, it did not diminish the resentment still felt in the Netherlands, France and Italy. However, it was in Scandinavia, where the British had hoped to find a real basis of support for the FTA, that the price for agricultural exclusion was exacted. Although Denmark was the most deeply affected, it was Norway that effectively derailed any hopes for an early start to negotiations. When the OEEC met in February 1957 to decide which course to take, Norway declared that its participation was dependent upon the creation of a study group rather than a fully fledged negotiating committee.[34]

The UK position was resented on two grounds. Firstly, by trying to push agriculture almost completely off the agenda, the British were seemingly indifferent to the possibility that others might want to reach some understanding among themselves. In particular, they deprived the Danes of the possibility of using the industry-agriculture link as a means of leverage to advance an agreement with the Six. Secondly, whereas there was some understanding (though not much) of the UK's Commonwealth argument, there was none at all for its commitment to domestic protectionism. In May 1957 officials were "considering quite advanced changes of policy on the agricultural front". This changed with the decision to collude with the Six in suspending serious negotiation until the ratification of the Rome Treaties removed the immediate necessity: "we no longer feel under compulsion to go fast or to make concessions to others to go fast".[35] During the summer the cabinet did modify its stance. In the first instance this was to take the form of allowing the rest of the OEEC to conclude an agricultural agreement from which the British themselves would seek exemptions. If they failed, so much the better. Neither the suggestion to offer a freeze on future levels of protection nor the option of offering specific product concessions was implemented. There was a recognition that something would eventually need to be done, but:

> "We have borne constantly in mind that the further we move at the October meeting the less we have to play with in actual negotiation later on and the further we shall ultimately be pushed. We must clearly move in this matter, but we must not move one step further

at this meeting than is absolutely necessary in order to start off serious negotiation."[36]

Whereas, in the summer the French had suggested that all they wanted was some reassurance that they could keep their share of the UK market plus "a little douceur on individual products"[37], the British intransigence led to a hardening of attitudes. For example, it so annoyed the Scandinavian countries that they issued a joint note endorsing the Danish standpoint on agriculture; a standpoint which they had never previously shown the slightest inclination of applying to themselves.

All in all it was a pretty gutless performance from a government that had seethed as the French had failed to curb the activities of the Patronat. Yet it would be unfair to pretend that the FTA failed on the point of agriculture – the position of the Six was too ambiguous for that to happen. However it afforded an easy position from which opponents could attack.

5. The inflexibility or "woodenness" in UK policy-making, as exhibited in the treatment of agriculture, was identified by Figgures as as an independent factor explaining the demise of the FTA. Another example cited was the reaction to the Carli Plan (see below) which Gore-Booth interpreted as evidence of insufficient sensitivity to the "vulnerabilities, vanities and susceptibilities" of difficult negotiating partners. All this puzzled Clarke, who had coordinated the interdepartmental effort. He thought that the Whitehall machine had "never operated more efficiently", dealing rapidly with issues of great complexity and, still, the UK always seemed tactically outmaneuvered by the French. He placed part of the blame on the few negotiating margins left by politicians but, equally, he recognised that the machine "will inevitably argue to convince itself and not the Europeans: it is sensitive to Departments' fears and not to the Europeans'". Bretherton distanced himself from too glowing an appraisal of the Whitehall machine, recalling the "deliberate obstruction" of the Commonwealth and Colonial offices. He went on, "But, apart from that, what impressed me….was the enormous proportion of our energies which had to go into the management of departmental differences and difficulties."[38]

The image of redrafts of redrafts as arguments were refined and redefined must stay with a researcher that ploughs through the swathes of documents in the European Integration Subcommittee of the Economic Steering Committee. That was the forum for the first rounds of policy coordination before policy documents were passed up and down the policy chain. It is easy to believe, but difficult to document, that this could lead to a false sense of perfectionism.

It is interesting that, in this connection, the Carli Plan was cited by two of the correspondents. The so-called origin question was the superficial cause of the failure of the Maudling negotiations. At its core were the practical difficulties involved in aligning the trading system of the Common Market with that of the FTA. French negotiators especially made a meal of the fact that, unless other measures were taken, the removal of tariffs on intra-area trade would lead to serious distortions, because countries enjoying access to cheaper (lower taxed) inputs would receive an artificial advantage in selling the end-products. They argued that the system could not work unless the external tariffs of the member states were closely aligned, if not identical. In March 1958 the Italian Minister for Foreign Trade, Guido Carli, suggested a compromise plan for a regime of tariff bands and compensatory duties charged on articles made up of inputs carrying lower tariffs. Carli described his proposals as "window dressing" and a "facade"[39] which had "great potentialities for hoodwinking Italian and French public opinion". French approaches appeared to confirm this. Foreign Minister Maurice Faure had accepted it because it was something he could use as a political platform and a senior French official suggested that "whether there were more exceptions to the rule than the rule itself was of no consequence".[40]

The British position had always been that this problem could be adequately tackled by a combination of rules of content and certificates of origin. The reaction to the Carli Plan was to secure the Plan's referral to a study group where, away from the spotlight of the negotiations, they proceeded to produce a report exposing the manifold inconsistencies and weaknesses.[41] The Six themselves did not abandon the plan altogether. They argued that for certain products rules of origin would need to be particularly restrictive if something like the Carli arrangements were not considered. As the Six were preparing their reply, Maudling urged UK ministers to relax the British negotiating position. The original British standpoint (complete freedom of trade within the area, complete freedom on tariffs and commercial policy outside) "would clearly have immense advantages for the United Kingdom...this is one of the reasons why it is very hard to achieve our objective in the negotiations." Possible modifications included accepting some tariff harmonisation or a combination of liberal origin rules and some compensatory taxes (but under the control of the FTA institutions) or agreeing to tariff harmonisation for one or two product groups.[42] These suggestions were blocked by the argument that they represented a radical departure from what had been agreed with the Commonwealth. Once any concession had been made on the external tariff, there was no telling where matters would stop. Despite Maudling's appeal to the effect that resolving the origin issue would do much for the negotiations' chances of success, ministers insisted on prior discussions with both with the Commonwealth and with the Federation of British Industry.[43] Maudling persisted. Most countries (except France and Italy) acknowledged the correctness of the UK's arguments but they were willing to countenance some tariff harmonisation if it would clinch an agreement.

If only the UK would move, he argued, it would provide the test whether the French really wanted an agreement.[44] This missive was never considered by the prime-ministerial committee to whom it was addressed. By September 1958, when the cabinet eventually made a gesture at least to study possible sectoral difficulties, the moment for seizing the initiative had long passed.[45] Figgures later suggested, "that we committed a major error....on the crucial, and almost the only crucial, question of origin, when we failed to take advantage of the gap which the Carli proposals were intended to open".[46]

6. Throughout the analysis in the previous paragraphs, it will be apparent that France continuously reappears as the main protagonist. It is no surprise, therefore, that most of those engaged in the post mortem isolated French opposition as a major factor in explaining the failure of the FTA. They disagreed, however, on the nature and timing of the problem. Figgures branded French Anglophobia as "the most powerful single force working against us" and he speculated whether its roots lay in the EDC debacle or after the Suez and Tunisia fiascos. Clarke, on the other hand, considered that the French factor only really became decisive when de Gaulle came to power. Wright also saw mid-1958 as crucial not so much because of de Gaulle but because the deteriorating economic situation would have forced the same reticence to conclude an FTA agreement on UK terms on any Fourth Republic government. Yet, he conceded, tactically they "left us miles behind". Coulson observed that the French had never made a secret of the fact that the Treaty of Rome had been accepted only with the greatest difficulty and that the problems with the FTA would be worse. He saw the French constitutional crisis as giving France a legitimate cause to stall and this was supported by the Six. Gore-Booth thought this simplistic. He thought Wormser had done everything to keep matters alive until something turned up, though, because it made the final breakdown more acrimonious than necessary, it had probably been a mistake. And that is the only mention that French policy had ever been anything other than incredibly clever.[47]

British officials were mesmerised by the French: always weak, always wrong, always unreasonable and always able to get their way. They watched in awe as UK allies within the Six such as Ludwig Erhard, Ernst van der Beugel and Baron Snoy et d'Oppuers counted for nothing when it came to the crunch. They were transfixed as France stitched together a coalition with Germany, Italy and the EEC Commission that only seemed to strengthen once de Gaulle took power; a coalition that not only swept all before it within the Six but that also ultimately vanquished British hopes. How this occurred will be analysed in the next article of this book.

* * *

As the FTA was dying, a solidarity arose among the seven 'non-Six' countries; a term, incidentally, which reflected the little else that was thought to keep them together. In the aftermath of the French veto they met regularly to coordinate their response to the further initiatives of the Six. Meanwhile, ideas of actually forming some sort of bloc among themselves, that had circulated since early 1958, began to gain more substance. At a meeting in Oslo, in February 1959, two officials from Sweden and Norway were authorised to explore the basis for an agreement. By May their work had advanced sufficiently for the Swedish government to issue invitations for the opening of intergovernmental talks to begin the following month. These, in turn, led to the Stockholm Convention, signed in January 1960, establishing the European Free Trade Association.[48] Clarke considered this the ultimate vindication of the learning capacity of the Whitehall machine:

> "Our performance since the end of 1958 has in my view shown a considerable improvement. The rapid decision to seek a European Free Trade Association of the Seven; the acceptance that there was an agricultural price to be paid – and ultimately a fisheries price too; the rapid negotiation of the EFTA Convention; the avoidance of alienating the Six during these proceedings – these have been considerable successes.... This suggested that we are learning from experience. In terms of history, however, this is the next chapter."[49]

In terms of this book, these events will be examined in a chapter below. In terms of history, however, this judgement would seem premature; there is little indication in an almost unbroken record of UK policy failures, culminating most recently in a decade of fumbling over the Exchange Rate Mechanism and political mismanagement of the Maastricht Treaty, that the British establishment and British politicians have learnt much over the intervening thirty-five years.

Notes

1. For recent archive based studies see: S. Burgess and E. Edwards, "The Six plus One: British Policy-making and the question of European economic integration, 1955", in *International Affairs*, Vol 64, No 3, 1988, 393-413; R. Bullen, "Britain and Europe, 1950-1957" in E. Serra (ed) *Il rilancio dell'Europa e i Trattati di Roma* Brussels/ Milan/ Paris/ Baden-Baden, 1989, 315-338; R.T. Griffiths, "La dinamica dell'inertia politica. La partecipazione ed il ritiro del Regno Unito nella conferenza Spaak, 1955-1956" in E. Decleva and A. Magliazza (eds), *Diplomazia e storia delle relazioni internazionali. Studi in onore di Enrico Serra*, Milan, 1991, 677-697; "The British Attitude towards European Integration" in *EFTA Bulletin* 2/91 (1991), 17-22; A.S. Milward, *The European Rescue of the Nation State*, London, 1992, 425-433; J.W. Young, "'The Parting of the Ways'?: Britain, the Mes-

sina Conference and the Spaak Committee, June-December 1955" in M. Dockrille and J.W. Young (eds) *British Foreign Policy, 1945-56* Basingstoke, 1989, 197-224.
2. Public Record Office, Kew (PRO), Foreign Office (FO) 371/122022, Thorneycroft to Eden, 20.1.1956.
3. PRO, Treasury (T) 234/190, *Record of Conclusions of a Meeting held in the Chancellor of the Exchequer's Room, Treasury, on 31st May 1956*.
4. PRO, T 234/190, *Initiative in Europe*, Memorandum by the President of the Board of Trade, 22.5.1956.
5. PRO, Cabinet (CAB) 129/82, *United Kingdom Commercial Policy* CP(56)191, 27.7.1956; Ibid., *United Kingdom Commercial Policy. Memorandum by the Chancellor of the Exchequer and the President of the Board of Trade* CP(56)192, 28.7.1956.
6. PRO, CAB 128/30, Minutes of cabinet, 20.11.1956.
7. See the Parliamentary debate in Hansard, 27.11.1956.
8. The Classic of this genre remains M. Camps, *Britain and the European Community*, London, 1964. See also by the same author *European Common Market and Free Trade Area*, Princeton, 1957 and *The European Free Trade Association; a Preliminary Appraisal* London, 1959, as well as E. Benoit, *Europe at Sixes and Sevens. The Common Market, the Free Trade Association and the United States*, New York, 1961; K. Kaiser, *EWG und Freihandelszone: England und der Kontinent in der Europäischen Integration*, Leiden, 1963.
9. A thorough treatment from the English position is H. Macmillan, *Riding the Storm, 1956-1959*, London/Melbourne/Toronto, 1971, 61-88, 431-459.
10. M. Charlton, *The Price of Victory*, London, 1983. P du Bois and B. Hurni, *L'AELE d'hier à Demain*, Geneva, 1987.
11. PRO, T 234/720, *Free Trade Area Negotiations: Post Mortem* (Figgures), 17.7.1959; Note (Clarke), 21.7.1959; *Thoughts in Retrospect on the Free Trade Area Negotiations: 1956-1959* (Clarke) 18.1.1960.
12. PRO, CAB 134/1030, *Statement by Sir Hugh Ellis-Rees*, 6 December 1955. For the furious reaction of the Benelux countries in the WEU see Ibid., *Economic Cooperation in Europe – Discussion in the Western European Council*.
13. PRO, T 234/200, Macmillan to Heads of Government of the Six, 28/29.11.1956. At the time the Six were anxious to complete the treaty while there was still a French government in power willing to ratify it. Also West German elections were due.
14. PRO, CAB 134/1855, Meetings of Subcommittee on Closer Economic Association with Europe, 17.4.1957, 29.4.1957. CAB 134/1859, *The Customs Union and the Free Trade Area. Next Steps. Report by Officials*, ES(EI)(57)119 Final, 30.4.1957.
15. PRO, CAB 134/1859, *Meeting of the Anglo-French Economic Committee Meeting in Conference Room A, Cabinet Office, on 16 April 1957*, ES(EI)(57)118, 15.4.1957.
16. PRO, FO 371/128343, *Record of Conversation between the Secretary of State and M. Pineau in Bonn on Friday May 3rd*. FO 371/128344, *The Rome Treaties and the Free Trade Area. Discussions with the German Government*.
17. National Archives and Records Administration, Washington, (NARA), Record Group 59, 440.02/1850, Adams to Department of State, 29.5.1957.
18. PRO, Prime Minister's Office (PREM) 11/2531, *Note by the Prime Minister in his discussion on the European Free Trade Area with Mr. Maudling on March 17; Record of Conversation at the Hotel Matignon after dinner on June 29*.
19. PRO, T 234/720, *Free Trade Area Negotiations: Post Mortem* (Figgures), 17.7.1959; Wright to Clarke, 27.8.1959.

20. PRO, FO 371/116038, Ellis-Rees to Foreign Office, 7.6.1955.
21. W. Asbeek Brusse, *West European Tariff Plans, 1947-1957. From Study Group to Common Market*, PhD European University Institute, Florence, 1991, 183-229. This was based upon a "common list" of products in which trade was predominantly intra-European. Tariffs on these items were to be cut by 25 per cent and the reduction was to be extended to other GATT members via the MFN clause.
22. PRO, CAB 129/82, *Organisation of European Economic Cooperation and tariffs. Memorandum by the Chancellor of the Exchequer and the President of the Board of Trade*, CP(56)172, 9.7.1956. See also PRO, CAB 128/30, Minutes of Cabinet, 12.7.1956, which approved these steps without discussion.
23. PRO, T 243/195, Bretherton to Cohen, 23.7.1956.
24. PRO, T 234/720, *Free Trade Area Negotiations: Post Mortem* (Figgures), 17.7.1959; Coulson to Clarke, 1.9.1959; Gore-Booth to Clarke, 1.9.1959.
25. PRO, T 234/720, Gore-Booth to Clarke, 1.9.1959.
26. PRO, FO 371/128343, *Record of Conversation between the Secretary of State and M. Spaak in Bonn on Friday, May 3*; see also FO 371/128344, *Visit of Baron Snoy on 13 May*.
27. PRO, T 234/720, *Thoughts in Retrospect on the Free Trade Area Negotiations: 1956-1959* (Clarke) 18.1.1960.
28. PRO, CAB 128/30, Minutes of Cabinet, 18.9.1956.
29. PRO, T 234/196, *The United Kingdom Commercial Policy* (Butler), 9.8.1956. See also CAB 128/30, Minutes of Cabinet, 14.9.1956.
30. PRO, FO 371/122034, Home to Macmillan, 3.9.1956.
31. PRO, CAB 128/30 Minutes of Cabinet, 18.9.1956.
32. PRO, PREM 11/2136, Stuart to Eden, 14.9.1956.
33. PRO, T 234/720, *Free Trade Area Negotiations: Post Mortem* (Figgures), 17.7.1959; Note (Clarke), 21.7.1959; Gore-Booth to Clarke, 1.9.1959; *Thoughts in Retrospect on the Free Trade Area Negotiations: 1956-1959* (Clarke) 18.1.1960.
34. HAEC (Historical Archives of the European Community) OEEC Archives, Meeting of Council of Ministers, 12-13.2.1957.
35. PRO, T 234/201, Clarke to Ellis Rees, 17.5.1957. See also CAB 134/1855, Meeting of the Subcommittee on Closer Economic Association with Europe, 14.5.1957.
36. PRO, CAB 128/89, *European Free Trade Area: Agriculture* C(57)219, 4.10.1957. ALSO GET CABINET DECISION
37. PRO, CAB 134/1861, *Record of Conversation between Mr. Maudling and Mr. Gaillard* ES (EI)(57)224.
38. PRO, T 234/720, *Free Trade Area Negotiations: Post Mortem* (Figgures), 17.7.1959; Note (Clarke), 21.7.1959; Gore-Booth to Clarke, 1.9.1959; *Thoughts in Retrospect on the Free Trade Area Negotiations: 1956-1959* (Clarke) 18.1.1960; Bretherton to Clarke, 3.2.1960.
39. PRO, T 234/375, *Note for the Record* (Figgures), 18.4.1958.
40. PRO, T 234/375, Ellis Rees to Foreign Office, 2.4.1958.
41. OEEC *Group of Trade Experts. Report on the Proposals by Mr. Carli* 25.3.1958 CIG(58)33 (HMG *Negotiations for a European Free Trade Area* 153-163) OEEC, *Proposals by Mr. Carli. Report by the Steering Board for Trade* 29.3.1958 CIG(58)35 (*Ibid.* 163-164).
42. PRO, CAB 129/93, *European Free Trade Area: Origin Problems. Note by the Paymaster-General* C(58)110, 16.5.1958.
43. PRO, CAB 123/130, Minutes of cabinet committee for a free trade area 15.5.1958 GEN 580/4th Meeting. The full cabinet was subsequently informed of this decision, CAB 129/93 *European Free Trade Area: Origin Problems. Memorandum by the Chancellor of the Exchequer* 20.5.1958 C(58)114.

44. PRO, CAB 123/130, *European Free Trade Area Negotiations. Memorandum by the Paymaster General* GEN 580/9, 19.7.1958.
45. PRO, CAB 129/94, *European Free Trade Area. Note by the Paymaster-General* C(58)184, 9.9.1958.
46. PRO, T 234/720, *Free Trade Area Negotiations: Post Mortem* (Figgures), 17.7.1959.
47. PRO, T 234/720, *Free Trade Area Negotiations: Post Mortem* (Figgures), 17.7.1959; Note (Clarke), 21.7.1959; Wright to Clarke, 27.8.1959; Gore-Booth to Clarke, 1.9.1959; *Thoughts in Retrospect on the Free Trade Area Negotiations: 1956-1959* (Clarke) 18.1.1960.
48. In addition to the literature cited in notes 8-10, see for a first archive-based account R.T. Griffiths, "The Importance of Fish for the Creation of EFTA", *EFTA Bulletin*, 1/92, 1992, 34-40.
49. PRO, T 234/720, *Thoughts in Retrospect on the Free Trade Area Negotiations: 1956-1959* (Clarke), 18.1.1960.

A Problem to Every Solution. The Six and the Free Trade Area

By Erik Bloemen

The negotiations on the Free Trade Area are remembered as being long and strenuous. They stretched from the autumn of 1956 when the British government first launched the proposal until December 1958 when negotiations finally terminated. From the point of view of the six members of the European Community, however, they lasted only one month, from the 17th of October until the 14th of November, 1958. Officially, that is. On the 17th of October the Six presented the so-called Ockrent Report to the eleven other members of the OEEC, giving the impression that the Six finally had reached a mutual position on how to tackle the Free Trade Area question. And on the 14th of November the French Minister of Information, Jacques Soustelle, held his famous press conference after which the British broke off negotiations. This happened just one and a half months before the Six, on the 1st of January 1959, would implement their first round of tariff cuts and quota liberalizations thereby initiating the 'discriminatory' praxis against the other OEEC members. The FTA story is thus impossible to disentangle from the creation of the European Economic Community.

In this connection two important questions can be raised. First, does the fact that de Gaulle consented to endorse the document mean that a free trade area solution was close to being accepted or, at least, still stood a chance of being accepted? And second, did the British overreact when they broke off the negotiations after the Soustelle statement?

In those days many political observers answered both of these questions negatively and with a little hindsight have even declared that the whole undertaking had been ill-fated from the start.[1] They have pointed to the fact that French public opinion, with the employers' organisations and the agricultural lobby up front, had rejected the plan from the outset and had fought against it till the bitter end. Why should de Gaulle, with general elections coming up, have risked his political future for a treaty that only entailed vague political benefits and many economic dangers?

Miriam Camps, on the other hand, is of a different opinion. In her very well-informed book, *Britain and the European Community*, written only six months after the French veto of British membership of the Common Market in 1963, she concludes: "Given all the difficulties that beset the negotiations, it is less surprising that they failed than that they came so close to succeeding. Although in retrospect the failure has seemed to many people to have been inevitable, it was touch and go, even at the end, whether the Six would, in fact, hold together and back the French up"[2] Camps, in fact, also blames the British, and not the French, for the failure. The British Government badly and repeatedly overstated its own bargaining power: "Had they initially put forward the kind of scheme they were ready to accept by the summer of 1958, the negotiations would almost certainly have succeeded", she concludes.[3]

According to Miriam Camps the main tactical error of the British decision-makers consisted in driving the "Europeans" and the "protectionists" into each other's arms. The "Europeans", she identifies as the federalists working to make the European Community a true political organisation with extended supranational powers reaching beyond mere economic cooperation, and who feared that the project of the Six would dilute in the broader framework of a free trade area. The "protectionists", on the other hand, were these economic pressure groups and their spokesmen in the state administration accepting the customs union idea as embodied in the Common Market only because it gave them a preferential access to the markets of their partners while at the same time guaranteeing that home markets would continue to be protected sufficiently against competitors outside the Six.

The problem with Miriam Camps' analysis is that both groups remain largely unidentified. The few names she actually conveys are mostly French. In her view, the free trade negotiations were a showdown between the French and the British. The other five members of the European Community, the six future partners of the UK in EFTA, let alone the so-called 'peripheral' members of the OEEC, Greece, Iceland, Ireland and Turkey, do not get the attention they deserve. Within the group of the Six, it is not hard to find "protectionists" on the French side. The French Ministry for Industry was full of them. But that does not set them apart from their Italian colleagues who also had high tariffs to defend.

The major problem, however, is to define the "Europeans". According to Camps, the structure of the Community and the elaboration of the Community doctrine have been, preponderantly, the work of Frenchmen.[4] This statement raises several questions. It is hard to see how the French "Europeans" could have exercised much influence over de Gaulle who was known for his aversion to the principle of supranationality. Camps does not in any way give a clue to solving that mystery. More problematic still, it is very doubtful whether it is correct to make the West European political project so singularly a French project.

These objections, however, should not overshadow the fact that Miriam Camps actually makes an interesting point when she claims that the whole first year of the negotiations was wasted by the combined obstruction of the French "protectionists" and "Europeans" helped by the British reluctance to make concessions. One must just take the analysis one step further and try to identify more precisely who were the "Europeans" and why the "free traders" in the Six could not break the opposition to the free trade area idea. With archives from the period now open this endeavour has become easier. Today we may, therefore, attempt to find new answers to these questions in order to test to what extent Miriam Camps' interpretation still stands firm.

The first reactions by the Six after the launching of the British plan were very similar: on the one hand, suspicion that the real aim of the British government was to frustrate the negotiations on the Common Market and, on the other hand, irritation that the proposal seemed to be one-sided in favour of the British.[5] A great deal of resentment was concentrated on the twin facts that agriculture was completely left out in the plan and that the British wanted to keep their preferences in the Commonwealth for themselves. British ministers who toured the capitals of the Six were everywhere told that it was absolutely necessary to be flexible in these two areas if the Free Trade Area was ever to materialize. However, the British themselves never displayed such flexibility although sometimes vague allusions were made that "something" could be done about agriculture.

When agriculture and the preferences were discussed for the last time during the last meeting of the Maudling Committee in November 1958, the British arguments were still the same as in early 1957; namely that the Commonwealth preferences were part of a bilateral bargain which could not be suspended by the British alone, and that the Six would have to negotiate directly with the Commonwealth countries if they wanted similar arrangements. During this last meeting, provoked by the leader of the French delegation Olivier Wormser, the chairman of the Committee, Reginald Maudling, made his position clear by ironically asking these three questions: 1) Is France prepared to accept the principle of free trade in agriculture? 2) Is France prepared to let the other OEEC members share in the preferences of the Six in their overseas territories? 3) Is France prepared to give Australian wheat and textiles from Hong Kong free access to its market?[6]

Wormser did not react, but the answer would have been "no", as Maudling very well knew. The same would have held true for most of the other delegations. The point is, that neither agriculture nor preferences were the real issue, although many people at the time thought so. These questions were only kept on the agenda because some token concessions were expected from the British.

In April 1957 the French Foreign Ministry at Quay d'Orsay had already produced a report explaining that preferences were a thing of the past with no importance for the future, and that hopefully the other five and may be even the British would realise that soon.[7] More important still, the French Foreign Ministry was not the least interested in letting British competitors enter France's own overseas territories. This view gained support within the Six except by the Dutch who exported more to the British colonies than to the French. This opposition, however, never became very serious as the Dutch delegate responsible for the negotiations, Undersecretary of State for Foreign Affairs, Ernst van der Beugel, in September told Maudling that personally he did not care[8]; and the fact is that divergencies on this topic within the group of six were never allowed to weaken their position during the negotiations.

The question of agriculture must be seen in a similar light. Within the Six agricultural pressure groups were originally shocked by the initial attitude of their governments. The German, Belgian and Luxemburg farmers were already seriously worried about what the Common Market would bring and were definitely not enthusiastic about the prospect of even more competitors entering their national markets. The Dutch, the French and the Italians, on the other hand, cherished high hopes of increasing their exports, especially to Germany, and for precisely that reason they were eager to limit market access to Germany for themselves.

The Netherlands was the country stuck in the worst dilemma. It was reluctant to sacrifice its market share in the British market, but on the other hand, securing access to the German market without facing competition from the Danish farmers who produced a similar basket of agricultural products would be a tremendous advantage for Dutch Agriculture. Pondering how to square this circle the Dutch Ministry of Agriculture zigzagged its way through the negotiations, even changing sides in the middle of a meeting of the Ockrent Committee.[9] The Dutch had the luck, however, in that the man responsible for agriculture in the European Commission was the Dutchman Sicco Mansholt. Despite all the efforts of the Danish Foreign Minister J.O.Krag – for a short time he managed to secure the half-hearted support of the Germans – to achieve Danish participation in the talks on a common agricultural policy, Mansholt did not yield. Krag was told time and again, he was welcome to join but only if Denmark was prepared to become a full member of the European Community and share all the burdens relating to full membership. This would also mean that Dutch and Danish exports would be on equal footing in the British market.

As demonstrated above, thus, agriculture and preferences were not the hot issues within the group of six, but the very concept of a free trade area was. The classical (and the GATT) definition of a free trade area is a construction whereby the participating countries reduce tariffs and quotas among themselves while remaining free to fix trade conditions with third countries. But this distinction remained somewhat blurred. The French spoke in their plan of February 1958 of an "economic union". The Ockrent Committee changed that into "economic association". But already in

1957, when everybody used the term 'free trade area', they all meant something different by it.

The British had proposed to found a free trade area of the classical type – although with agriculture and the colonial preference question left out. The Six, however, were at the time deeply involved in negotiations on a customs union – official definition: no internal barriers and common external barriers – and had learned that in practice definitions did not count for much. When the Six entrusted the precursor of the European Commission, the so-called Interim Committee (headed by baron Jean-Charles Snoy et d'Oppuers, who had been the Belgian representative at the Spaak Committee), with the task of producing a common stance towards the British proposal, they did not live under the illusion that this would be an easy job. One reason was, of course, that they had just experienced how difficult it was to reach an agreement among themselves; another was that they found it hard to make up their minds on the merits of the British proposal.

The first moment for producing a joint inventory of the positions of the Six came in the summer of 1957. A working party, headed by the high-ranking German civil servant, Hans von der Groeben, had made a short list of four different types of "free trade areas".[10] The first one, plan A, was a copy of the Common Market on a bigger scale. The political problem with this option, according to the French ambassador in Brussels, Raymond Bousquet, was that "the Six" would dilute into "the Seventeen". The other options were all weaker. Plan B involved coordination of monetary and employment policies in order to maintain an equilibrium of the the individual countries' balances of payments. There would be only a soft paragraph on agriculture, there would be unanimity voting and no strong commission. The problem here was that transition from stage one to stage two would not be automatic, but depend on the development in the balances of payments. Tariffs and quotas were to be abolished although within a different structure than the one regulating the Six, so that the procedure laid down in the Rome Treaties would not be endangered. Plan C was more or less the British plan: the abolishment of tariffs and quotas among members, whereas OEEC rules would be applied towards non-members. It was added, however, that such a construction would imply a liberal use of escape clauses. Plan D was the most minimalistic plan of the four. Von der Groeben and his group had not worked it out in detail, but all in all it boiled down to: 'wait and see, no fixed timetables, no fixed goals and hope for the best'.

It is interesting to note the first reactions of the representatives of the Six.[11] The French, supported by the Italians, could imagine a free trade zone only along the lines of plan A, but admitted that this was unrealistic because the UK would never accept it. The Germans and the Dutch opted for plan B expecting, however, that the final result would end up somewhere between B and C. The Belgians showed an interest in plan D.

A Problem to Every Solution The Six and the Free Trade Area

What was the background of these different reactions? At first sight, the French choice for plan A might seem to be the most peculiar one. This is especially true if one recalls Miriam Camps' hypothesis about the coalition between French "Europeans" and "protectionists", because the implications of plan A would be the dilution of the Six into a wider framework. One could, of course, argue that the French position was only tactical and aimed at delaying the negotiations. Although this interpretation holds some truth, the picture that emerges from the French archives – that is to say, the archives that have been opened until now – does not support Miriam Camps' view. The danger of dilution of the Six is rarely mentioned, and certainly not in the important economic department of the Ministry of Foreign Affairs where Olivier Wormser wielded his sceptre. Wormser was the civil servant responsible for the conduct of most of the French negotiations on the free trade area, both before and after de Gaulle came to power. There are two documents from his section, dated 8th and 24th of June 1957, which stress the political importance of a treaty with Great Britain. The second memorandum states: "Without any doubt it would be a grave error to neglect the French-British friendship at a moment when there is a rapprochement without historical precedent between France and Germany. The Atlantic Community could be damaged. Above all, we would throw ourselves into the arms of a partner whose dynamism cannot be denied and we would destroy the bridges, refusing the counterweight and the support of England."[12]

While the Ministry of Foreign Affairs wanted to play a constructive role, not out of idealism but for simple political reasons, others did not. Opposition from the Ministries for Industry and Agriculture is often singled out. The reason for their scepticism was rooted in the fact that public opinion, the "Patronat" (the employers), the agricultural organisations and the trade unions, were all against the free trade area. In fact, in January 1957 the French Parliament had already adopted a resolution stating that France should become a member of the Free Trade Area *and* that it should obtain the same guarantees and advantages in the Free Trade Area as in the Common Market. This second qualification was quite an impossible task to achieve, but the government could hardly ignore it. If it tried, electoral defeat was the probable outcome; a risky affair in the shaky Fourth Republic. One could object, on the other hand, that in those days, it was the civil servants rather than the political top who masterminded French policy. And were these civil servants not just a group of plain protectionists?[13]

To a certain extent the answer is yes. However, the word 'protectionism' has different connotations. One is arrogance; we do not care about the others. The impression you get from the French archives, however, is that fear rather than arrogance dominated. There was already fear about the competitiveness of French industry in the Six despite all the escape clauses and other safeguards written into the Rome Treaties. An OEEC-wide free trade area was considered more than France could cope with.

The French civil servants never got rid of this, probably unjustified, fear. It helps to explain the final collapse of the Maudling negotiations in November 1958. The interesting question, therefore, is much more why they lasted so long before breaking. The reason for this was rooted in another fear which even de Gaulle took seriously: what if the European Economic Community would not survive the breakdown of the Free Trade Area negotiations? The French knew perfectly well that their five partners were all in favour of a free trade area although in different shapes and for individual reasons.

The principal opponent to the French position came from the West German Minister for Economy, Ludwig Erhard. Erhard, normally described as the architect of "der Wirtschaftswunder" and a true believer in liberal market economy, put his full weight behind the free trade plan.[14] Unfortunately for him and for the British who had placed high stakes on him, Erhard encountered opposition from an even more formible member of the Federal Government, Bundeskanzler Konrad Adenauer. Although Adenauer is seldom ranked among the true "Europeans", the founding of the European Community, nevertheless, constituted the ultimate success of his foreign policy which aimed at integrating the Federal Republic firmly into the West, securing safety against the East and keeping the door open for reunification with the German Democratic Republic in the future on West German terms. Adenauer was appalled by Erhard's 'radicalism' which at times went so far as to risk the Common Market of the Six if that was necessary to establish the Free Trade Area.

During the first stage of negotiations Adenauer left it to the Foreign Office to contain Erhard. This resulted in a long struggle over the question which ministerial domain had jurisdiction over the free trade area question. If the whole incident was regarded as third countries joining EEC, it was the responsibility of Foreign Affairs. If it was defined as a reconstruction of the OEEC, the Ministry for Economy should be in charge. Because of this unclear position none of the ministries was entrusted with full responsibility (until Adenauer finally interfered in September 1958). This made it very difficult for everyone involved in the discusssions to interpret the German position, and it led to a certain amount of wishfull-thinking that Erhard would get his way in the end, especially on the British and the Dutch sides.

From an economic point of view – in 1957 Germany's export to the Seven almost equalled the export to the EEC countries – Erhard's standpoint could be regarded as the logical German position, and the efforts of the Foreign Office to find a compromise with the French as sacrificing vital economic interests on the alter of wider political considerations. However, keeping the ultimate collapse of the negotiations in mind, one could also argue differently. In the autumn of 1957, when none of the Six had developed a firm strategy to pursue, the French started to push the idea of a *décalage*, giving the Six a lead of, for example, four years over the others in order to give the European Community time to get off the ground. In their bilateral talks with the French, the Germans played with this idea but did not offer more than a short initial advantage. What would have happened if the Germans had supported the French on this point instead of concentrating all their energy during the following months on convincing the French to drop the whole idea? Nothing much maybe, but it is interesting to note that after the breakdown of the FTA-negotiations the Germans and then the others offered the French all sorts of *décalage*, trying to lure them back to the conference table.

The official German explanation for its hesitation to meet the French demands was that it would be unacceptable for the others. The German worries were especially focused on the reactions of the Dutch. But as is often the case, it is dangerous to think for others. In a meeting of the Dutch Coordination Committee in February 1958 Van der Beugel schemed about the possibility of a general treaty for the FTA with elaborated rules only for the first four years. Transition to the next stage would depend on a unanimous decision by the governments, thus offering France the opportunity of demanding a *décalage* after those four years had passed.[15] The backbone of Van der Beugel's reasoning was the conviction that the much-feared trade distortions would not materialize; that, in fact, not much would happen at all in those four years and that in this way the French hesitations would be overcome.

This option was never elaborated. Instead, the Dutch as well as their Benelux partners opted for a fully developed free trade zone. Trying to achieve this, they used different diplomatic styles. In the beginning the Dutch had kept quiet, but in October 1957 they changed their tactics. Noticing that the French were successful by being unreasonable, the Dutch negotiators also decided to become awkward.[16] They consciously accepted the risk that this behaviour probably meant that "in the next months, if not years" the Netherlands would become rather isolated within the Six – a prediction that proved to be correct. The Belgians followed the opposite tactics, attempting to soothe the French into a compromise and reprimanding the Dutch for not doing the same. Benelux cooperation was not always without tension.

The fact that the Belgians first opted for plan D can be explained by a strong "European" influence in their delegation and a certain fear that the ideas animating the Rome Treaties would vanish in the broader free trade construction. By crossing over to plan B very swiftly, however, the Belgian Government proved that such concerns only played a marginal role. The

Dutch Government, on the other hand, was much more sceptical about the benefits of the Common Market, but even here the possibility of giving up the EEC was at no time during the negotiations seriously considered.

There is not much to convey about the Italian position at this stage. The Italians were considered by the others to be full-fledged "protectionists". During the negotiations they usually sided with the French while leaving the hard work to them. Different from France, however, they were not happy at all to see the negotiations collapse although mainly for political reasons. They were worried about the strengthening of the axis between Paris and Bonn and their own limited influence on policy-making within the Six. Being a power not quite at the same level as France and Germany, but much bigger than the Benelux countries taken seperately, the Italian Government often felt somewhat lost in the middle. Nonetheless, an Italian plan – the so-called Carli-plan – would play an important role during the final stage of the negotiations.

When, in the fall of 1956, the original British FTA-proposal had been launched, the Six decided they would answer 'unisono' and, besides, that there was no hurry. The Belgian foreign minister and 'architect' of the Common Market, Paul Henri Spaak, made it already then clear to the British that the Treaties of Rome had to be realized first.[17] After the signing of the Rome Treaties in March 1957, attention shifted to the ratification procedures in the national parliaments. The negative experience with the European Defence Community (derailed in the French Parliament in August 1954) still haunted the Six. The fear grew that the prospect of free competition in an OEEC-wide free trade area would make French public opinion – as well as the political parties – shrink back from entering the admittedly much more regulated, but also ambitious Customs Union of the Six. Low-key discussions amongst the seventeen continued until the French Parliament ratified the Rome Treaties in the summer of 1957. However, this accomplishment did not help very much to kickstart the FTA-negotiations either. When the Maudling Committee started its work in November, the Six had barely made any progress in finding a compromise among themselves. The main problem was that the French Government – when there was a government in these late days of the Fourth Republic – could, or would not, present a clear position on the question.[18]

In February 1958, at last, the French Government came forward with its own proposals. In advance it had promised the other five governments that it would be a reasonable document. In fact, it was not much more than a compilation of all possible objections to the Free Trade Area as envisaged by the British and their allies inside the camp of the Six. Ludwig Erhard, the German Minister for Economy, and a major protagonist of a free trade area English-style, became so infuriated that the French had to refrain from publishing the document.[19] To break the deadlock, a special committee was installed, chaired by the Belgian representative to the OEEC, Rogier Ockrent. The work of this committee, as well as initiatives taken by the European Commission and bilateral talks, especially between the French and the Germans, led to the endorsement of the Ockrent Report in October 1958. Meanwhile, the Fourth French Republic had given way to the Fifth. On June 1st general Charles de Gaulle had been accepted as the new leader of France and he, to say the least, was a man who was able to make up his mind.

In March 1958, after the very negative French plan had been launched and France as a consequence seemed to become completely isolated, the Italian Minister of Foreign Trade, Guido Carli, formulated a proposal to levy compensatory duties.[20] In principle the Six agreed on the fact that preferably the external tariffs of the members of the Free Trade Area should be harmonized, but only Italy and France had insisted on this. According to Carli's plan the first thing to do was to establish a minimum and a maximum external tariff. Countries which for a certain product opted for the maximum tariff were not allowed to impede the import of that same product from a country within the Free Trade Area operating the minimum tariff. However, they were allowed to levy higher tariffs than the so-called maximum and impose duties compensating the difference between their tariff and the official maximum. This would reduce the risk that products, let us say, from Canada were exported to Great Britain which had a low tariff, and from there reexported to France or Italy which had high tariffs, thereby employing the arrangements of the free trade zone to get access as a third country to the markets of France and Italy on conditions not normally open to Canada. It would, however, also mean that if the same product were produced in Great Britain itself, compensatory duties would also have to be paid. Whatever the merits of this proposal, the semantic content of the words 'free trade zone' was becoming rather vague.

The French clung to the Carli plan until the very end of the negotiations. Frustating as this was for some of the other countries, one should remember that France was in deep political crisis at this moment, caused by the uprising in Algeria. Therefore there were no more real negotiations during the last months of the Fourth Republic, and when de Gaulle entered the scene it took some time before he and his new government were ready to dedicate full attention to the question. However, in July 1958 the new government met to revise the French position on the free trade area. It was decided to make the long-awaited concession and to drop the demand of a décalage. But, as the Minister of Foreign Affairs Maurice Couve de Murville warned his colleagues – and more importantly, de Gaulle made clear to Adenauer – it would be in vain to try to push the

French any further. The Six should rather support France in her remaining demands. These concerned the invocation of safeguard clauses and their continued application under specific conditions after the termination of the transition period. Secondly, automatic transition from stage one to stage two in the implementation process of the Free Trade Area was ruled out because France wanted to see the impact on her economy before she decided to move any further. The French demand, therefore, was that this pasage only could be effected by unanimous vote by the member states.[21]

During the fall the German delegation operated under the strict orders to support the French view and so in fact did the Belgians and Italians. During this process even the Dutch realized they were fighting a loosing battle, and in October a joint formula among the Six was finally found by endorsing the Ockrent Report. However, the French Government was by no means overenthusiastic about the result. To the despair of the other delegations it launched a further demand: a standstill of the external tariffs.[22] This struck at the heart of the idea of a free trade zone, and it is very unlikely that the British or the Scandinavians would have ever accepted it. But there were more confusing developments. The Six had agreed to leave the Carli plan and everything that had to do with distortions and origin rules out of the Ockrent Report. During the July meeting of the Maudling committee it had been decided, at the request of Couve de Murville, to study the specific problems which various vulnerable industrial sectors might face under a free trade regime. This task had been delegated to the Steering Board for Trade of the OEEC. The French would provide them with a list of the sectors expected to be hurt by increased competition.[23]

When the Steering Board met in September, there was no list. The French delegation declared it had not been able to make such a list because, as long as the Carli plan had not been studied well enough, there was no real basis for such sector studies. This was, of course, sheer nonsense, and the Steering Board decided to go ahead and study five sectors, textiles, chemicals, non-ferro metals, machinery, and pulp and paper. The meeting took an unpleasant turn for the French delegation because other countries interested in a succesful result asked for speedy procedures. The Swedish representative Hubert de Besche (thinking of pulp) demanded that the studies be restricted to the question of origin rules and trade distortions and that national competition problems be taken into account if a country asked for it. The French, for their part, had envisaged general studies of European industries and their competition problems, a much more time-comsuming procedure. The Swedish proposal was declined – it would have forced the French to expose their own industrial weaknesses - and a French list was, therefore, never handed in. A solution to this fundamental question was nowhere in sight as the 14th of November 1958 dawned.[24]

The way the French managed to put part of the blame for the collapse of the negotiations on the British side was a diplomatic piece of art. In early November Couve de Murville had privately told the British that the French government could never accept a free trade zone which was not an image of the Common Market – in essence taking back all the concessions the French had made so far. On the 14th of November a letter by de Gaulle with the very same message landed on the desk of the British Prime Minister, Harold Macmillan. The same day, Jacques Soustelle, a lower ranked Minister of Information, held a press conference in which he made the same statement but without any reference to the letter of the General. Soustelle was known as one of the fiercest opponents of a free trade zone and all the others except the British thought at first that he had just spoken for himself. The British government committed the blunder of only referring to these statements of a minister with no responsibility for the negotiations at all, when explaining their official reasons for breaking off further negotiations. The British reaction was understandable, but to France's partners within the Six it definitely looked as if it was the United Kingdom that was skating on thin ice. France could hardly be blamed, if the British government simply looked for a pretext to defect.[25]

Besides, the French had their contingency policy ready. They had planned to underline their commitment to the European Community and to soothe the other OEEC members by letting them share, to a certain extent, in the tariff cuts and the liberalization of quotas of the Six by 1 January 1959. After some fine-tuning with Adenauer at a summit in Bad Kreuznach, the other four were informed about the French proposals. They all accepted this plan because they had feared much worse.[26] France's most difficult hour came in mid-December during the OEEC meeting where Maudling handed back his mandate. In 1957 France had de-liberalized its trade because of balance of payments problems and had let the day pass when according to the rules the French tariffs were due to be re-liberalized again. Now they promised to fulfil their obligations in the EEC without doing the same towards the OEEC. This move was also sanctioned by the other five, once again because of British clumsiness in threatening economic retaliation. Such economic war-mongering was simply unacceptable. The problem itself was solved later in December, when de Gaulle agreed to devalue the franc. With German financial support, France could now fulfil its obligations towards the OEEC and join the others by making the franc convertible with the dollar.[27] Meanwhile, the Germans also removed the main Danish worries by concluding a three year deal which gave the Danes the guarantees they had sought for their agricultural exports.[28]

The devaluation of the franc was, in fact, part of a plan to reorganize the French economy which had been prepared in utmost secrecy since the summer of 1958.[29] It took careful preparation because of the serious social implications of this move at a time when de Gaulle still had to consolidate his power. Much is still unclear regarding what happened behind closed doors, but it is probably not too far-fetched to link the increasing French boldness at the conference table during the FTA-negotiations with the growing realization that the economic reorganization and stabilization policies would work.

With short-term problems out of the way, the question remained how the future relations between the Six and the other OEEC members could be arranged. The Six had entrusted the European Commission with the task of formulating a proposal. In late January, members of the Commission toured the capitals to discuss their preliminary findings. They presented two options. Plan A started from the Ockrent Report, but envisaged a more realistic approach taking the economic disparities between the countries into account and implying a sector-by-sector approach rather than a general solution. In fact, Plan A came close to the French standpoint during the last months of the Maudling negotiations. Plan B – a majority in the Commission seemed to support this plan – envisaged a worldwide solution. It argued that a free trade area would entail discrimination against the United States whereas the situation in the world required a liberal attitude in the wider forum of GATT. The only 'European element' left in Plan B concerned negotiations and consultations between the Six and the other OEEC countries on various minor topics.[30]

Having stated that Plan A was close to the old French standpoint, it can hardly be a surprise that France itself now favoured Plan B, while the former opponents of Plan A, now supported it. When the Commission finished its memorandum, the so-called Hallstein memorandum, the governments of the five quashed the idea insisting that the Council of Ministers should pronounce upon it first. Another special working party was the result – with no result at all. The French very well knew that time was on their side with the Seven building their own organisation (EFTA) and the Commission favouring Plan B.[31]

As 1959 progressed, the drift of thinking of the Commission went more and more in the direction of a worldwide solution foreclosing any special arrangements within the OEEC and involving the United States in the plans instead. Despite opposition by the Benelux countries, Italy and the West German Ministry for Economy, the Commission proceeded undeterred. In September it finished a new memorandum expressing its original preferences quite openly. This time it made sure that the memorandum was leaked to the press before somebody could stop the initiative.[32]

Was this outcome, then, the result of a coalition between the "Europeans" and the "protectionists", as Miriam Camps has suggested, and was it indeed touch and go, whether the Six would hold together or not?

A Problem to Every Solution The Six and the Free Trade Area

The archives do not support this thesis. In spite of all their frustrations and anger, none of the Six ever considered giving up the European Community. Even the Dutch, the most ardent supporters of the Free Trade Area, did not want to jeopardize the Treaty of Rome. A "great coalition" between "Europeans" and "protectionists" was not needed. The European Community could not exist without France. De Gaulle who was neither a European nor a protectionist was the decisive factor. At a yet unknown moment he must have reached the conclusion that a wider free trade area was not in France's interest and everything points in the direction that he had secured Adenauer's support to drop the FTA-idea as early as September 1958. However, as long as France was both politically and economically weak as she was in most of 1958, de Gaulle had to tread carefully to avoid receiving all the blame for the collapse of FTA-negotiations. In this he was succesful because the British Government eagerly seized the opportunity to become the prime scapegoat.

Notes

1. London, Public Record Office, Treasury, T234/200 Telegramme Labouchere to FO 8.12.1956.
2. Paris, Archive Ministère des Affaires Exterieures, Direction des Affaires Economiques et Financières, 753, note a.s. zone de libre échange 9.1.1958.
3. Bonn, Archiv Auswärtiges Amt, 200, Freihandelszone, 189, Hartlieb an Carstens, 18.1.1958; ibid. 13.3.1958.
4. Miriam Camps, *Britain and the European Community, 1955-1963* (Princeton/London 1964) 169.
5. ibid.
6. ibid.
7. ibid. 507.
8. Leon N. Lindberg, *The political dynamics of European economic integration* (Stanford/London 1963) chapter VIII.
9. Den Haag, Archief Ministerie Buitenlandse Zaken, 996, 613, *Verslag van de vergaderingen van de Ministerraad van de EEG en van de Intergouvernementele Commissie voor de Vrijhandelszone op 13 en 14 november 1958.* In this archive one can find the minutes of the meetings of the Maudling committee and the preparatory meetings of the Six.
10. Paris, Ministère des Affaires Etrangères, Direction des Affaires Economiques et Financières, 740, note pour le sécretaire d'état (not signed), 11.4.1957.
11. Den Haag, Ministerie van Financiën, no inventory, *Verslag van de vergadering van de coördinatiecommissie voor de integratie en de vrijhandelszone op 5 september 1957.*
12. Den Haag, Ministerie van Buitenlandse Zaken, 610.20, 142, werkgroep Ockrent. DVO aan T, 25-6-1958.
13. Bonn, Auwaertiges Amt, 401, 30, aufzeichnung des Referats A3 nach dem Stande vom 7.9.1957, gez. Schulte-Meermann; Paris, Minstère des Affaires Etrangères, 759, Bousquet a Pineau, a.s. Comité intérimaire du 22-24 Juillet, 25.7.1957.

14. Bonn, Auwaertiges Amt, 401, 30, Von Hardenberg, Aufz. Tagung des Interimausschusses, 29.7.1957.
15. Paris, Ministère des Affaires Etrangères, Direction Générale des Affaires économiques et financières, 752, Comité mixte franco-britannique, note 8.6.1957; ibid 24.6.1957.
16. There is a nice (apocryphal) anecdote about Donnedieu de Vabres, the very influential chairman of the Interministerial Committee, responsible for coordinating French policy. When he told a colleague he would resign and enter private enterprise, the logical question was: "In what line of business?" Donnedieu answered that he was going to build dams and his colleague said: "Well, that is what you have been doing all the time."
17. The German Foreign Office warned that Erhard had said that the FTA was a matter of life or death and they had to sacrifice the EEC if necessary. Bonn, Auswaertiges Amt, 200, Freihandelszone, 149, Hartlieb an Carstens, 22.3.1958.
18. Den Haag, Ministerie van Financiën, Coördinatiecommissie 12-2-1958.
19. Ibid. Coördinatiecommissie 8.10.1957.
20. Bonn, Auswärtiges Amt, 200, 149, FHZ-verhandlungen, not signed, 14.3.1958.
21. Bonn, Auswärtiges Amt, 200, 149, Harkort an Hartlieb, 25.7.1958.
22. Bonn, Auswärtiges Amt, 401, 286, Diplom Paris an AA, 16.10.1958.
23. Koblenz, Bundesarchiv, 102, 29382, Bericht des stellv. Mitglieder, 13.9.1958.
24. Ibid, 27.9.1958; 29.9.1958; 3.11.1958.
25. Bonn, Auswärtiges Amt, 401, 286, Harkort an ss, 17.11.1958.
26. Bonn, Auswärtiges Amt, 200, 1, Aufzeichnung Harkor, FHZ, no date; ibid. Carstens an Min, 28.11.1958.
27. Paul M. Pitman, 'Le programme de réforme financière francais et le rétablissement de la convertabilité en éurope occidentale', *Du franc Poincaré à l'écu*, colloque tenue 3 et 4 dec. 1992 (Paris 1993) 449-470.
28. Den Haag, Ministerie van Financiën, no inventory, Verslag van de vergadering coordinatiecommissie, 5.1.1959.
29. Pitman, op. cit.
30. Koblenz, Bundesarchiv, 136, 2597, Vialon an Kanzler, 28.1.1959.
31. Ibid, Meyer Cording, FHZ, 2.4.1959.
32. Den Haag, Ministerie van Buitenlandse Zaken, 6, 627, Linthorst aan BZ, 25.9.1959.

The Creation of EFTA

By Mikael af Malmborg & Johnny Laursen

In the autumn of 1958 it appeared as though Western Europe was being recast into a system of three economic and political blocs: the British sphere, the EEC and the Nordic Common Market. In October 1958, the Nordic Council convened at what, with hindsight, might appear to be the high point of Nordic cooperation. After four years of investigations, an inter-Nordic Civil Servant Committee for a Nordic customs union submitted a five volume report to the Council for a political decision.[1] However, instead of throwing its political authority behind the plan for a Nordic customs union, the Council referred it back to the Governments, thereby consigning it to further examination and eventual obscurity. A year later Europe found itself divided into only two competing market blocs: the European Economic Community (EEC) and the European Free Trade Association (EFTA). This particular configuration of the European market split was to have a significant impact on the subsequent attempts to combine the blocs anew, i.e. during the first applications for membership of the EEC 1961-63, in the enlargement of the EEC 1972/73, and in the contemporaneous intricacies of widening and deepening European integration within the context of the European Community. How, then, did this particular amalgamation of a European great power and the Scandinavian group come about, and what was the basis of this most uneven alliance?

To pose the question is in itself slightly unusual. Most accounts of EFTA have drawn heavily on the "natural" and "unproblematic" nature of this group. It has been asserted that Scandinavia and the UK shared the same political traditions, shared the same opposition to federal and supranational ideas and also had quite compatible economies. There is much truth in this. At the conference of The Hague in May 1948 and at the establishment of the Council of Europe a year later, the Scandinavians and British formed a "functionalist" bloc against the "federalist" school which had support in Continental Europe. This coincidence of interest also held good at the creation of the OEEC and throughout the many plans for European unification in the mid-1950's. The British and the Scandinavians identified themselves with the aims and goals of OEEC-Europe, and had little understanding for the concept of European unification as developed by Continental federalists. They paid scant attention to the plans for a European Defense Community and a European Political Community, and it was therefore with a great deal of scepticism that they witnessed how the Six, meeting at Messina in June 1955, launched a plan for a customs union. The UK tended to intervene in European discussions mainly in order to water down the federalist plans, or where matters of security were involved. Scepticism in Scandinavia towards ceding national sovereignty to supranational institutions was strong enough even to handicap the efforts for Nordic unity set in train in the late 1940's. Thus, in 1950, in a response to the drive for regional integration plans, Norway, Sweden, Denmark and the UK established the minimalist Uniscan.[2] In 1952, the creation of the Nordic Council demonstrated the same careful approach to the question of national sovereignty.

During the 1940's and 1950's, a preference for "soft" structures and shared attitudes towards sovereignty and European idealism largely conditioned the first responses of the Uniscan-countries to the plans for European unification. However, after the initial reconstruction of the European economies, Western Europe in the 1950's faced new, tangible challenges of cooperation in such "hard" fields as trade, payments and security. Not least because of the weak institutional setup of the OEEC, trade liberalization was a slow and uneven process which concentrated on the removal of quota restrictions. Trade barriers such as tariffs, state trade and subsidies were largely left out of the process. This meant that areas like agriculture and many industrial sectors (e.g. the high tariff sector of chemicals) suffered from heavy protectionism. The system also created an imbalance between high and low tariff countries.

For the UK, the particular design of trade liberalisation in the OEEC had many advantages, quite apart from the political one of avoiding ceding power to international institutions. In this setting the UK preserved Commonwealth links, maintained the system for the protection of domestic agriculture, and at the same time, gained advantages on the European industrial market. The OEEC impasse in the mid-1950's, however, posed substantial problems to the growth and modernisation of the economies of the smaller European states. It was largely as a response to these developments that the Scandinavian countries started serious investigations in 1954 for a Nordic common market.[3] At the same time, the Scandinavians were part of a group of low tariff countries within GATT and the OEEC which were pressing for a program of tariff reductions.[4] The decisive assault on this problem did not come from this group, however, but from another one strongly influenced by the low tariff Benelux; namely the Six. Basically, it was the breakthrough of the Coal and Steel Community countries in 1956 towards forming a Customs Union that forced both the British and the Scandinavians to react. The British reaction came in the form of the abortive initiative for an OEEC-wide free trade area (FTA) linked to the EEC.

The Scandinavian reaction to, and later support for, the FTA to a large extent reflected their position in the previous OEEC-system and their own problems in setting up a balanced compromise on the Nordic Common

Market. The FTA initiative indeed occurred at an intricate moment in the discussion of the Nordic plans and forced some of the most delicate issues in the Nordic talks to the surface. Nevertheless, the FTA also held out substantial promises to the Scandinavians. Firstly, it offered a solution to the European tariff problem. Secondly, the Scandinavian states were all trading nations, for which the Nordic plan was only a partial solution. Thirdly, the FTA might neutralise the dangers of the emerging Six-state bloc for Scandinavian exports. Therefore, at the OEEC-Council meeting in July 1956, they joined the chorus of agreement that such a plan should be investigated by the OEEC.[5]

However, the free trade proposal also involved significant risks. The issues raised in the European context thus threw explosive questions into the Nordic investigations, which at the time were moving through some very difficult issues. For one thing, Finland (not a member of the OEEC) had just joined the Nordic investigations. She was most apprehensive about opening her home market to Nordic cooperation and was also concerned about her precarious relationship to the Soviet Union. Also, from the beginning of the Nordic negotiations, Norway had been reluctant to expose her domestic industry to competition. During 1956 Denmark and Sweden applied strong pressure on the Norwegians in order to make the Nordic market for industrial goods as broad as possible, and its realisation as quick as possible, to allow the Nordic market to have a significant impact. On the other hand, Norwegian and Danish pressure for substantial institutions capable of encouraging production cooperation in, for example, the steel industry, met with strong Swedish resistance. The Swedes also resisted the Norwegian claim for a Nordic Investment Bank able to facilitate industrial adaption to the Common Market. The Danes, caught in severe economic growth problems because of the dominance of agricultural exports, were eager to establish a Nordic market as a platform for the Danish export industry and as a tool for economic modernisation.[6] In June 1956 at a Scandinavian trade union congress, the Danish Minister for Economic Affairs, J.O. Krag, gave a severe warning that, if a Nordic market were not established within two years, Denmark would have to associate herself with the Continental integration plans. Otherwise it would be impossible to maintain economic growth and welfare.[7]

Even though Denmark was the largest exporter of agricultural products in Europe, from the outset the Danish negotiators had accepted the exclusion of agriculture from the Nordic talks. The free trade proposal, however, reopened this painful question, since Denmark now insisted that agriculture be introduced in the free trade discussions. In late 1956 and early 1957 Denmark claimed support from the Scandinavians in this question, and also wanted agriculture to be included in the Nordic investigations, as this would otherwise prejudice its position in OEEC. Norway and Sweden supported the claim for non-discrimination of agricultural goods, but refused to accept a claim for reduced protection. Consequently, in April 1957, Denmark established contact with the EEC-Interim Committee and initiated talks for association with that group.[8] The industrial sector also faced severe problems. The free trade negotiations made the Norwegians even more reluctant to support to the Nordic project. They now proposed pursuing a Nordic free trade area instead of a customs union since this would allow them to retain their own relatively high tariff wall instead of a common Nordic one that would be lower. Norway also introduced the claim to incorporate fish in the Nordic plan.

The Nordic negotiations, therefore, entered a full-scale crisis in early 1957. In Denmark in that year the Nordism of the coalition government, led by the Social Democrats, coincided with the interests of industry and labour in a drive for industrialisation. Together they gained the upper hand over the demands of the bourgeois opposition and agriculture for assent to EEC-membership. Also, the Swedish Government invested much political authority in the Nordic plan. Thus, from the summer of 1957, an adaptation of the Nordic plan into a comprehensive part of the FTA slowly emerged as a common Nordic platform. The common external tariff was renegotiated, fish and certain processed agricultural products were discussed and, after much bargaining, the Scandinavians were able to present a compromise memorandum on agriculture to the OEEC in October 1958.[9]

The plan presented to the Nordic Council in October 1958 was therefore a precarious compromise, based on uncertain external conditions. When the Council decided not to support the plan, it was against the background of an impending OEEC-crisis on the FTA, a retreat which exposed the Nordic market to substantial risks.[10] The truth of this became abundantly clear at a Nordic Government conference in Oslo at the end of January 1959, called to discuss the future of the Nordic plans. At the meeting, Finland and Norway presented radical changes to the plans. The Norwegians repeated their idea of a Nordic free trade area, and both countries wanted a broad range of commodities exempted and a very long transition period. At the same time, the Swedish Minister of Commerce, Gunnar Lange, with the support of the Norwegians, presented the idea of an outer free trade area.[11] Since neither the Danes, nor the Finns, could tolerate this, it was decided to await the European development and only to proceed with some sectoral talks on, for example, Swedish concessions on Danish agricultural exports.[12] This final impasse of the Nordic plans coincided with a turn of Swedish and Norwegian interests towards a smaller free trade area as a response to the EEC.

From the beginning of the OEEC-negotiations, the Six had formed a separate bargaining group. This group became more institutionalised with the establishment of the Interim-Committee in early 1957 and the inauguration of the EEC Commission in 1958. As the EEC made headway towards the establishment of their preferential market, the "Non-Six" OEEC-countries found themselves responding with frequent ad hoc consultations. The dominant impetus to coordination among the Non-Six, however, came from the approach of 1 January 1959, the date for the first EEC tariff cuts and, thus, the beginning of the preference system within the Common Market. The consultations therefore increasingly turned into a discussion of alternatives and claims for temporary arrangements, if and when the OEEC-negotiations should founder, or if no solution should be found before the above-mentioned date. In autumn 1958, the Maudling negotiations were slowly sliding into a crisis. When in mid-November 1958 the French Minister for Information, Jaques Soustelle, explained in a press statement that France doubted the feasibility of the free trade area, the crisis gained its full force and gave an impetus to separate considerations among the Non-Six. The first discussions were conducted between the heads of delegations of the Six Non-Six at the OEEC in November.[13] A first real meeting of what was now called the "Six Non-Six" was arranged with great discretion in Geneva on December 1-2, in order to consider possible alternatives. The selection of states attending this meeting was in itself an indication that a development from consultations to something more tangible was under way. The "peripherals", i.e. the less industrialised countries in the OEEC, were thus delicately but unmistakably left out.[14] This decorous dumping of the economic responsibility for the "peripherals" was not least a reflection of the awareness of an impending trade conflict with the Six.

The urge to hit back at EEC exports was strong in Switzerland and Sweden, both of which had large industrial exports to the EEC, and both of which conducted a policy of neutrality which conflicted with the integrationist approach of the Six. As early as October 1957, Switzerland had hinted at the possibility of an outer free trade area. The Swedish Minister of Commerce, Gunnar Lange, approved of the idea, since such an arrangement would not threaten the credibility of Swedish neutrality, and would keep the Nordic countries together. Norway, with her close political and economic links to the UK, was also rather favourable to the idea.[15] In the United Kingdom and Sweden, the industrial federations had long considered a small free trade area, in case the Maudling negotiations failed. They had already started discussing the issue in early 1958, and when it was later raised at a political level, politicians and diplomats could count on their support.[16]

The Danes, on the other hand, were far from enthusiastic. With their agricultural exports equally distributed between the Continental and the British markets, it was of crucial importance for Denmark to avoid a split. In the British Government a "Uniscan-Plus" solution (i.e. Uniscan plus Switzerland, Austria and Portugal) was subjected to serious consideration in November and December 1958.[17] Her Majesty's Government hesitated, however, to engage in a new and daring project so shortly after the collapse of the first one, with the imminent risk of finding itself at the centre of a new fiasco. There was also opposition against the concessions this would imply to Danish agricultural and Norwegian fishery interests. On the other hand, there was the risk that the UK would become entirely isolated if a Nordic common market was established and subsequently associated with the EEC.[18] UK policy, therefore, in late 1958 began to orient itself towards a loose arrangement with the Uniscan-countries, and Austria and Switzerland. The main aim, though, remained a solution with the EEC. This was pursued in bilateral contacts with mainly the French Government during the following months.

Whereas the UK assumed a reserved position, Sweden, Norway and Switzerland provided the Non-Six Six, or "the Seven", as it was called when Portugal was allowed to enter the group, with momentum. At a meeting of the Seven in Oslo on February 21, 1959, these countries expressed their determination to proceed with the creation of an outer free trade area. Denmark and Austria, though, expressed apprehensions about a trade split in Western Europe. In late February 1959, the EEC-Commission submitted a memorandum on multilateral association to the EEC Council of ministers; a memorandum which dashed the hopes of coming to a multilateral association within a few years.[19] Later that month, Denmark tried to reestablish the 1930s' Oslo Convention in the form of consultations between the Nordic countries and Benelux, with a view to supporting the Benelux compromise proposals. This initiative foundered on resistance in Norway and Sweden, as well as on the EEC-side.[20] At the same time, the British Government lost faith in achieving a solution via their bilateral negotiations with the EEC-countries.

The stage was thus set for a new initiative and this came from Sweden, which now provided the Seven-group with a determined leadership in close consultation with Norway and the UK. A broad agreement had already been reached in early March, when Swedish and Norwegian officials visited London. It was then agreed that a Nordic customs union should keep the same phasing as the free trade area, and that Finnish membership of the latter would create too many difficulties.[21] At the following meeting of the Seven in Stockholm in mid-March there was a preliminary discussion on the content of a free trade area, and the Swedish representative was commissioned to prepare a draft document.[22] In late April and early May the Swedish and Norwegian officials H. De Besche and S. Sommerfeldt toured the capitals of the Seven, and on the basis of these visits the Swedish Government issued an invitation to a conference on the establishment of a free trade area.

The Stockholm Convention was largely moulded in the crucible of the civil servants' talks at Saltsjöbaden, outside Stockholm on June 1-13. The intergovernmental negotiations in the Maudling Committee had prepared the ground in many respects for the Seven once they decided to go ahead with serious treaty negotiations. Most of the potential problems had already been spotted during the OEEC-talks, and many of the civil servants had actually taken part in these negotiations. Thus, once the talks started they could proceed quite quickly with the establishment of the general principles of an agreement and with the removal of the already well-known disagreements.

The report from the civil servants outlined the raw basis for an economic compromise. To a large degree the report drew heavily on the British concepts during the OEEC-negotiations e.g. with the proposed rules of origin (see below). Opposition from Denmark, Austria and Norway against a short transition period, which would burden the relationship to the Six and rapidly expose domestic industry to foreign competition, on the other hand, soon led the talks towards a long transition period like that of the Six. The UK, Swedish and Swiss delegations, which had initially demanded an aggressive and quick removal of trade barriers, gradually came to accept this. The removal of quantitative restrictions was to be left mostly to the member states themselves, with some minimum provisions. Both these provisions represented a possibility to play down the tensions towards the EEC. The troublesome agricultural question was temporarily surmounted, by leaving it to bilateral talks between Denmark and her trade partners, primarily the UK. The talks, thus, accomplished a shift of emphasis in the relationship to the EEC from that of pressure to a bridge-building concept.[23]

Having created a platform for agreement, some decisive political mine-sweeping manoeuvres remained before the agreement could proceed. In two rounds of negotiations in late June and early July, Denmark and the UK agreed on a set of bilateral agricultural agreements, which were to be attached to the trade agreement. Shortly after this, Denmark achieved a similar concession from Sweden.[24] Equally important were the consultations of the Danish Government with the Federal Government in Bonn. Ludwig Erhard's blessing of the plan and the assurance that the Federal Government would not retaliate against Danish agricultural exports played an important role in the Danish decision to proceed.[25] Thus, the road was slowly clearing for Denmark to enter EFTA, while at the same time retaining close bonds with Continental Europe.

The Nordic plan, however, remained. Not until the Nordic meeting at Kungälv, Sweden, on July 10-11, did the Nordic countries agree that these plans had to recede into the background in favour of the European development. This was a most delicate and difficult decision. The Civil Servant Committee, which had been preparing a Nordic customs union for five years, stressed the importance of establishing a Nordic common external tariff inside the Seven or at least of strengthening Nordic economic consultation and cooperation within the Seven. It proposed establishing a Nordic Council of Ministers and a Committee of high officials to strengthen the cooperation.[26] Furthermore, there remained the sensitive question of the fate of Finland. Due to overt Soviet pressure, the Finnish Government had to withdraw its intention to seek full membership in EFTA, as declared at Kungälv. The Nordic Prime Ministers agreed to try to proceed with a Nordic market inside EFTA, and to establish an arrangement between Finland and the Seven.[27] Before the ministerial meeting of the Seven in Stockholm on July 20-22, ministers of the four Nordic countries met to discuss a common position. They discussed their wishes for a special status for agriculture and fish, a special committee to negotiate with the Six when the time became ripe, and a mutual statement to the effect that the Nordic countries reserved the right to proceed with the development of Nordic economic cooperation. The Finnish Minister of Commerce, A. Karjalainen, made it clear that the Finnish Government had not reached a final position on EFTA, but nevertheless wished to follow the negotiations closely. It was agreed that the Nordic countries would try to achieve observer status for Finland, and would try to include Finland in the communiqué.[28]

At the ministerial meeting of the Seven in Stockholm on July 20-22, the Saltsjöbaden report finally established the basis of agreement. This was not easy, however. There remained discussions on the liberal or restrictive character of the rules of origin and the process and raw material lists (see below). The UK wanted a full and complete system of rules of origin in order to demonstrate to the EEC that the system would work, and in order to secure a substantial preference. The Danes continued to exert pressure in order to get an agricultural agreement incorporated into the convention. Norway claimed that industrially processed fish should be considered as an industrial product, but met with UK opposition. The Nordic statement that Denmark, Norway and Sweden reserved their freedom of action with regard to Nordic cooperation provoked strong opposition from the others, who could not accept that the Nordic countries had removed the trade barriers among themselves faster than among the rest of the group. The Finnish problem, presented by the Swedish minister Lange, met with some sympathy, but a special status as observer was rejected, primarily by the British representative with reference to possible claims from, for example, Ireland for equal treatment. Karjalainen was, however, invited to give a statement to the meeting. It was agreed that the Finnish Government should be kept informed within the context of Nordic cooperation with a view to later association.[29] As EFTA was now set in motion, the Nordic customs union was left behind as the sole casualty. During the autumn of 1959, the civil servants struggled with the formulation of the rules

The Creation of EFTA

of origin, process and raw material lists and other technical provisions of great importance for the actual economic effects of the Convention.

The Stockholm Convention eventually established a free trade area with a minimum of institutions. Decision-making was based on unanimity except for complaints procedures and escape clauses. Political authority rested with the Council. The organisation was equipped with a minimum secretariat in Geneva and supported by a small cluster of technical committees. Contrary to the EEC, EFTA had no parliamentary assembly, Commission or Court of Justice.

This minuscule institutional structure was matched by somewhat more deliberate and complicated economic provisions. The basic principle of the Convention was to establish a free trade area without tariffs and quota restrictions before 1970, and in order to accomplish an act of economic bridge-building EFTA aimed at maintaining the same pace of tariff reductions as the EEC. The philosophy behind this policy was that by freeing trade among themselves, the Seven would not only exert a moderate economic pressure upon the EEC, but also facilitate a subsequent arrangement between the two market blocs (as it is easier to unite two big markets than eleven national markets). This formula was part of the compromise at Saltsjöbaden. Here, the Danish attempt to initiate negotiations with the EEC on the basis of the Benelux proposals had been rejected by the others, who wanted to be able to negotiate from the position of an existing free trade area. On the other hand, they had all agreed to issue a press communiqué stating that the aim of the new agreement was to promote the creation of a multilateral agreement comprising all OEEC-members. When the ministers gathered anew in Stockholm on November 19-20, to give their final approval to the Convention, they adopted a resolution confirming that EFTA was only a temporary solution, and that they were determined to achieve a multilateral association with the EEC. This affirmation was even anchored in the preamble of the Convention stressing the determination of the signatories to: *"facilitate the early establishment of a multilateral association for the removal of trade barriers and the promotion of closer economic cooperation between the Members of the Organisation for European Economic Co-operation, including the Members of the European Economic Community."*[30]

A prerequisite and part of the logics of the bridge-building concept was, however, that the two blocs develop in a relatively parallel manner. A piece of potential bridge-building on behalf of the individual countries was contained in the clauses on liquidation of quota restrictions. There were fairly detailed rules about the rhythm in which this liberalisation should proceed, but it is noteworthy that member states in the end obtained the right to globalize their quotas and also make them accessible to EEC-exporters.[31]

Many of the problems which had marred the Maudling negotiations were solved by omission or by being left open to later decision in the Council. This established the setting for the subsequent development, with issue-linkage and political package bargains by the Council of Ministers during the 1960's. One particular provision working to that effect was the one which established that EFTA could accelerate the internal tariff reductions. When the EEC began an acceleration of their tariff scheme, this opened up bargains in EFTA between countries keen on keeping close to the EEC, and countries apprehensive of the effect of the tariff reductions on their industries.

During the OEEC-talks trade distortion owing to the different tariff levels had been a problem of particular importance.[32] In EFTA this was simply solved by a right to claim consultations. This not only reflected the virtues of liberalism, though. The UK, in particular, could hardly provide for tariff harmonisation within EFTA, without weakening her opposition to the same idea vis-a-vis the EEC. The problem of the different tariff levels was further dealt with in a set of rules of origin, which regulated the definition of commodities qualifying for area treatment. In a set of process lists and lists of basic materials, the industrial commodities and processes were carefully defined. Commodities produced entirely in EFTA or containing 50 per cent value added in EFTA could, thus, claim EFTA treatment.

The commodity range of the Convention limited its liberal and pragmatic character also in other respects. The Convention contained separate clauses on fish and agricultural products, a matter which was to create significant problems during the 1960's. The strict rules on trade did not apply to these sectors, but there were, on the other hand, tangible stipulations and obligations anchored in the Convention. For agriculture the organisation was committed to the removal of agricultural export subsidies, and both sectors were covered by the general consultation and complaint procedures. In both sectors the organisation was committed to consultations with a view to a general expansion of trade. Thus, in these areas the Stockholm Convention reproduced the shortcomings of the OEEC.[33]

It is tempting to look at the minimalist trade arrangement as mere technicalities, or as an expression of the pragmatic commonsense character of the cooperation of the Seven. The technical provisions of how trade was to be liberalized among the Seven were, however, of great consequence for the division of benefits and burdens among the EFTA partners and, what is more, for their relationship both bilaterally and collectively to the EEC.

Firstly, by confining trade to industrial goods the Convention was primarily tailored to the needs of the advanced, industrial states, i.e. the UK, Sweden and Switzerland. These were countries which had had strong hopes of the OEEC-wide trade negotiations during 1956-58. To them the

EFTA-preference was not only important in itself, but also in the pressure that it put on the EEC-states having industrial export interests in the EFTA area. Weaker and later-industrialized countries such as Denmark and Norway, on the other hand, wanted to cushion the impact of foreign competition. This was, for example, reflected in their wish to strengthen the escape clauses for sectoral problems. The same conflict of interest was expressed in the vain Norwegian claims for liberalisation of capital movements within EFTA in order to secure financial support for the adaption of Norwegian industry to competition.

When studied in detail the Stockholm Convention reveals itself as a most deliberate economic compromise. Why would the UK thus join a free trade area which only took 10 percent of the total British exports in 1959? Firstly, the export to the EEC covered only 13.2 per cent of the British exports compared with 43.8 per cent to the Sterling area. EFTA allowed the UK to keep a foothold in the Continental industrial goods market and possibly conquer market shares from EEC exporters. The EEC in 1958 disposed of exports worth $4970 million, equivalent to 21.8 per cent of its total export, in the EFTA area. These EFTA markets might either be taken over by British industry to some degree, or at least exert a moderating influence on the EEC according to the British view. The weakness of this strategy was that the "liberal" EEC-countries, West Germany and Benelux – not France – were the most vulnerable in this respect. It would also seem likely that the EFTA countries with stronger dependency on EEC-markets would seek separate solutions in order to soften the preference. Whereas only 13.2 per cent of British exports were dependent on the EEC-market, 34.9 per cent of the other EFTA-countries' export went to the EEC.[34]

A sectoral perspective might be even more informative. The Convention held out particular promises to the British automobile and textile industries. The process list had a separate, very restrictive list for textiles. This meant that other EFTA-producers of garments had to buy British textiles, if they wanted to avoid tariffs on their imported raw materials.[35] The automobile question was demonstrated in the hard bargaining employed by the two producers of motorcars, Sweden and the UK, in order to have the other EFTA-countries define their fiscal duties on automobiles as protective duties. As such they would be abolished within EFTA, thus creating a preference for EFTA car producers.[36]

EFTA offered particular opportunities to the specialized and competitive manufacturing industry in Sweden. For Sweden automobiles, paper and pulp and metal manufacture were of particular importance.[37] Pulp and paper products with an export of $363.4 million accounted for 17.4 per cent of Swedish exports in 1958. The most important export was, however, commodities within SITC 7-8 (i.e. machines, transport equipment and manufacture) worth $680.7 million, equivalent to 32.6 per cent of total exports. This range of commodities, together with chemicals, was traditionally protected by high tariff walls in Europe, and therefore more likely to offer trade advantages within a free trade area. Sweden, furthermore, had a strong interest on the EEC-market which took 31 per cent of her exports in 1958.[38] It was, therefore, no wonder that Sweden provided the Non-Six Six with initial leadership, in order to apply pressure on the EEC. Being a strong industrial exporter, Sweden had no interest in wider, more detailed obligations, not to speak of strong institutions. With the UK they shared the interest to accelerate industrial trade without complicating compensatory measures. In a political sense the EFTA-solution was optimal to the sine qua non of Swedish foreign policy, i.e. neutrality.

The advantages to a country like Norway were much fewer. Norway had a small and relatively weak domestic manufacturing industry. Semi-fabricated goods such as base metals etc. accounted in 1958 for 23.6 per cent of Norway's exports, whereas only 9 per cent, i.e. $67 million, fell within SITC 7-8. Like Sweden, Norway had a strong export of pulp and paper products amounting to 19.5 per cent of total exports. A special feature was the strong export of fish and fish products equivalent to 13.8 per cent, i.e. $102.6 million. As her main export was raw materials and semi-fabricated goods, which already had nil or low tariffs, she would not reap full benefits of the tariff reduction. The exception to this trend was chemicals (SITC 5), a traditional high tariff product, where Norway had a competitive export industry covering 10 per cent of total exports.[39] This was the reason why Norway claimed and received a décalage for a range of industrial products, and in the end applied strong bargaining pressure on the UK in order to have frozen fish fillets considered an industrial product.

The country which experienced the imbalance of the Convention the most was Denmark. The Danish case exemplifies the complexity of the relationship between the EEC and EFTA. In 1958 Denmark had a staple export (covering a range of specialized food products, such as bacon, butter, eggs, cheese and cattle) worth $746 million representing 60 per cent of all exports. At the same time Denmark's export was divided, with 31.2 per cent of total export being disposed of in the EEC and 40 per cent in EFTA.[40] Denmark's problem was that her agricultural export constituted such a large part of intra-European agricultural trade that any arrangement with her would tend to prejudice a future agricultural arrangement between the EEC and the UK. As previously mentioned, Denmark had received some compensation for the exclusion of agriculture, in the form of bilateral agricultural agreements with other EFTA-members. These guaranteed a large share of Denmark's agricultural exports to the UK, in particular, but yielded little in the way of expanding markets. The agreements, however, covered enough trade to ensure that EFTA was able to claim GATT-recognition for liberalising over 90 per cent of intra-EFTA trade.[41] Furthermore, the failure of EFTA to deal effectively with the dumping of subsidised food surpluses from EFTA-countries with regulated farming policies was a substantial problem to Denmark.[42] In 1958, therefore, whereas Denmark exported $76.2 million worth of butter, the other Nordic countries sold surpluses from their subsidised home production worth $26.6 million.[43] Bilateral agreements with West Germany in 1958-65 gave important guarantees for Denmark's agricultural export. On the Danish side this was reciprocated with a considerate commercial policy with regard to West German industrial exports, when the new tariff reform was passed 1959-60 in connection with EFTA-membership. The reason why Denmark nevertheless joined EFTA was that the Government had committed itself to shift the structure of the economy from agriculture to industry, based on export. Thus, Danish exports within the highly processed industrial manufactures in SITC 7-8 amounted to $280.3 million in 1958. Furthermore, Danish industry had long been aiming at the Nordic industrial market as the first target for an export drive.[44]

The association of Finland to EFTA implied, in many respects, an effort to patch up what had been broken with the failure of the Nordic Market. Soon after the Convention was signed, discussions between the Seven and Finland were initiated on the terms of an associations agreement. This so-called FINEFTA agreement was finally signed on 27 March 1961. Finland's main export interest was pulp and paper products which in 1958 were worth $352.6 million and accounted for 45.5 per cent of all exports. Wood and lumber amounted to 24.7 per cent of total exports, and SITC 7-8 products to a mere 12 per cent, i.e. $93.3 million.[45] The economic basis of the agreement was the extension of the economic and commercial clauses of the Convention to Finland, but with substantial exceptions in the form of partial décalage in the tariff reduction and maintenance of quantitative restrictions on a range of industrial goods.[46] The main effect was that Finland secured access to EFTA for her timber and paper exports on equal terms with Norway and Sweden. The political embarrassment of compromising the policy of neutrality was avoided by a careful institutional arrangement. The FINEFTA agreement thus created a Joint Council absolutely parallel to the normal EFTA-Council. All matters relating to Finland were discussed here, whereas Finnish participation in the Committees and working parties were managed in a much more pragmatic manner.[47]

The history of the creation of EFTA and the eventual outcome of these negotiations demonstrate a remarkable continuity in the problems of the OEEC and the issues of the Nordic Common Market. In certain areas the Stockholm Convention supplied the eventual solution to the problems. The gradual removal of tariff and quota barriers for industrial goods thus solved one important problem of the 1950's. Other areas, such as agriculture, saw a change of context, as Denmark's agricultural export was regulated in the form of bilateral agreements, particularly with the UK,

Sweden and West Germany. EFTA, nevertheless, did not bring a long-term solution to agricultural protectionism, and this fact together with the development of the Common Agricultural Policy within the EEC, left the issue an unresolved area of conflict in EFTA during the 1960's.

In many respects EFTA can actually be seen as the eventual creation of a Nordic market, and inter-Nordic trade did indeed surge in the wake of the Stockholm Convention. However, at the same time, Nordic co-operation suffered a heavy blow, as the strengthening of political and institutional Nordism had lost its main locomotive. During the following years Nordic cooperation went through vain efforts to regain momentum, but from 1961-63 the lack of strong institutions and the temporary character of EFTA-cooperation claimed its price for Nordic cooperation, in the form of three EFTA-members applying for membership in the EEC.

One might speculate whether the pragmatic, no-nonsense character of EFTA was not primarily a reflection of the widely varying aims of the partners within the association. One of the acclaimed virtues of EFTA was that it had no political substance. This would indeed have been inimical to the existence of this alliance between the minimalist neutrals and potential EEC-candidates such as Denmark and the UK. Thus, whereas EFTA provided a solution to the dilemma of economic integration with political and institutional non-commitment for the neutrals, it was for the UK, in Miriam Camps' words, primarily a "holding operation".[48] Thus, in certain respects the most important article of the Stockholm Convention was article 42, which allowed any member state to withdraw from the association with 12 months notice. One can therefore only in a general manner say that EFTA (constructed as it was on the traditional UNISCAN-axis between Great Britain and Scandinavia) was a UNISCAN-Plus alliance.[49] The continuity was certainly there, but the 1960's posed different challenges than those of the 1950's: the weakness of the British economy and the Pound Sterling, the development of the EEC, agricultural protectionism, the protectionism in areas other than tariffs and quotas, monetary cooperation and plans for political cooperation in Europe. All these issues pointed towards the eventual break-up of EFTA, with the British and the Danish gaining EEC-membership in 1973.

Notes

1. *Nordisk økonomisk samarbejde. Beretning fra det nordiske økonomiske samarbejdsudvalg*, vol. 1-5, Copenhagen. 1957; *Nordisk økonomisk samarbejde. Tillægsberetning fra det nordiske økonomiske samarbejdsudvalg*, Copenhagen. 1958.
2. Uniscan simply provided for consultative meetings on the level of civil servants and, when necessary, between ministers on economic and financial questions of mutual concern.

3. Nordiska Rådet, 3. session 1955, Ekonomiska utskottet förslag no. 5, p. 571; Protokol fra Harpsund-mødet den 30-31. oktober 1954, in: Rigsarkivet(RA)(Danish National Archive, Copenhagen)/Ministry of Economic Affairs/Official archive of Kurt Hansen/Cabinet Economic Committee (Regeringens økonomiudvalg) (henceforward Cabinet Economic Committee), vol. 6, box. 5.
4. Benelux, Denmark, Norway, Sweden and Switzerland. Wendy Asbeek Brusse, *West European Tariff Plans 1947-1957. From Study Group to Customs Union*, PhD thesis, European University Institute 1991, see also in the present volume Griffiths, R., The United Kingdom and Free Trade Area: A Post Mortem.
5. Archive of the OEEC/Historical Archive of the European Union, Florence, 23/3(63): 334th Council of Ministers, 17.-19.7. 1956.
6. The Nordic common market plans in: Johnsson, Per-Olaf: *The projected Scandinavian Customs Union, 1945-59*, Ph. D. Thesis Florida State University 1964; Stråth, B.: *Nordic Industry and Nordic Economic Cooperation. The Nordic Industrial Federations and the Nordic Customs Union Negotiations 1947-1959*, Stockholm 1978; Wendt, F.: *The Nordic Council and Cooperation in Scandinavia*, Copenhagen 1959, p. 101-115.
7. Göteborg Handels- och Sjöfartstidning, 18.6. 1956.
8. Udenrigsministeriet (UM)(Danish Foreign Ministry): 73.B.66.c: Referat af mødet med Interimkomitéen tirsdag den 16. april 1957; Ibid: Referat af møde med Interimkomitéen den 17. april 1957.
9. Svenska Utrikesdepartementet (UD) (Swedish Foreign Ministry, Stockholm), H 77 D, vol 80, Press Release 25.10.58
10. Nordisk Råd, 6. session, Oslo 1958: Economic Committe report p. 1828-1831, Council recommendation 26 p. 1890-1891, Council recommendation 27 p. 1892-1893, plenary debate p. 79-93, 186-197.
11. UD H 77 D, vol 86: PM from de Besche 3.2.1959, with appendix.
12. RA/Statsministeriet (Prime Ministers Office)/Official Archive of Viggo Kampmann 24: Referat af det nordiske statsministermøde i Oslo 24-25.1. 1959.
13. Public Records Office, Kew (PRO)/Foreign Office (FO) 371/134515: Ellis-Rees to FO, 25.11. 1958.
14. PRO/FO 371/134515: Coulson to Barclay, 3.12. 1958.
15. UD, H 77 D, vol 68: PM from de Besche 21.10.1957, and Hägglöf, I., *Drömmen om Europa*, Stockholm 1987, p 161-162.
16. Camps, M.: *Britain and the European Community 1955-1963*, Princeton 1964, p. 213, and Stråth 1978, p. 156.
17. PRO/Cabinet (CAB) 130/123: European Free Trade Area. Alternative Courses. Note by the Chancellor of the Exchequer, GEN 580 21.11. 1958; PRO/CAB 130/123: Meeting of the Cabinet Committee for a European Free Trade Area, GEN 580/9th, 4.12. 1958.
18. PRO/CAB Meeting of the Cabinet Committee for a European Free Trade Area, GEN 580/10th, 12.12. 1958.
19. First Memorandum from the Commission of the European Economic Community to the Council of Ministers of the Community, EEC Commission, 1959; For the swedish reactions see: af Malmborg, M., *Den ståndaktiga nationalstaten. Sverige och den västeuropeiska integrationen 1945-1959*, Lund 1994, s. 358.
20. RA/Budgetdepartementet (Budgetary Department)/Official Archive of Erik Ib Schmidt 7: Notits, 29.5. 1959, Notits 1.6. 1959 (concerning Krag's talks in Oslo and Stockholm).
21. CAB 130/135: UNISCAN: Closer Cooperation, 4.3. 1959, GEN 613/52.
22. EIS 7: Notits: De syv landes møde i Stockholm 17-18.3. 1959.
23. Erhvervsarkivet, Århus (Business Archive, Århus)/Archive of the Federation of Danish Industry (FDI) 178-59(185): Rapport vedrørende forhandlingerne i

Saltsjöbaden om en europæisk frihandelssammenslutning mellem de 7, UM 17.6. 1959.
24. Erhvervsarkivet/Landbrugsrådets Arkiv (Danish Agricultural Council Archive) 16.A.: Notat, 14.7. 1959.
25. Auswärtiges Amt (Foreign Ministry of the Federal Republic, Bonn) Referat 410/Bd. 173: Besprechung des Herrn dänischen Aussenministers mit Vertretern des Bundesregierung im Hause des Herrn Bundesministers von Brentano am 25.6. 1959, 26.6. 1959.
26. EIS 7: Nordic Economic Cooperation Committee: P.M. ang. förhållandet mellan den nordiska marknaden och ett frihandelsområde för "de yttre sju", Stockholm 22.6. 1959.
27. Törnudd, K., "Finland and Economic Integration in Europe", in *Cooperation and Conflict*, 1/1969, p 64
28. EIS 7: Note by Schmidt (nd.).
29. FDI 178/59(185): Referat af møderne i Saltsjöbaden den 20-21. juli 1959 vedr. oprettelsen af en europæisk frihandelssammenslutning, UM: 73.B.66.f/9; also: R.T. Griffiths, The Creation of the European Free Trade Association, in *EFTA Bulletin* 92/1.
30. *Documents on Swedish Foreign Policy 1959*, Press Release, 20th November, p 102-103.
31. Quota restrictions is a very potent form of trade protection. A country applying quotas to its imports could thus use the quotas as bargaining chips with her trade partners. Global quotas open to exporters gave the same level of protection, but not the same leverage in trade policy.
32. Whereas the EEC was covered by an external tariff wall, the projected free trade area would have different external tariff levels, which could open for re-export from one member country with low tariffs to another one with high tariffs.
33. The Stockholm Convention is printed in: *Lovtidende*, C, 1960: Konvention om oprettelse af den europæiske frihandelssammenslutning, p. 3ff.
34. UN Yearbook of International Trade Statistics 1959, New York, 1960, p. 20-21.
35. Curzon, V.: *The Essentials of Economic Integration*, London 1974, p. 162-64.
36. EFTA-Bulletin, July 1961: Patterns of Production and Trade. Motor Cars, p. 5-6, 10.
37. *EFTA Trade 1964*, Geneva 1964, p. 72-74, 76-78.
38. UN Yearbook of International Trade Statistics 1958, vol. 1, New York 1959, p. 472, 476-77.
39. UN Yearbook 1958, p. 401, 405-407.
40. UN Yearbook 1958, p. 172, 176-77.
41. Building EFTA 1968, p. 72. GATT was built on the principle that the contracting parties gave most-favoured-treatment to each other, i.e. that any tariff concession given another country, should be given to all GATT-members. Customs unions and free trade areas could be exempted from this rule, if they covered a substantial share of trade between the members.
42. Curzon 1974, p 141-142.
43. UN Yearbook 1958, p. 176, 207, 405, 476.
44. Laursen, J.: "Mellem Frihandelzonen of Fællesmarkedet. Dansk markedspolitik, 1956-58" in: B. Nüchel Thomsen (ed.): *The Odd Man Out? Danmark og den europæiske integration 1948-1992*, Odense 1993, p. 66-69,79-81.
45. UN Yearbook, 1959, p. 203, 207-209.
46. Building EFTA 1968, p. 52.
47. Building EFTA 1968, p. 53-56.
48. Camps 1964, p. 229-30.
49. UNISCAN was dissolved after the creation of EFTA in order to avoid any fears of a special group.

The Influence of European Federalists in the 1950s

By John Pinder

Two Kinds of Federalists; Varieties of Influence

The classical federalist doctrine foresees the creation of a federation in one step, by the act of a constituent convention. Horrified by the degradation of Europe in two world wars, federalists drafted at least ten constitutions in the period 1948-53.[1] Almost all provided for a house of the people and a house of the states, an executive responsible to the federal parliament, and a federal judiciary; and the federal powers included human rights, security and economic policy. Federalist organisations in the 1950s campaigned to this end successively for a Federal Pact, a European Political Community, and a Congress of the European People to initiate the constituent process. The archetypal federalist leader in these campaigns was Altiero Spinelli. Each of them failed to achieve its objective. But they had their influence on the opinions and commitments of individuals and groups, on public opinion and on the development of ideas. These things are hard to measure. There are many other influences on opinions, commitments and ideas; and in the 1950s the survey industry in Europe was still embryonic. But things that are hard to measure are not necessarily unimportant; and this paper will seek to illustrate the significance of such influence.

The second kind of federalist sees federalism as a 'series of transitional steps'; and in Europe in the 1950s they saw the European Coal and Steel Community as a 'step in the direction of launching ... an effective federalising process'.[2] The European Community became the focus for such federalists in the 1950s and has remained so since. The federal elements in its institutions included the judiciary (Court of Justice), independent executive (High Authority, then Commission), house of the people (European Parliament, then called Assembly) and house of the states (Council, which may be seen as a federal element when it votes by majority). The relationships between these institutions were not properly federal. For example, the European Parliament had virtually no legislative powers, which were reserved to the Council. But the essential point, for these federalists, was that the institutions had a degree of independence from the governments of member states and a direct relationship with citizens or legal entities in the member states, thus giving the Community a capacity for action without the unanimous agreement of the governments and enabling it to be more than just their creature. Federalists placed their 'emphasis on the supranational character' of the institutions[3] because they believed that this would both make them more effective and lay the basis for further steps in the federalising process. Such steps could take the form either of more federal elements in the institutions or additional federal competences, leading eventually to a federal destination as defined above.

The principal steps in the 1950s were the establishment of the ECSC in 1952 and of the European Economic Community and Euratom in 1958. The attempt to create the European Defence Community and European Political Community proved a step too far and came to grief when the treaty was shelved by the French National Assembly in 1954. Evidence will be given later that Jean Monnet, the chief instigator of the Community process, was a federalist of the second kind: moving by steps towards a federal outcome. Other principal actors in the establishment of these Communities – Alcide De Gasperi, Walter Hallstein, Robert Schuman, Paul-Henri Spaak, Konrad Adenauer – were more or less sympathetic to this kind of federalism. The principal federalist organisation of the early 1950s, the European Union of Federalists (UEF), also envisaged, on its foundation in 1947, a federalism which 'grows bit by bit'.[4] But it soon moved to a one-step policy, which it retained until in 1956 it split, in the wake of the failure of the EDC, into two organisations, one of which remained committed to the one-step constituent approach, with the other supporting the step-by-step Community concept. The latter was, of course, also the policy of Monnet's Action Committee for the United States of Europe, founded, likewise following the collapse of the EDC, in 1955.

Monnet, the archetype of the step-by-step federalists, operated by bringing his influence to bear on governments. Spinelli did this too. For example, he strongly influenced the Italian government in the first half of the 1950s. But since governments were not usually susceptible to the constituent approach, the one-step federalists generally sought to influence public opinion, including politicians and other people deemed influential. The 'political class' was, indeed, a target for both kinds of federalist. Here, particularly in Britain and France, they had to do battle against those who preferred the intergovernmental method of cooperation, whether, like General de Gaulle, based on an ideology of the nation-state, or because of a more bureaucratic inertia.

The word "functionalist" was used in the early 1950s to describe those who wanted to stick to the intergovernmental method rather than to participate in the Community. But this can be confusing. Functions can be performed by either the intergovernmental or the Community method. The difference, for federalists, is that intergovernmentalism is neither effective nor a step in a federalising process. Alternatively, functionalists have been described as those who argued that 'supranational solutions should be reserved for those ... problems which could only be resolved that way'.⁵ But federalists would argue the same, as their use of the term "subsidiarity" underlines. It is true that federalists envisage reform of the supranational institutions so that they become democratic, based on the principles of representative government as well as the rule of law; and those who would resist democratisation of the institutions in this sense will not be called federalist in this paper. In order to avoid misunderstanding, the term functionalist will be used only sparingly.

The Federalists by 1950

At the end of the war, the only significant federalist organisations in Europe were Switzerland's Europa Union and Britain's Federal Union. Although the latter had gained substantial influence in Britain in the period leading up to 1940, neither country was inclined to pay much attention to federalists after the war. But in the autumn of 1946, both groups convened international federalist conferences; and this led to the foundation of the UEF in 1947, based largely on countries whose wartime experience had predisposed many people to federalism.⁶ The leaders came from the Resistance. Henri Frenay had been the founder of Combat, the major French Resistance group. Hendrik Brugmans was from 1942 to 1944 in a Nazi hostage camp, and subsequently active in the Dutch Resistance. Eugen Kogon was arrested by the Gestapo in 1938 and in Buchenwald concentration camp from 1939 to 1945. Altiero Spinelli was imprisoned under Mussolini from 1927 to 1943.⁷ These people were well placed to express the aspirations of their generation in countries that had suffered so much from the war; but they lacked political experience of the sort that federalists were going to need in seeking to influence countries with democratic governments. Count Richard Coudenhove-Kalergi, who had founded an organisation called Paneuropa in the 1920s, was closer to the political class and founded, likewise in 1947, the European Parliamentary Union, which also supported the idea of the United States of Europe.⁸ None of these, however, had the political clout of the United Europe Movement, founded in Britain in 1947 by Winston Churchill and his son-in-law Duncan Sandys, which wanted to confine European cooperation to intergovernmental methods.⁹

Sandys, armed with Churchill's prestige, organised the great Congress of Europe at The Hague in May 1948. Organisationally, and as political tacticians, the federalists were no match for him. He sought like-minded people on the Continent who also wanted to shape Europe on intergovernmental lines. Although on the opposite side in British politics, the Labour government took the same view. But a different wind blew in a number of Continental countries. There, the federalists found that they were not without powerful support, particularly from the countries that were soon to establish the ECSC.

The Hague Congress brought together some eight hundred people, including several score present or former ministers. Among the past and future heads of government were Adenauer, De Gasperi, Spaak, François Mitterrand and Paul Reynaud. Reynaud, who was Prime Minister up to the fall of France in June 1940, had warmly welcomed Churchill's last-minute offer of an Anglo-French union on quasi-federal lines, but had been overruled by his Cabinet and replaced by Pétain. He was the leading political figure on the federalist side at The Hague.[10] The outcome, in the political resolution of the Congress, was a draw. The intergovernmentalists were then using the word 'union' to represent the kind of Europe they wanted; and the resolution used the term 'union or federation' no less than four times, leaving open which kind of Europe the Congress wanted.[11]

The British delegation of federalists was led by R.W.G. Mackay, who had recently secured nearly two hundred signatures for a motion that he, as a Labour MP, had proposed in the House of Commons with the Conservative Robert Boothby, which precisely defined a European federation and called for a constituent assembly to draft its constitution, while an identical resolution was supported by 169 members of the French National Assembly.[12] The British Prime Minister, Clement Attlee, told the House that he agreed with the idea of a European federation for the long term, but that a slow approach to it would be required. The British government was less sympathetic than the Prime Minister. It was determined to give no ground to the federalists and to stick to the concept of union that Sandys had promoted at The Hague. As pressure grew, following The Hague, for the establishment of the Council of Europe, Ernest Bevin, the Foreign Secretary, said to his UnderSecretary of State: 'We've got to give them something and I think we'll give them this talking shop in Strasbourg'.[13]

The drift on the other side of the Channel was in the other direction. Reynaud, following The Hague, pressed the French government for action; and French policy favoured the creation of a European parliamentary assembly to give a political impulse to the unification of Europe. Robert Schuman, the French Foreign Minister, on signing the treaty establishing the Council of Europe in May 1949 in London, spoke of laying the foundations for a 'vast and durable supranational union'.[14] The Council of Europe comprised two institutions: a Consultative Assembly of parliamentarians in response to the aspirations of the French and other Continentals, though with the word "consultative" underlining the British reservations; and a Committee of Ministers, voting by unanimity, which the British were determined would have the whip hand. Thus the lines were drawn for the battles that were to begin at the Assembly's first session, later in 1949, between the federalists and the intergovernmentalists, spearheading the subsequent conflict between the six founding countries of the Community and other European countries, led by Britain.

Council of Europe and Federal Pact

The first session of the Council of Europe's Assembly opened in August 1949. The British delegation included Churchill and other illustrious Conservatives, then in opposition. From the Labour side it included Mackay, who had been chairman of the Federal Union and had already in 1940 written a book, entitled Federal Europe, which contained his draft of a European constitution,[15] He immediately set to work with Pierre de Félice, a French federalist Deputy, to formulate a federalist aim for the Council of Europe. The formula they devised was a 'European political authority with limited functions but real powers'.[16] A resolution based on this was proposed to the Assembly together with André Philip, another federalist French Deputy, who had been minister of economics and finance in de Gaulle's first cabinet following the liberation, and who served as President of the Socialist Movement for the United States of Europe. The resolution was passed almost unanimously. But, together with much else, it was rejected by the Committee of Ministers, prompting an indignant Reynaud to say 'On ne pouvait ignorer avec plus d'insolence les voeux de l'Assemblée'.[17]

The principal leaders of the UEF were in Strassbourg, following the proceedings with the closest attention. They took up the campaign that had been initiated by Mackay, with a project for a 'Federal Pact'. At the end of October their Central Committee resolved that such a Pact should provide the classic powers and institutions of a federation: foreign policy, defence, human rights, tax, trade, currency and economic policies, with a two-chamber legislature and a federal executive and judiciary. The new development was their proposal that the Pact should enter into force when ratified by states bringing together 100 million citizens or more.[18] They were well aware by now of the British obduracy and this was intended to enable a core of more federalist countries to proceed without the British – foreshadowing Monnet's initiative in launching the Schuman plan the following spring.

The European Movement had been set up, following the Hague Congress, under British leadership with Sandys as Chairman of its Executive Committee. But the Movement's organisations in Belgium, France, Germany, Italy and the Netherlands had rapidly become federalist, as were its Socialist and Christian Democrat party groups – the Socialist Movement for the United States of Europe (SMUSE) and the Nouvelles Equipes Internationales (NEI). At the Movement's Executive Committee in January 1950, and against the opposition of the British, these all supported the

UEF's proposal.[19] The support for federal developments among these founding members of the Community offered a basis for the success of Monnet's first federal step, the ECSC. Meanwhile, the UEF tried to rally the Continentals at the Council of Europe with its campaign for a Federal Pact.

This campaign aimed at the session of the Council of Europe in the second half of 1950. It was headed by a high-powered international committee, which included three French former Prime Ministers (Léon Blum, Paul Ramadier, Paul Reynaud) and German political leaders, such as Heinrich von Brentano, founder of a German federalist organisation and later Foreign Minister, and Carlo Schmidt, a prominent Socialist who had become a Vice-President of the principal German federalist organisation, Europa Union Deutschland, in 1949.[20] The aims of the campaign, along the lines laid down by the UEF, were approved by the Bundestag in July 1950, with the votes of all the democratic parties. Thousands of French mayors signed the appeal.[21] In Italy the sponsoring committee included cultural and political stars ranging from Benedetto Croce and Ignazio Silone to Luigi Sturzo and Ugo La Malfa. By November 1950, the appeal had been signed by over half a million Italians; and in that month it was signed by Prime Minister De Gasperi and Foreign Minister Count Sforza, in the presence of President Einaudi, at a public meeting organised in Rome by the Movimento Federalista Europeo (MFE). Both houses of parliament passed a resolution with the same words.[22]

Italy has, since then, been a bastion of European federalism. But this was not a foregone conclusion. At the start of the Italian federalists' campaign, De Gasperi had asked them to remove the federalist aspects from their demands and to limit their activity to collecting signatures for 'European unity in peace'. Spinelli recalled that they parted 'on cold terms' after a meeting with him.[23] But by November, at the end of that year's campaign, he was telling the Senate that 'European federation ... is the road that we must follow'.[24]

The Assembly of the Council of Europe met at Strasbourg in August 1950. Just before, the federalist youth movement had undertaken frontier actions nearby, burning the barriers in a non-violent symbolic protest.[25] They obtained enormous publicity; and the participants included some who were to be influential in the future, among them, as he still proudly affirms, the young Helmut Kohl. But the debate in the Assembly on the Federal Pact was lost. Delegates from the Continental core countries mostly voted in favour. The British and the Scandinavians, however, tipped the scales against.

Before the Assembly's meeting in November, the federalists renewed their efforts. Five thousand young people demonstrated in Strasbourg for a European parliament, government and citizenship. The UEF held a congress which called for a constituent convention to draw up a Federal Pact among those countries that were willing.²⁶ This was immediately followed by a Congress of the Peoples of Europe, in which the UEF delegates were joined by others, including numerous delegates to the Assembly. It was chaired by Senator Fernand Dehousse, a Belgian professor of law who was Vice-President of the UEF and was to play a notable part in subsequent events. Other speakers included de Félice and Spinelli. An appeal was issued, signed by many of the Assembly delegates, again demanding a Federal Pact for a European parliament and government.²⁷ But the federalists again failed to gain enough votes in the Assembly for the project. The resolution was transmitted to the Committee of Ministers, which buried it.²⁸

This was the end of the road for the attempt to use the Council of Europe as a launching pad for a European federation. The position of the British and Scandinavians in the Assembly, and of the British government in the Ministers' Committee, was too strong. But the exercise had demonstrated the strength of political support for federal Europe among the core countries of the Continent. Sandys told the House of Commons in November that almost all Continental parties and most governments had 'declared themselves in favour of some kind of European federal system'.²⁹ The federalists' campaign had played its part in this; and the favourable political reception of the Schuman plan in the six founder states was thus assured.

Monnet and the ECSC

Monnet had played a creative part in the launching of Churchill's offer of union with France in June 1940.³⁰ It was natural that, after the war, he should explore the possibility again. In April 1949, together with Etienne Hirsch and Pierre Uri, two of his closest collaborators who were to make notable contributions to the development of the Community, he met Sir Edwin Plowden, the nearest British official equivalent to Monnet who was then head of the Commissariat du Plan, for intensive discussions about possible economic integration. Monnet was to recall that he had in mind 'the idea of a Franco-British union' as a 'first step towards a European federation'.³¹ But it was clear from Plowden's reactions that the British government would not countenance any such notions. Monnet drew the same conclusion as the federalists: union would have to start among Continentals.

By April 1950, Monnet was working on a first draft of what was to be the Schuman Declaration. The federal aim was explicit: 'Europe must be organised on a federal basis.' A Franco-German union was 'an essential element in it'.³² A number of drafts later, the declaration went to Robert Schuman through his Chef de Cabinet, Bernard Clappier, who, like Hirsch and Uri, was also subsequently to play an important part. Schuman never articulated a clear concept of federation. But as a man of the border lands between France and Germany, he felt profoundly the need for 'a union, a cohesion, a coordination' which would contain the 'historic reality' of the European states;[33] and, as we have seen, he had hoped that the Council of Europe would lead to a 'supranational union'. Monnet's draft responded to his European faith. He embraced it willingly and held tenaciously to the concept of the Community.

The declaration, which Schuman issued on 9 May 1950, mentioned the federal goal no less than twice. The essential first step was, for Monnet, the independent High Authority which was to be responsible for the government of the coal and steel industries of France, Germany and the other member states: in the event, Italy and the Benelux countries. Monnet had much experience of international organisations, as Deputy Secretary-General of the League of Nations and in charge of joint allied procurement boards during both world wars. This experience had convinced him that organisations which depended on the agreement of the member governments for every move could not transform the relations between France, Germany and other states in the way that was now required. It was an independent executive that he held to be the key; and the High Authority was the only institution mentioned in the declaration, although the need for 'channels of appeal against its decisions' was also noted. It was thanks to a particular federalist intervention that the Community's institutions began to resemble more closely those of an emergent federation.

Hirsch recalls in his memoirs how André Philip came to him during the brief period between the Schuman Declaration and the opening of negotiations on the ECSC treaty, to suggest that 'an element of democratic' structure should be added.[34] Philip, in addition to being President of the SMUSE and co-sponsor of Mackay's federalist resolution at the Council of Europe, was active in various federalist contexts;[35] and Hirsch was later to be President of the UEF. He went to Monnet with the proposal and, after an initial rebuff, Monnet became enthusiastic about the idea and it found its way into the French paper on which the negotiations were based. The channel of appeal had likewise become the Court of Justice. The Council of Ministers came from another source. During the negotiations the smaller countries proposed it in the belief that it would safeguard their interests; and Monnet, as leader of the French delegation, accepted it as a useful means of coordination with the governments. Its role as the Community's main legislature was not then foreseen, partly because most of the legislation for the ECSC was contained in the treaty, rather than being subsequently enacted by the institutions.

It has been suggested that 'the first origins of the Schuman Plan were really in the Quai d 'Orsay'.[36] The French Foreign Office was undoubtedly preparing for an international organisation to provide the framework for the resurgent heavy industries of the Ruhr. But naturally enough, the diplomats envisaged 'ministerial committees' with 'regular meetings' and a 'common ministerial organisation'.[37] It is hardly to be expected that they would have designed the Community with an independent executive and a basis for federal parliamentary and judicial institutions. Federalists, on the other hand, place 'emphasis on the supranational character' of the institutional forms.[38] It is the federalist view that the Community's institutions, with their elements beyond the purely intergovernmental, have given the Community its durability and capacity for presidential development; and Monnet was among the first to underline this, in his inaugural address to the High Authority when it first met in August 1952.

In this address, Monnet emphasised the institutions' federal characteristics: an independent High Authority, responsible to a European Assembly; the Assembly, with its power to dismiss the Commission, its independence of member governments and the provision for eventual direct elections; the Court of Justice, independent of the member states' courts; and the direct relations with legal entities in the member states, including the power to tax enterprises.[39] This address was drafted by Spinelli. Monnet had asked him to do it because he had been impressed by the power and clarity of Spinelli's writing. After the inaugural address, he asked Spinelli to accept the formal responsibility for the High Authority's press relations, actually with the intention, Spinelli noted in his diary, that Spinelli should write for Monnet a series of political speeches, equivalent to what the American founding fathers had written in *The Federalist Papers*.[40] This was not so surprising. Already in 1943, Louis Joxe, later a prominent French politician, had been given *The Federalist Papers* to read by Monnet, who said 'Read it from end to end; it is good throughout'; and Joxe remarked that it was 'the missal' of Monnet's faith. One of Monnet's close collaborators since the period at the High Authority has affirmed that the book was always on his desk.[41] But Spinelli was not a natural ghost writer; on the contrary, he was obsessively his own man. His attempt soon after to draft Monnet's opening speech to the Assembly went against the grain and Spinelli left Luxembourg to continue his federalist activity in Italy and in the UEF.

Spinelli was convinced that Monnet, even if he had 'no idea how to make a constitution' and thought that 'a few shreds of improvised ideas were enough', 'certainly' wanted 'to arrive at a federation'.[42] Since Monnet has often been seen as an arch-functionalist, in a sense antithetical to federalism, it is worthwhile to dwell on this. There is the evidence of Spinelli, of Joxe, of The Federalist Papers on his desk, of the inaugural address. There is the Action Committee for the United States of Europe, which Monnet founded in October 1955, inviting its members to join with a letter which stated that 'it is indispensable for States to delegate certain of their powers to European federal institutions'.[43] There is evidence that he understood the difference between a federal and a unitary state, emphasising in an article in *Le Monde* in the same year that the need was for the former, not the latter.[44] The federal aim is reiterated passim in his memoirs.

It is perhaps because he was more interested in the steps than the constitution that Monnet has been seen as a functionalist. He was indeed the pioneer of the step-by-step approach to federation. His first draft for the Schuman Declaration, which started by announcing the federal aim, went on to say that the proposal had 'an essential political objective: to make a breach in the ramparts of national sovereignty which will be narrow enough to secure consent, but deep enough to open the way towards the unity that is essential to peace'.[45] The success of this approach was due to its ability to attract support from interests which, without necessarily being committed to the federal elements in the institutions, wanted the benefit of the functions that they could perform, In the case of the ECSC, these were political and strategic interests of the French and German governments; for the customs union, the single market and the economic and monetary union, economic interests became more prominent.[46] Without the input from federalists, the institutions would have lacked most of their federal elements – and hence, in the federalist analysis, their capacity to become a framework for the Community's growth. Without the support of these interests, federalists would not have been able to successfully initiate the step-by-step development of the Community's institutions and powers.

Despite Monnet's instinctive preference for one step at a time, which enabled him to start the process that has brought the Community so far in the subsequent four decades, the challenge of the Korean War to western defence and the response in the proposal for a European Army 'touched', as Monnet was to put it, 'on the core of national sovereignty', so that 'federation would', in the autumn of 1950, 'have to become an immediate objective'.[47]

Spinelli, the Constituent and the EDC

In June 1950, as the negotiations to establish the ECSC were beginning, North Korea invaded South Korea. This was believed in the West to have been instigated by Stalin. It required the commitment of substantial American forces, thus weakening the western capacity to meet any similar Soviet challenge that might be mounted in Europe. The United States insisted on the need for a German contribution to western defence. Europeans, so soon after World War II, were sensitive about such a prospect; and their response took the form of proposals to accommodate German troops in a European Army. At the Council of Europe's Assembly in August 1950, while the Federal Pact project failed to prosper, Churchill moved a resolution which called for 'the immediate creation of a European Army, under the authority of a European minister of defence, subject to European democratic control'; and he said that it was an enterprise 'in which we should all bear a worthy and honourable part'.[48] The reference to democratic control was apparently added by Reynaud and other federalists.[49] But Churchill moved the resolution all the same, and it was passed by an overwhelming majority. When Churchill soon after became Prime Minister in the newly elected Conservative government, it became evident that Britain's 'honourable part' was not going to be participation in a European Army; and the old statesman said to one of his ministers: 'I really meant it for them and not for us'.[50] But it soon became clear that 'they' were taking the idea more seriously. Monnet proposed it to Schuman in September, then to Prime Minister Pléven, who had been another of Monnet's close collaborators, in October,[51] whereupon Pléven made a declaration proposing a European Army, with a minister of defence responsible to member governments and to a European Assembly, who would execute general directives from a Council of Ministers.[52] With this scarcely promising institutional proposal, negotiations among the six prospective member states of the ECSC began in February 1951.

Already in October 1950, Spinelli had identified the opportunity for federalists. A common army required a common budget and a common foreign policy, in the framework of democratic institutions: in short, a European federation,[53] Spinelli persuaded the UEF congress in Strasbourg in November 1950 to adopt the proposal for a constituent assembly, even if Europa Union Deutschland, at its own congress the following month, was said to have supported this as a propaganda action rather than as a realisable political demand.[54] The UEF, with the SMUSE and the Congress of the European Peoples as co-sponsors, then made preparations for a conference to be held in Lugano in April 1951, in order to draw up detailed proposals for a constituent assembly and a Federal Pact. The steering committee for this purpose was chaired by Germaine Peyrolles, Vice-President of the French National Assembly, and its secretary was Henri Frenay, who had, like André Philip, been a minister in de Gaulle's first government and who was by then the chairman of the UEF's ExecutiveCommittee. There was also a juridical committee, chaired by Fernand Dehousse and including, in addition to Spinelli, distinguished lawyers and scholars such as Piero Calamandrei (founder of a famous anti-fascist journal, rector of Florence University and a member of the MFE since 1947), Hans Nawiasky (Munich University) and Georges Scelle (Paris University).[55] Based on this committee's work, the Lugano conference produced draft statutes for a constituent assembly and principles for a constitution or Federal Pact.[56] It also appointed Spinelli as the UEF's delegate-general to organise the campaign to promote these proposals. This campaign secured, among other things, the support of about eight hundred members of parliament from the six ECSC states. It also enjoyed substantial American support. General Eisenhower, who took up his duties as Nato Supreme Commander in that year, advocated in July in a speech in London, with both Attlee and Churchill present, 'The establishment of a workable European federation', which 'cannot be attacked successfully by slow infiltration, but only by direct and decisive assault, with all available means'; and soon after, in an interview with *Paris-Match*, he was more explicit in advocating a European constituent assembly.[57]

By July 1951, the Intergovernmental Conference on the European Defence Community (EDC), as the European Army proposal was now called, produced an interim report; and Spinelli sent a memorandum on it to Ivan Matteo Lombardo, the new head of the Italian delegation to the IGC.[58] In it Spinelli analysed the contradictions of an army without a state and concluded that there was a need for a clear definition of the institutions and their powers, including a directly elected European parliament and an executive responsible to it, the whole to be designed by a constituent assembly. Lombardo was a considerable political figure: a former secretary-general of the Partito Socialista Italiano, who had resigned the post when Pietro Nenni, the party's leader, took it into alliance with the Communists. Lombardo was also a member of the MFE since 1947; and Spinelli had been close to him when working for a short time in the ministry of external trade, where Lombardo was at that time the minister. In October, the month after receiving Spinelli's memorandum, Lombardo sent one to the other delegations to the IGC, which closely followed Spinelli's argument, explaining the need for a constituent assembly to draw up a constitution for a directly elected parliament with legislative powers, with an executive responsible to it and with the power to tax in order to be effective in its defence and other functions.[59]

In November, Lombardo told Spinelli of his idea that the constitutional problems could be confided to the Assembly of the ECSC, and Spinelli found it good; he had indeed been given a similar suggestion by Monnet a few weeks earlier.[60] By January 1952, the UEF's Central Committee took up the idea.[61]

Meanwhile, the foreign ministers of the ECSC Six had, in October, addressed the Council of Europe Assembly about the EDC. De Gasperi, who combined the function of Foreign Minister with that of Prime Minister, emphasised the need for a European parliament, with a European executive responsible to it and a European budget.[62] His speech, Spinelli observed, had 'certainly' been prepared by Lombardo.[63] De Gasperi had by then become pronouncedly federalist. A few weeks later he conveyed his thoughts on the subject in a broadcast to the Italian people. 'A federal Europe' would be 'a kind of great Switzerland': pacific, prosperous, based, as in Switzerland and the United States, on a common defence of liberties.[64] A federal Europe evidently fitted his conception of Italian interests.

With the Italian economy then still much weaker than the others, he saw the need for economic as well as military solidarity; and he wanted to deflect opposition from the left which was to be expected against purely military actions.[65] A broad federal framework, favouring liberty and prosperity as well as defence, made sense to him.

Adenauer, who also combined the posts of foreign minister and head of government, stressed the need for 'a federation', with unification for those activities that required it, while member states kept their powers over the rest.[66] He was a pragmatist and seldom referred to federation as such; but he was convinced of the dangers of nationalism and had affirmed as early as 1946 that his aim was the United States of Europe.[67] Schuman, likewise discreet about precise constitutional proposals, said that decisions to go to war could not rely on unanimity among member governments, A more decisive procedure would be required, in the form of majority voting. This would impinge on the sovereignty of member states and parliaments, and the consequently shared power could not be left solely in the hands of the executives.[68]

The Council of Foreign Ministers of the Six met again in December and De Gasperi insisted that the IGC must decide to create common political institutions for the EDC, including a parliamentary assembly. Schuman agreed in principle, but said that it would be better left to a later stage – although he understood that the Italian parliament might not ratify a treaty without some assurance about political union. The Council met again at the end of the year and Adenauer proposed a convenient compromise, whereby the EDC treaty would contain an article 38, giving the 'preconstituent' role to the Assembly that would be established under the EDC treaty.[69]

Thus the ECSC Six appeared to be moving towards political union as well as defence community. Spaak, as President of the Assembly of the Council of Europe, was becoming increasingly frustrated by the inability to secure any substantial European commitment from the British. He had had high hopes of the new Conservative government, as Conservative delegates, including Churchill, had spoken fair words about Europe in the Assembly when their party was in opposition. But on 28 November Sir David Maxwell Fyfe, speaking for the now governing Conservatives, disappointed Spaak with a speech in which, although intending to be helpful, he criticised the federalist aspirations of many delegates as 'illusory'; and Anthony Eden, the new Foreign Minister, further undermined Maxwell Fyfe's helpful intentions with a speech in Rome where he uncompromisingly slammed the door on any British participation in the EDC.[70] Spaak concluded that 'moderate delegates' could no longer wait for the British.[71] On 10 December he asked Reynaud, de Félice and Pierre-Henri Teitgen, a federalist French Deputy who was President of the French Christian Democrat party (the MRP) and had been a close colleague of

Frenay's in the Combat resistance group, to propose to the Assembly that night a resolution drafted by Frenay and Spinelli, calling for the ECSC Six to go forward to a European political authority.[72] This they did and, with the British and Scandinavians again opposing, lost by 41 votes to 47. Spaak resigned after a passionate speech. He felt that he had waited long enough for British leadership. But British commitment was not forthcoming. The Council of Europe was 'no longer ... in the forefront of the struggle.'[73] As Spinelli put it, Spaak had decided to 'cross the federalist Rubicon'.[74]

Spinelli, Spaak and the EPC

In the period that began in 1952, when the future seemed to lie in the project for a European Political Community, Spaak did indeed espouse the federalist cause with all his considerable energy and talent. He had not previously been a committed federalist. 'Although I have never belonged to the federalists', he told the Assembly after his resignation, 'I voted yesterday in the same spirit and with the same will for the resolution of de Félice'.[75] Spinelli, who then worked closely with him, found this neophyte 'very ignorant of all federalist problems', but with an 'instinct for the right path'.[76] Later, after a discussion with Monnet, Spinelli was to note in his diary their agreement that 'Spaak is with us, but he won't press the battle to the end'.[77] Like Schuman, he felt the need to renounce national sovereignty; but he would accept whatever method of cooperation appeared to offer the most likely prospects of action.[78] This brought him to act as a federalist between 1952 and 1956. During the first part of that period, as President of a federalist European Movement, he was for the constituent, the European Political Community (EPC), and hence something close to a one-step view of European federalism. Spinelli, found then that 'the tandem Spaak-federalists' functioned 'benissimo',[79] In the latter part of the period, as Belgian Foreign Minister, he performed great service for the step-by-step approach, in driving forward the project of the Treaties of Rome. From 1957, when he became Secretary-General of Nato, he disappeared completely from the federalist scene.

Already in mid-January 1952, a month after Spaak's resignation from the presidency of the Council of Europe's Assembly, Spinelli visited him in his capacity as President of the European Movement. Spaak had assumed this function at the end of 1950, after Sandys had resigned following the Movement's rejection of the British intergovernmentalist policy. Spaak told Spinelli that he wanted a 'showdown' with the British in the next meeting of the Executive Committee. In February, Spaak and Spinelli agreed that they should establish a Committee of Initiative for the campaign for the constituent.[80] This met for the first time in March, with

Spaak as chairman, Frenay as secretary, and Spinelli, Kogon and Philip as members together with seven others, for the most part federalists.

As the UEF had done for the Lugano conference, the Committee of Initiative established a Committee of Jurists for the European Movement, later renamed the Study Committee for the European Constitution, whose task was to prepare draft resolutions for the Assembly that was to draw up the constitution of a European Political Community.[81] Spaak was the chairman. Dehousse, who had chaired the juridical committee for Lugano, and who was also chairman of a Committee of Jurists of the Council of Europe Assembly which was to report on proposals for a European constitution, was the secretary-general. The members were Calamandrei, Nowiasky and Spinelli, each from the Lugano juridical committee, de Félice, Frenay and five others, almost all federalists as well as distinguished lawyers. Two Americans were coopted as advisers: Robert R. Bowie, who had just returned to Harvard from being Legal Counsel to the US High Commission in Germany and hence au fait with the ECSC negotiations and the people involved, and who was later to be Director of the State Department's Policy Planning Staff; and Carl Joachim Friedrich, a professor at both Harvard and Frankfurt, and the leading exponent of federalism as a process.[82]

The Study Committee worked intensively from April to September 1952. Meanwhile, the EDC Treaty was signed in May, with its article 38 which had resulted from the intervention of De Gasperi and Lombardo. This article required the Assembly of the ECSC, with the addition of nine more members, to propose the definitive constitution of the EDC's Assembly, in the context of a 'federal or confederal structure'.[83] Spaak and the federalists pressed for this task to be given to the ECSC Assembly as soon as it was itself to be established, in September 1952, rather than awaiting ratification of the EDC Treaty, which would bring the European Army into being before the democratic structure to contain it; and at their meeting in September, the Council of Foreign Ministers of the Six did indeed decide to ask the Assembly, duly enlarged with the nine extra members and thus called the Ad Hoc Assembly, to produce the constitutional draft within six months. The ECSC Assembly met the following day and elected Spaak as its President, and hence also President of the Ad Hoc Assembly. Monnet made his speech – the second one on which Spinelli had collaborated before deciding that ghost-writing was not for him. But Monnet, while noting the federalist aspirations regarding the Ad Hoc Assembly, wanted to concentrate on building up the ECSC. 'I too believed we must build a federal Europe', he was to write, but he wanted to lay 'solid foundations for this first enterprise, which would later make possible all the rest'.[84] Thus Monnet took no part in the project for a European Political Community (EPC), as the Assembly was to call it.

Spaak and Dehousse, who had according to Friedrich made an 'outstanding contribution' to the work of the European Movement's Study Committee, presented its draft resolutions to the Ad Hoc Assembly. The resolutions had been drafted by Spinelli, again according to Friedrich one of the Committee's 'most active and effective members', who had also been the rapporteur at its final session at the end of September.[85] The Assembly transmitted them to its own Constitutional Committee, which it set up with von Brentano as President. The rapporteur for its sub-committee on institutions was Dehousse, and for its sub-committee on powers and competences, Ludovico Benvenuti, an Italian federalist who had played a leading part in the campaign in the Council of Europe for a Federal Pact and had been a member of the European Movement's Study Committee.[86] Thus federalists were in the key positions in the Constitutional Committee; and others, particularly Spinelli, were also active behind the scenes.

Six months later, on 10 March 1953, the Constitutional Committee presented its draft Treaty for an EPC constitution to the Ad Hoc Assembly. Friedrich analysed it as partly federal and partly confederal.[87] The EPC was to have federal competences for human rights, defence (though the power of war and peace remained with the member states), tax, and the field of the ECSC. A common market and foreign policy could be added incrementally to the competences by unanimous agreement among the member states. There were to be the normal federal institutions, but also a Council of Ministers whose assent would often be required, sometimes unanimously. Spinelli noted that, although it was not a federation, the federal structures would make possible a victorious struggle against the nation states – within fifty years.[88] While we still do not know whether the Community will eventually arrive at a federation, the timescale was perhaps prophetic as far as the Community and the step-by-step approach are concerned!

The Ad Hoc Assembly adopted the draft Treaty by fifty votes to none, with five abstentions. One who did not vote in favour was Michel Debré, a prominent Gaullist and subsequently one of de Gaulle's Prime Ministers. Debré had voted against the text in the Constitutional Committee and had indeed tabled a counter-proposal in confederal form. Although Debré had in November 1950 signed the appeal of the Congress of the Peoples of Europe demanding a Federal Pact, and de Gaulle himself had a few weeks before that pronounced in favour of direct elections to European institutions to which some part of sovereignty in the fields of the economy and defence would be delegated, the Gaullists had turned resolutely against all things federal.[89] Debré's opposition in the Ad Hoc Assembly was a warning signal of trouble ahead in France. Georges Bidault, by then French Foreign Minister and no great friend of the federalists, said, when Spaak presented the draft Treaty to him in his capacity as President for the time being of the Council of Foreign Ministers, that governments would have to take the measure of the difficulties, 'car des hommes irréprochables s'inquiètent de l'effacement des patries'.[90]

It was not only inside France that events were drifting against the EDC and hence the EPC which depended on it. Four days before the Ad Hoc Assembly approved the draft Treaty, Stalin died; and Spinelli, with a strong sense of political realism, noted that this 'could mean the end of the present attempt to unite Europe'.[91] Four months later, the Korean war came to an end. Until that period, things had gone quite well for the EDC Treaty. Germany and the Benelux countries had ratified it. By April 1953, the federalists had demonstrated the prevalence of public support by collecting over 1.6 million signatures for the Federal Pact, which could be held to comprise the EDC and EPC.[92] Italy was waiting on France to ratify. But in France, the political climate was deteriorating. The long-drawn-out war in Vietnam was grinding to an unhappy end. The urgency of defence integration seemed reduced by Stalin's death. Not only were the Communists and Gaullists irreconcilably opposed to the European Army, but by mid-1954, half the Socialists and some centrists were also against. One factor that weighed heavily was fear of German rearmament in a Community in which Britain was not to be involved. On 30 August 1954, the National Assembly voted by 319 votes to 264 to remove the EDC Treaty from its agenda; and that was the end of the affair, Germany was rearmed, but in the context of Nato and a toothless Western European Union, not in a Community with federal characteristics.

It has been argued that the National Assembly would have ratified the Treaty if it had been presented in 1952 or even 1953. The French government must have been confident of this when it signed the Treaty in May 1952; and not without reason, because in February the Assembly had approved, by 327 votes to 287, the principle of a European Army, though with the condition of its subordination to a 'supranational political authority'.[93] Edouard Herriot, the greatly respected Radical, 82 years old and Honorary President of the Assembly when he helped to persuade the Deputies to vote the EDC Treaty out in August 1954, had in July 1952 signed a letter, jointly with Spaak, calling for a 'supranational political authority' to be created through a European constituent assembly, clearly in the context of the EDC. Jacques Fauvet, editor and subsequently general director of Le Monde, was to write that the Treaty would have been ratified at that time.[94] Federalists had grounds to claim that if the EPC Treaty had been ready at the same time as the EDC, in May 1952, both could have been ratified together in that year. As it was, the EPC was sunk with the EDC; and the delay until such a bad political conjuncture for France certainly had not helped.

Federalist influence on the EPC Treaty had been strong. The European Movement had worked for the federalists' ideas. Federalists had instigated the Italian government's push for article 38. They had provided the principal sources of initiative in the Ad Hoc Assembly, even if the caution of others had compelled them to put some water in their wine. They were bitterly disappointed when the EDC went down and the EPC with it. Yet the EPC campaign can be seen to have brought the federalists influence over the longer term.

Historians of the federalist movement have suggested that, despite its immediate failure, the campaign helped to put political union on the map as something that could come about in the future, and more specifically, that it raised public expectations regarding political integration in a way that contributed to the relance that led to the Treaties of Rome.[95] From the Federal Pact to the EPC, the MFE acquired considerable influence on Italian politics. De Gasperi's adoption of federalism was an immediate triumph; but the federalists' ideas were to remain a significant factor in Italy up to the present time. In Germany it could be claimed that Europa Union, which gave staunch support to Adenauer's federalist policies, was *the* political movement in the period 1950-53.(96) Among the many individuals whose future activity in favour of a federal Europe was made more effective by the experience of the campaign, two in particular stand out. Spinelli consolidated his political stature in Italy, thus laying the ground for his future appointment as a member of the Commission of the EC and then as a Member of the European Parliament in the 1970s. The EPC campaign gave him the ideas and the experience, as well as the reputation, that enabled him to persuade the European Parliament, starting after its first direct elections in 1979, to draw up and pass, with a large majority, its Draft Treaty establishing the European Union, which has remained as a benchmark for federalists' subsequent efforts to develop the Community and was, meanwhile, together with the single market programme, one of the two main impulses behind the Single European Act. Spinelli, moreover, undoubtedly influenced Spaak to adopt the federalist cause for the crucial period up to the signing of the Rome Treaties in March 1957. The experience of the EPC surely focused Spaak's mind on the question of European unification and helped give him the commitment to see the difficult process of drafting the Treaties through to its successful conclusion as a step of historic importance in the direction of a federal Europe.

De Gasperi died ten days before the French National Assembly buried the EDC Treaty. He was deeply concerned, and one of his last political actions before he died was said to be a phone call to try to save what he feared could be the last chance to unite Europe.[97] How sad that he did not live to see the remarkably rapid relaunching of the process of unification, this time by the step-by-step method, even if with a really big step.

Monnet, Spaak and the EEC

In November 1954, less than three months after the collapse of the EDC project, Monnet announced his resignation as President of the ECSC's High Authority. He recalled telling his colleagues that 'the work must be continued until it culminates in the United States of Europe'; and when some of them evidently wondered whether he was doing the right thing, Enzo Giacchero, the Italian member of the High Authority of whom Monnet wrote that 'all his enthusiasm went to federalist ideals', said 'We're a citadel under siege. The most fearless among us is making a sortie'.[98] A few days later, he told Spinelli that he was resigning in order to be able to induce governments to make new delegations of sovereignty, as in the ECSC.[99] The aim of the 'sortie' was, indeed, to establish the Action Committee for the United States of Europe, assembling the political leaders of all the main democratic parties and trade unions of the Community countries, with the exception of the Gaullists, in order to press for the delegation of powers, as we saw earlier, 'to federal institutions'.

Meanwhile, Monnet was busy considering which sectors should be the next to receive the Community treatment. His first inclination was to add energy, in particular atomic energy, and transport to the competences of the ECSC. He agreed to a draft to this effect with Spaak, now the Belgian Foreign Minister. Energy seemed to him a sector in which European collaboration was likely to attract support in France, where, as the Suez operation the following year demonstrated, there was deep concern about the security of Middle East supplies. An energy community would surely not suffer the same fate as the EDC.

All plans for unification had reverted to the economic field. It was to be over a third of a century before proposals were again made to involve the Community in defence. But the sectoral approach was not the only possibility. Johan Beyen, as Netherlands' Foreign Minister, was convinced of the merits of a general common market. Only a few days after he became Foreign Minister, in September 1952, he persuaded the Council of Foreign Ministers to add consideration of general economic integration to the request it was about to make to the Ad Hoc Assembly to draw up the EPC constitution. He himself proposed a common market in December of that year; but it was not until he sent a memorandum to Spaak in April 1955, while Spaak had been discussing sectoral integration with Monnet, that his idea began to take off.

Beyen was, like Adenauer and Schuman, another prudent statesman who was not inclined to use the word federal. But he was against loose association based on intergovernmental cooperation; and he favoured an authority independent of the member states, gradually taking up the economic responsibilities of government, with 'a supranational parliament possessing real powers of control'.[100] Like Adenauer and Schuman, he appeared to prefer a federal reality to the federal word.

Although not popular in France, the idea of the common market found much favour in Germany. Monnet was soon persuaded that Germany would not accept an atomic energy community without it being combined, in a Junktim, with the common market.[101] Not that Monnet was unaware of the merits of general economic integration. He had told Uri in 1950 that the Schuman plan could not remain an isolated step and that more general integration would have to come before long.[102] As early as 1943, he had written in a memorandum that the states of Europe 'must form a Federation or 'European entity' which will make them a single economic unit'.[103] His problem in 1955 was his fear that France might reject a general common market and thus, repeating the experience of the EDC, set back the process of integration indefinitely. But when he understood that the common market was necessary to keep the Germans on board, he accepted that the risk had to be taken.

Moved by these considerations, Spaak, who had initially treated Beyen's proposal with reserve, also accepted it; and, together with their Luxembourg colleague, Spaak and Beyen drew up a Benelux memorandum which led to the convening of the Messina Conference on 1-2 June 1955. The resulting resolution approved by the six Foreign Ministers accepted the proposals for a common market together with an atomic energy community. They gave the task of drawing up detailed proposals to a committee chaired by Spaak.

The Spaak Committee started work in July 1955. Its principal drafter was Uri, who had been an intellectual power-house in Monnet's team since before the launching of the Schuman plan. Spaak was to write that the Spaak report which the committee produced was 'largely the fruit of his efforts' and that he was 'one of the principal architects of the Treaty of Rome'.[104] One of the strongest points of the Spaak report was the logical connection between the process of establishing the common market and the character of the Community institutions. Spaak told Spinelli in January 1956 that 'all in the small group see the need for a supranational authority and parliament – but the big three governments are cold' about the institutions.[105] Uri, who was later to explain that he preferred the term "federal" to "supranational" because it implied both cooperation and the division of powers,[106] saw how the common market project could be tied in with the existing Community institutions, more or less as designed for the ECSC. The role of the Council was, admittedly, enhanced, in line with the greater need for 'secondary' legislation beyond what was specified in the Treaty and hence to be enacted by the Community institutions, to wit the Council on a proposal from the Commission. The Commission was, conversely, to be somewhat less powerful than the High Authority, although its legislative role would be considerable when the Council moved from unanimous voting to a majority procedure. The Court of Justice was to have the same decisive powers. The provision for the European

Parliament to be directly elected following a unanimous decision by the member states was retained. In short, the institutions were broadly the same as in the ECSC, with similar scope for their development – which has in fact occurred. The principal powers included those to establish the customs union, the common commercial policy, the common agricultural policy and the general common market; and there was provision for a wide range of further economic cooperation: in all, a pronouncedly general rather than sectoral economic integration.

The Treaties of Rome, establishing the European Economic Community and Euratom, were signed on 25 March 1957; and they were ratified in the second half of the year by all six states so that they could enter into force on 1 January 1958. One of the purposes of Monnet's Action Committee was to mobilise the party leaders to prevent any recurrence of the EDC debacle; and it did indeed contribute to the successful ratification in France as well as the other countries.

The first Commission of the EEC, which took office in January 1958, was led by very able federalists. Its President, Walter Hallstein, had led the German team in the negotiations to establish the ECSC; and he had seen that Community as a first step which 'in its constitution-type structures already intentionally anticipates the structures of the future complete European federation.'[107] Thus he expressed Monnet's idea of a step towards federation in the language of a law professor who knew exactly what a federal constitution was like: a 'joining together with a state constitution, which preserves the state character of the participants'. He explained his concept of the process whereby this comes about as a 'creatio successiva'.[108]

Spinelli found Sicco Mansholt, the Dutch Vice-President responsible for agriculture, 'very federalist' in discussing with him the plan for a constituent assembly; and in 1961 Jean Rey, the Belgian Commissioner who was later the Commission's President, told Spinelli he thought that Commissioners should propagate federalism.[109] Robert Marjolin, the French Vice-President, had played a key part in steering the project for a common market through the hazardous waters of the French civil service where, according to his account, only Clappier, by then director of external economic relations at the Quai d'Orsay, was inclined to support it.[110] Marjolin, who had been another of Monnet's close collaborators at the Commissariat du Plan, was to write that he 'leant, almost instinctively, towards the idea of European federation', but felt in the Commission in the years following 1958 that it was not actual.[111]

There was one convincing reason for that, in the person of General de Gaulle, who became President of France in June 1958. He was God's gift to the realist school of international relations as against the federalists. For him, 'there is and can be no Europe other than a Europe of the States – except, of course, for myths, fictions and pageants'.[112] There were to be few steps towards federation while he remained President, for over a decade up to 1969. He succeeded in delaying the introduction of majority voting for some twenty years; and he would doubtless have wished to cut out all federal elements from the Community institutions. But the French voters indicated, in presidential elections towards the end of 1965, that they did not care for his attacks on the Community; and the same was clearly true of the Germans, alliance with whom was important to de Gaulle. Indeed, the Community and its institutions proved too well-founded to be brushed aside. They demonstrated the capacity to survive de Gaulle's hostility in the 1960s and the economic difficulties plus British awkwardness in the 1970s and early 1980s. The Community's powers have been extended, as Monnet expected; and its institutions have been reformed in a federal direction, with a majority procedure by now applying in the Council for almost all legislation; direct elections and increased powers for the European Parliament; and some additional authority for the Court of Justice, on top of the steadily growing respect that has been engendered by the quality of its work in establishing the rule of law in the Community. If the Maastricht Treaty comes fully into effect and the economic and monetary union is completed, the remaining essential steps to a federal system will be few, if hard to take, with full co-decision between Parliament and Council as perhaps the most crucial. The Community will then be not so far from the point at which the step-by-step approach coincides with the one-step idea, because one more major step would be enough to arrive at a federal system.

But the views of the step-by-step and of the one-step federalists were far from coinciding in the late 1950s. On the contrary, there was bitter conflict between the followers of the Monnet and of the Spinelli approaches.

Federalists Divide: AEF and Congress of the European People

For some weeks after the sinking of the EDC by the National Assembly in August 1954, federalists were in a state of shock. Before long, however, two opposing tendencies emerged. One agreed with Monnet that the federalising process should be continued by building on the Community idea. The other, led by Spinelli, took a more radical view.

When Monnet told Spinelli, at the end of November, that he was resigning in order to induce governments to continue that process, Spinelli's reaction was, on the contrary, that the federal idea should be promoted as 'an idée force' to turn people against the sovereign state.[113] For a time he nurtured the thought that the UEF, acting as a radical opposition against the nation-state, should propagate the idea that states could no longer justify the obedience of citizens as regards foreign policy, defence and economic matters, because of their inability to satisfy the citizens' needs in these fields. He had been impressed by the Indian example of securing constitutional change, in the form of independence, with the help of nonviolent civil disobedience. But he soon converted this into the more positive formula of popular mobilisation to press the politicians and governments to accept the idea of a constituent assembly. Influenced, again, by the example of the Indian National Congress, he put this proposal to the UEF under the title of a Congress of the European People.[114] The name is confusingly similar to that of the Congress of the Peoples of Europe, which the UEF set up in 1950 in order to promote the Federal Pact. But while the aim was simillar, the method of the CEP was more radical. It was to organise, without the help of governments, primary elections wherever possible, to send representatives to a permanent congress, which would 'represent European legitimacy' in promoting the constituent; and as a means of political action while awaiting success in this, 'cahiers des doléances' were to be presented to the congress, bringing forward the complaints of citizens and local governments regarding problems that arose as a result of the lack of effective government for Europe.

Spinelli felt, after August 1954, that nothing more could be expected of governments unless they were to be driven by popular pressure. He was not impressed by the preparations for the relaunching of the Community at the Messina conference. Immediately after the agreement of the Foreign Ministers in the first days of June 1955 to start negotiations that were to result in the EEC and Euratom, he thought that Monnet had lost his battle and the Benelux memorandum had led to nothing. He continued to meet Monnet for discussions from time to time during that period and found him 'very friendly' and 'benevolent' to Spinelli's action.[115] It seems that the two archetypes viewed each other with mutual sympathy, though each was sceptical about the merits of the other's approach. By the end of 1955, Spinelli had realised that Messina might produce something; but he remained convinced that a real relaunching would require a non-conformist attitude and a struggle on the political-intellectual plane.[116]

Meanwhile, those in the UEF who supported Monnet's approach were developing their ideas. Ernst Friedländer, who had become President of Europa Union Deutschland in October 1954, rejected the thesis of what he called the 'all-or-nothing federalists'. While agreeing upon the end, he criticised their method, preferring to build on the EC's success by moving forward step by step with those countries that were willing. He was temperamentally averse to what he regarded as emotional appeals to the public, and was more at home seeking to convince, with practical arguments, people with political and economic responsibilities.[117]

Most German federalists were reasonably content with the German government's European policy and saw no need to go into radical opposition against it. So Friedländer's line was supported by Europa Union. Dutch federalists took the same view. So did some of the federalist organisations in other countries, including La Fédération, a major group in France. With Spinelli, backed by the Italian federalists and a number of others, including significant French support, driving determinedly in the opposite direction, a collision was inevitable.[118] The first battle took place at a UEF Congress in January 1956, with Spinelli's radical policy opposed by supporters of the step-by-step Community method – who were encouraged by a speech that Robert Schuman, by now President of the European Movement, contributed in their favour. But the issue was not resolved and another Congress had to be convened in March. Here there were three tendencies: the Spinellists; the Monnetists, who envisaged, as an observer was to put it, 'a series of federal pacts of limited scope';[119] and those who wanted both of them to continue working together in the UEF. But the split was too deep for that. Spinelli was not willing to compromise; and before long the Germans, Dutch, La Fédération and some others pulled out and established their own organisation, the Action Européenne Fédéraliste (AEF).

The Spinellists went ahead with the Congress of the European People. In the period 1957-61, some 650,000 votes were cast for delegates to the congress, about a quarter of a million of them in Lombardy and Rome alone. But this was not enough to put any pressure on governments. Spinelli lost interest and the CPE died. Italian federalists who have since been influential in developing Italy's markedly federalist stance did, however, obtain their political formation in that campaign. Spinelli himself, after working as a professor and founding an international affairs institute in the 1960s, ironically enough became a Commissioner in 1970; and that helped to give him a standing, when he became a member of the European Parliament in 1976, to carry through his project for a European Union Treaty. While the efforts of Spinelli and his followers in the Congress of the European People had not been sufficient to secure a credible body of representatives elected by the people, Monnet's Community Treaties and the member governments did that job for him when the first direct elections were held in 1979. So he lived to see his dream of the 1950s come true, and to lead the elected representatives in drafting a European constitution.

Meanwhile the step-by-step federalist organisations developed their line of action. The founding congress of the AEF was held in September 1956.[121] The aim was the United States of Europe, with federal institutions and powers including foreign policy, defence, currency and other economic matters. The difference from the Spinellists was that the means were to be any steps useful for its realisation. The organisations in the Community member states worked, first to secure ratification of the Rome Treaties, then to demand further Community development. The British Federal Union, which also supported the AEF, worked, rather, towards British entry into the Community. The British federalists' efforts in the late 1950s contributed to the decision to seek negotiations for accession which were brought to an end by de Gaulle's veto in January 1963; but they continued with successive campaigns until British accession was achieved in 1973.[122]

The AEF's most spectacular event was a conference in Wiesbaden in January 1959.[123] The participants included von Brentano, by then German Foreign Minister, Hallstein, Marjolin, Schuman, as well as former UEF notables such as Brugmans and Dehousse. The British delegation was led by Lord Attlee, who showed more commitment to world than to European federalism. Among its members, however was Roy Jenkins, then a relatively young Labour MP, who was to become a Vice-Chairman of Federal Union – presaging the commitment he was later to show when, as President of the Commission, he relaunched the project for monetary union, seeing it as the way to take Europe 'over a political threshold', and setting in train the process that was to lead to the European Monetary System and later the project for economic and monetary union.[124]

Brugmans presented the conference with 'theses' including the strengthening of the European Parliament and Commission, with direct elections as an early objective; progress towards a European constitution was to be made when that should be possible. The conference resolved to press for the direct elections as well as 'own resources' for the Community and the coordination of foreign policy, within the perspective of eventual federal institutions.[125]

Thus the AEF was prepared for the long haul of developing the Community and its institutions, while the Spinellists ended the 1950s concentrating on the idea of the constituent assembly and the constitution. Over a decade was to pass before they united again in a revived UEF in the early 1970s.

Federalists' Influence

For federalists who saw federalism as a step-by-step process, the 1950s ended on a high note. Federalists together with relevant interests, political or economic, had launched the process of economic integration, first sectoral then general. Monnet and his team had been seminal. But sympathisers with the step-by-step approach, such as Schuman, De Gasperi, Adenauer, Beyen and Spaak, had played an essential part, as had numerous other federalists as the process got underway. Federalists, particularly Monnet and his associates, had been responsible for the federal elements in the Community institutions – the Court, Parliament, independent executive and provision for majority voting in the Council – on which federalists expected to base the development of a federal system, through institutional reforms and the addition of other necessary competences.

John Pinder

The end of the decade was not so cheerful for one-step federalists. The campaign in the Council of Europe for a Federal Pact had been frustrated by British opposition. The EDC, which according to Monnet had made federation an 'immediate objective', had been sunk by French opposition; and the EPC, which was largely the work of federalists – Spinelli, Lombardo, De Gasperi, Dehousse and, as a federalist for the time being, Spaak – had gone down with it. The Congress of the European People was far down the road to failure. But it would have been naive to be confident of early success with such a radical project as federation in one step. Many federalists remained convinced that events would sooner or later demonstrate its necessity and a more favourable political conjuncture would enable it to be brought about. The campaigns had engendered strong commitments among individuals and organisations, and, it was held, implanted the idea of a federal political union in the minds of very many people.

Spinelli, the most notable exponent of this view, was to demonstrate the staying power of the idea by reviving the project in the 1980s. The European Parliament's Draft Treaty for a European Union was the product of his commitment, together with the backing of numerous federalists, including in particular those MEPs associated with the Italian MFE and with Europa Union Deutschland. The immediate result was one of the major impulses that led to the Single European Act, and in particular to the strengthening of the role of the Parliament. But the Draft Treaty also established the idea of a European federation again as a political project, which was to lend power to further steps in the federalising process as well as to efforts to secure a federal end to it.

As the example of Spinelli and his supporters shows, commitments formed in the 1950s, or even earlier, gave this stamina to the constitutional approach. The same was true for the step-by-step federalising process. Monnet and his Action Committee remained active, as did the AEF and its strongest component, Europa Union. Hallstein, Mansholt, Marjolin and Rey continued their striking endeavours in the Commission into the 1960s, for long enough to ensure that the customs union, the common agricultural policy and the common commercial policy would be secured as considerable federalising achievements. After a pause during which de Gaulle blocked other movement, the federalising steps recommenced, again with the help of people who had acquired their commitments in the 1950s. Jenkins, who had held office in Federal Union in the late 1950s, was the one who launched the idea for the EMS with an explicitly political aim. Jacques Delors, who has given such a strong impulse to the federalising process since 1985, must have been influenced by the strong federalist current that prevailed in France in the early 1950s and continued, among those who sympathised with Monnet's approach, through the following years; and he sympathised with the Christian personalist school of thought, whose chief postwar exponent was Alexandre

Marc, and which had a pronounced federalist commitment. Helmut Kohl, who evidently found his youthful participation in the federalists' frontier demonstration memorable, was the principal exponent of the need for political union in the negotiation of the Maastricht Treaty.

Such people, motivated not just by particular interests but by a more general commitment to the federalising process, played an important part in the transfer of competences to the Community; and the contribution of federalists was essential in the establishment and subsequent strengthening of the federal elements in the institutions. It has been suggested that the logic tying one step to another in the development of the Community has been 'undetected and unexplained'.[127] These federalists and sympathisers, who have shown considerable continuity from the 1950s to the present, may be part of that logic. But an explanation based on personalities would be inadequate. It may also be affirmed that the process of federalisation reflects a secular movement towards interdependence in the economy, environment and security, whose result is that crucial problems can 'no longer be resolved by national means'.[128] Joint action among closely interdependent states is therefore required if the problems are to be resolved. The federalists' case is that they will not be satisfactorily resolved without federal institutions: an executive independent of member states' governments in order to secure effectiviness; a parliament for democracy; and a court for the rule of law. Otherwise some of the principal problems facing these countries will not be resolved; or, if resolved, in a way that is not acceptable to constitutional democracies.

The federalists' achievements in the creation and development of the Community have been due, not so much to their personal qualities, as to their understanding, more or less complete and more or less consistent, of this underlying logic of the processes of interdependence, integration and federalisation. This, it is suggested, is a much more powerful explanation of the process of the Community's development than the neo-functionalist spillover from one field of integration to another. It can be convincingly argued that such spillover had an important influence on moves to monetary union, following the integration of capital markets under the single market programme. But even here, and certainly in most other instances, the underlying forces of interdependence that make separate nation-states incapable of dealing with the problems, and the determination to master them through a process of unification, have been more important. The significance of the Community's acquis of institutions and competences has been that, once the impulse for a federalising step has been given, the already existing framework makes it easier to take.

It is a gross error to suppose that continuation of the federalising process to a federal end is inevitable. First de Gaulle, then the British, now perhaps the Danes, have shown how it can be obstructed and could be reversed. What federalists are entitled to claim is that, if the process is reversed, it is inevitable that crucial problems will become increasingly insoluble. The story of the 1950s, however, with the success of the Schuman plan followed by the failure of the EDC and EPC, in turn followed by the relaunching with the Treaties of Rome, shows that the logic indicated above can prevail. The Community has now proceeded so far that, if the economic and monetary union is accomplished, the principal reform remaining to make it a federal system for the economy is the one critical step of full co-decision between the Council and the Parliament. That could occur in the 1990s. The further main step to make it a federal state would be the staged incorporation of the competences for defence and related foreign policy into the federal Community system. But that is probably for another millennium. The story of the 1950s tells us not to be too sanguine about it.

Notes

1. Walter Lipgens, *45 Jahre Ringen um die Europäische Verfassung: Dokumente 1939-1984: Von den Schriften der Widerstandsbewegung bis zum Vertragsentwurf des Europäischen Parlaments* (Bonn: Europa Union Verlag, 1986), pp. 202, 209 n.38.
2. Carl J. Friedrich, 'Federal Constitutional Theory and Emergent Proposals', in A. W. Macmahon (ed.), *Federalism, Mature and Emergent* (New York: Doubleday, 1955), pp. 526, 528. For other works on the same theme, see Friedrich, *Trends of Federalism in Theory and Practice (London: 1968)*; Friedrich, *Europe: An Emergent Nation?* (New York and Evanston: Harper & Row, 1969); John Pinder, *European Community: The Building of a Union* (Oxford: Oxford University Press, 1991), chapter 10; Pinder, 'The New European Federalism: The Idea and the Achievements', in Michael Burgess and Alain-G. Gagnon (eds), *Comparative Federalism and Federation: Competing Traditions and Future Directions* (Simon & Schuster, 1992 forthcoming).
3. Richard T. Griffiths, *Challenge and Response in Western Europe: The History of European Integration*, EUI Research Project Report (Florence: European University Institute, December 1991), p. 7.
4. Lipgens, op. cit. (n. 1, above), p. 220; Andrew and Francis Boyd, *Western Union* (London: Hutchinson & Co., undated 1948?), p. 142.
5. Griffiths, op. cit. (n. 3, above), p. 5.
6. Walter Lipgens, *A History of European Integration 1945-1947: The Formation of the European Unity Movement* (Oxford: Clarendon Press, 1982), pp. 303-14, 571-99; Richard Mayne and John Pinder with John Roberts, *Federal Union: The Pioneers* (Basingstoke: Macmillan, 1990), pp. 1-29, 53-5, 89-90.
7. Each of them wrote an autobiography: Hendrik Brugmans, *Wij Europa: Een halve eeuw strijd voor emancipatie en Europees federalisme* (Amsterdam: Meulenhoff, 1988), especially pp. 118-28; Henri Frenay, *La nuit finira* (Paris, 1973); Eugen Kogon, *Der SS-Staat: Das System der deutschen Konzentrationslager* (München: Kindlerverlag, 1974); Altiero Spinelli, *Come ho tentato di diventare saggio: Io, Ulisse* (Bologna: il Mulino, 1984).
8. Lipgens, op. cit. (n. 6, above), pp. 607-14. Coudenhove-Kalergi's basic book was *Paneuropa* (Wien: Pan-Europa Verlag, 1923), published in English as Paneurope (New York: 1926).

9. See Mayne and Pinder, op. cit. (n. 6, above), pp. 94-5.
10. Brugmans, op. cit. (n. 7, above), p. 192; John Pomian (ed.), *Joseph Retinger: Memoirs of an Eminence Grise* (London: Chatto & Windus, 1972), p. 222; Mayne and Pinder, op. cit. (n. 6, above), p. 28.
11. Boyds, op. cit. (n. 4, above), pp. 159-61; Lipgens, op. cit, (n. 1, above), pp. 240-2.
12. Lipgens, op. cit. (n. 1, above), pp. 196, 236-8; Mayne and Pinder, op. cit. (n. 6, above), pp. 99-100, 103.
13. Michael Charlton, *The Price of Victory* (London: BBC, 1983), p. 77.
14. H. Brugmans, *Prophètes et Fondateurs de l'Europe* (Bruges: College of Europe, 1974), pp. 343, 348 n.7.
15. R. W. G. Mackay, *Federal Europe* (London: Michael Joseph, 1940).
16. Mayne and Pinder, op. cit. (n, 6, above), p. 103.
17. Jean-Pierre Gouzy, *Les Pionniers de l'Europe Communautaire* (Lausanne: Centre de Recherches Européennes), p. 65.
18. Lipgens, op. cit. (n. 1, above), pp, 280-4,
19. Gouzy, op. cit. (n. 17, above), pp. 64-5; Lipgens, op. cit. (n. 1, above), pp. 285-92.
20. Sergio Pistone, 'Il ruolo del Movimento Federalista Europeo negli anni 1948-50', in Raymond Poidevin (ed.), *Histoire des débuts de la construction européenne* (Brussels: Bruylant, 1986), p. 305; Lipgens, op. cit. (n. 6, above), p, 653.
21. Gouzy, op. cit. (n. 17, above), p. 65; Lipgens, op. cit. (n. 1, above), p.296.
22. Pistone, op. cit. (n. 20, above), pp. 305-8.
23. Ibid., p. 308; Sergio Pistone, 'Il ruolo di Altiero Spinelli nella genesi dell'Art. 38 della Comunitá Europea di Difesa e del progetto di Comunitá Politica Europea', in G. Trausch (ed.), *La construction de l'Europe, du Plan Schuman aux Traités de Rome: Projets et initiatives, déboires et échecs* (Brussels: Bruylant, 1992 forthcoming), p. 20 n. 5 of ttypescript; Edmondo Paolini, *Altiero Spinelli: Appunti per una biografia* (Bologna: il Mulino, 1988), p. 80. For the development of De Gasperi's views, see also John Pinder, 'Federalism in Britain and Italy: Radicals and the English Liberal Tradition', in Peter M. R. Stirk (ed,), *European Unity in Context: The Interwar Period* (London and New York: Pinter Publishers, 1989).
24. Brugmans, op. cit. (n. 14, above), p, 329.
25. E. G. Thompson, 'Frontier Incident – for Peace', *Federal News* no.186, October 1950, cited in Mayne and Pinder, op. cit. (n. 6, above), pp.104-5; Karlheinz Koppe, *Das grüne E setzt sich durch: 20 Jahre Europa Union Deutschland 1946-1966* (Köln: Europa Union Verlag, 1967), pp. 46-7; Claus Schöndube and Christel Ruppert, *Eine Idee setzt sich durch: Der Weg zum vereinigten Europa* (Hangelar bei Bonn: Verlag Heinrich Warnecke, 1964), pp. 164-5.
26. Gouzy, op. cit. (n. 17, above), p. 67; Lipgens, op. cit. (n. 1, above), p. 299; Schöndube and Ruppert, op. cit. (n. 25, above), pp. 165-6.
27. Gouzy, ibid., pp. 162-4.
28. Schöndube and Ruppert, op. cit. (n, 25, above), pp. 166-7.
29. Walter Lipgens and Wilfried Loth (eds), *Documents on the History of European Integration, Vol. 3: The Struggle for European Union by Political Parties and Pressure Groups in Western European Countries 1945-1950* (Berlin and New York: Walter de Gruyter, 1988), p. 754.
30. Jean Monnet, *Memoirs* (translated by Richard Mayne. London: Collins, 1978), pp. 21-35; Mayne and Pinder, op. cit. (n. 6, above), pp. 25-9.
31. Monnet, ibid., p. 280.
32. Ibid., p. 295.
33. Cited by Dieter Dettke, 'Pionier der europäischen Integration: Robert Schuman', in Thomas Jansen and Dieter Mahncke (eds), *Persönlichkeiten der Europäischen Integration: Vierzehn biographische Essays* (Bonn: Europa Union Verlag, 1981), p. 240.

34. Etienne Hirsch, *Ainsi va la vie* (Lausanne: Fondation Jean Monnet pour l'Europe and Centre de Recherches Européennes, 1988), p. 107.
35. Lipgens, op. cit. (n. 6, above), pp. 126, 130, 219.
36. Alan S. Milward, *The Reconstruction of Western Europe 1945-51* (London: Methuen, 1984), p. 396.
37. Ibid., pp. 310-11.
38. Griffiths, op. cit. (n. 3, above), p. 7.
39. Jean Monnet, *Les Etats-Unis d'Europe ont commencé: Discours et allocutions 1952-1954* (Paris: Robert Laffont, 1955), pp. 55-60.
40. Altiero Spinelli, *Diario europeo 1948/1969*, edited by Edmondo Paolini (Bologna: il Mulino, 1989), pp. 142-5.
41. Louis Joxe, contribution in Henri Rieben, *Des guerres européennes á l'Union de l'Europe* (Lausanne: Fondation Jean Monnet pour l'Europe and Centre de Recherches Européennes, 1987), pp. 352-3; and personal information.
42. Spinelli, op. cit. (n. 40, above), p. 163.
43. *Action Committee for the United States of Europe: Statements and Declarations 1955-67*, European Series No. 9 (London: Chatham House and PEP, 1969), p. 11; also reproduced in Rieben, op. cit. (n. 41, above), p. 314.
44. *Le Monde*, 16 June 1955, cited in Henri Rieben in *L'Europe en Formation*, printemps 1987, p. 10.
45. Monnet, op. cit. (n. 30, above), p. 296.
46. See John Pinder, *The Building of a Union* (n. 2, above), pp. 91, 206-17,
47. Monnet, op. cit. (n. 30, above), p. 343.
48. Cited in Mayne and Pinder, op. cit. (n. 6, above), p. 106,
49. H. Brugmans, *L'idée européenne 1918-1965* (Bruges: De Tempel for the College of Europe, 1965), p. 142; Paul-Henri Spaak, *The Continuing Battle: Memoirs of a European 1936-66* (London: Weidenfeld and Nicholson, 1971), p. 217.
50. Charlton, op. cit. (n. 13, above), p. 137.
51. Monnet, op, cit. (n. 30, above), pp. 342-6.
52. The declaration is reproduced in Roberto Ducci and Bino Olivi, *l'Europa incompiuta* (Padova: CEDAM, 1970), pp. 183-8.
53. Pistone, op. cit. (n. 23, above), n. 6.
54. Koppe, op. cit. (n. 25, above), p. 44; Spinelli, op. cit. (n. 40, above), p. 65.
55. Gouzy, op. cit. (n. 17, above), p. 81.
56. Lipgens, op. cit. (n. 1, above), reproduces these on pp, 299-303.
57. Gouzy, op. cit. (n. 17, above), p. 82.
58. Pistone, op. cit. (n. 23, above), pp. 9-11.
59. Ibid., p. 11; Spinelli, op. cit. (n. 40, above), p. 100.
60. Spinelli, ibid., pp. 84, 102.
61. Gouzy, op. cit. (n. 17, above), p. 88.
62. Cited in Brugmans, op. cit. (n. 14, above), p. 324.
63. Spinelli, op. cit. (n. 40, above), p. 114.
64. Cited in Brugmans, op. cit. (n. 14, above), p. 326; see also Pistone, op. cit, (n. 23, above), n. 22; Monnet, op. cit. (n. 30, above), p. 382.
65. Pistone, ibid., p. 2.
66. Werner Weidenfeld, *Konrad Adenauer und Europa: Die geistigen Grundlagen der westeuropäischen Integrationspolitik des ersten Bonner Bundeskanzlers* (Bonn: Europa Union Verlag, 1976), p. 340; the whole speech is reproduced in pp. 335-43.
67. Cited in Brugmans, op. cit. (n. 14, above), p. 274; see also Werner Weidenfeld, 'Seine Sorge hiess Europa: Konrad Adenauer', in Jansen and Mahncke, op. cit. (n. 33, above), pp. 315-6, 319-20, 322.
68. Altiero Spinelli, *L'Europa non cade dal cielo* (Bologna: il Mulino, 1960), pp. 132-3.
69. LuigiVittorio Majocchi and Francesco Rossolillo, *il Parlamento europeo* (Napoli:

Guida Editori, 1979), pp. 180, 182, 188; a complete record of the first meeting is given on pp. 173-91.
70. See Mayne and Pinder, op. cit. (n. 6, above), p. 106.
71. Spaak, op. cit. (n. 49, above), pp. 219-21.
72. Gouzy, op. cit. (n. 17, above), pp. 83-4; Lipgens, op. cit, (n. 1, above), p.91
73. Lipgens, op. cit. (n. 1, above), p. 311; Spaak, op. cit. (n, 49, above), pp. 224-5
74. Spinelli, op. cit. (n. 40, above), p. 117.
75. Cited in Schöndube and Ruppert, op, cit. (n. 25, above), p. 167.
76. Spinelli, op. cit. (n. 40, above), p. 135.
77. Ibid., p. 140.
78. Beate Schneider, 'Propagandist und Staatsmann: Paul-Henri Spaak', in Jansen and Mahncke, op. cit. (n. 33, above), p. 427.
79. Spinelli, op. cit. (n. 40, above), p. 130.
80. Ibid., pp. 124, 126, 130.
81. Carl J. Friedrich, 'Introduction', in Robert R. Bowie and Carl J. Friedrich (eds), *Studies in Federalism* (Boston and Toronto: Little Brown and Company, 1954), pp. xxv-xlii. Friedrich's Introduction tells the story of the Study Committee and the book contains the documents it produced, including the draft resolutions for the Assembly (pp. 819-27).
82. His books expounding this idea are given in n. 2, above.
83. The article is reproduced in Bowie and Friedrich, op. cit. (n, 81, above), p. xxviii and in Lipgens, op, cit. (n,1, above), pp. 314-5.
84. Monnet, op. cit. (n. 30, above), p. 383.
85. Friedrich, op. cit. (n. 81, above), pp. xxvii, xxix.
86. Schöndube and Ruppert, op. cit. (n. 25, above), p. 211,
87. Friedrich, op. cit. (n. 81, above), pp. xxxii-xxxiii. The draft treaty is reproduced in Bowie and Friedrich, op. cit. (n. 81, above), pp. 828-53, and in Lipgens, op. cit. (n. 1, above), pp. 335-60,
88. Spinelli, op. cit. (n. 40, above), p. 171.
89. Gouzy, op. cit. (n. 17, above), p. 67.
90. Ibid., p. 94.
91. Spinelli, op. cit. (n. 40, above), p. 168.
92. Koppe, op. cit. (n. 25, above), p. 66.
93. Gouzy, op cit. (n. 17, above), p. 100; Pistone, op. cit. (n. 23, above), p. 17; Schöndube and Ruppert, op. cit. (n. 25, above), p. 206.
94. Jacques Fauvet, 'Naissance et mort d'un Traité', in R. Aron and D. Lerner (eds) *La querelle de la CED* (Paris: Colin, 1956), cited in Gouzy, op. cit. (n. 17, above), pp. 100-1, in Lipgens, op. cit. (n. 1, above), p. 368, and in Pistone, op. cit. (n. 23, above), pp. 25-6.
95. Koppe, op. cit. (n. 25, above), p. 68; Pistone, op. cit. (n. 23, above), p. 18.
96. Koppe, loc. cit.
97. Brugmans, op. cit. (n. 14, above), p. 325.
98. Monnet, op. cit. (n. 30, above), pp. 374, 406.
99. Spinelli, op. cit. (n. 40, above), p. 223.
100. Jerzy Lukaszewski, *Jalons de l'Europe* (Lausanne: Fondation Jean Monnet pour l'Europe and Centre de Recherches Européennes, 1985), pp. 193-7, citation from p. 197.
101. Robert Marjolin, *Le travail d'une vie: Mémoires 1911-1986* (Paris: Robert Laffont, 1986), p. 296; Monnet, op. cit. (n. 30, above), pp. 400-4; Pierre Uri, 'Réflexion sur l'approche fonctionnaliste de Jean Monnet et suggestions pour l'avenir', in Giandomenico Majone, Emile Noël, Peter Van den Bossche (eds), *Jean Monnet et l'Europe d'aujourd'hui* (Baden-Baden: Nomos Verlagsgesellschaft, 1989), p. 77.

102. Uri, loc. cit.
103. Rieben, op. cit. (n. 41, above), p. 279.
104. Spaak, op. cit. (n. 49, above), p. 231.
105. Spinelli, op. cit. (n. 40, above), p. 285.
106. Uri, op. cit. (n. 101, above), p. 76.
107. Lecture given at Georgetown University, March 1953, cited in Lipgens, op. cit. (n. 1, above), p. 306 n. 2.
108. Wolfgang Ramonat, 'Rationalist und Wegbereiter: Walter Hallstein', in Jansen and Mahncke, op. cit. (n. 33, above), p. 348.
109. Spinelli, op. cit. (n. 40, above), pp. 242, 376.
110. Marjolin, op. cit. (n. 101, above), pp. 274-303; regarding Clappier, p, 283.
111. Ibid., p. 312.
112. Press Conference, 15 May 1962.
113. Spinelli, op. cit. (n. 40, above), p. 223.
114. Ibid., p. 210; Paolini, op. cit. (n. 23, above), pp. 101-3.
115. Spinelli, ibid., pp. 240, 260-1, 267, 269, 270.
116. Ibid., p. 280; Paolini, op. cit. (n. 23, above), pp. 106-7.
117. Koppe, op. cit. (n. 25, above), pp. 68, 71, 76-7, 105.
118. Koppe, ibid., pp. 84, 94-6; Gouzy, op. cit. (n. 17, above), pp. 138-41.
119. Gouzy, ibid., p. 140.
120. Paolini, op. cit, (n. 23, above), pp. 131-2; Pistone,
121. Koppe, op. cit. (n. 25, above), pp. 96-7; Lipgens, op. cit. (n. 1, above),p.455.
122. Mayne and Pinder, op. cit, (n. 6, above), chapters 10-12,
123. Ibid., p. 153, Koppe, op, cit. (n, 25, above), pp. ll4-7.
124. Roy Jenkins, *Europe's Present Challenge and Future Opportunity*, First Jean Monnet Lecture (Florence: European University Institute, 1977), cited in Peter Ludlow, *The Making of the European Monetarv System* (London: 1982), pp. 47-9.
125. Reproduced in Koppe, op. cit. (n. 25, above), pp. 212-3.
127. Griffiths, op. cit. (n. 3, above), p. 7.
128. Ibid., p. 11.

Notes on Contributors

Dr. Erik Bloemen, lecturer Dept. of History, Free University Amsterdam. His main fields of specialization are the history of management and European economic development and integration since 1945.

Dr. Wendy Asbeek Brusse, lecturer Dept. of History, University of Groningen. She works and publishes on European commercial policies after 1945 and on the history of European integration. She is presently writing a book on post-war European cartels.

Dr. Monika Dickhaus, lecturer Faculty of History and Philosophy, University of Bielefeld. Her research field is economic history in the 19th. and 20th. Century. Her primary focus has been on central banking, international monetary cooperation and questions relating to European economic and monetary integration in the post-war period. She is preparing a book on the international monetary policy of the German Central Bank during the period of the German Wirtschaftswunder.

Dr. Richard T. Griffiths, formerly professor of Contemporary History at the European University Institute (Florence); currently professor of Economic and Social History, University of Leiden. He has worked on 19th. and 20th. Century economic history and the history of European integration. He is currently working with the Arena Project (Oslo) on small states and European integration and is writing a book on the Creation of EFTA.

Dr. Flemming Just, senior researcher, Dept. of Agricultural and Co-operative Research, South Jutland University Centre (Esbjerg). His main research areas have been agricultural politics, the co-operative movement and local history. He is the coordinator of EU-projects on agri-environmental problems in western and eastern Europe. He is currently writing a book on Agriculture in Danish politics 1960-1990.

Dr. Johnny Laursen, senior lecturer, Aalborg University Centre; associated researcher to the Danish Research Council project, "Danish Politics in Transition 1945-1985". Has worked on labour history, European interwar history and Danish European policy after 1945. He is currently writing a book on Denmark's European policy in the 1950s and 1960s.

Dr. Mikael af Malmborg, researcher Dept. of History, Lund University. His main field of research is post-war European integration with special reference to Sweden. He is presently engaged in an interdisciplinary project on Sweden's long period of peace writing on Swedish international relations after the First World War.

Dr. Karl Molin is assistant professor Dept. of History, Stockholm University. His research has focused on industrial relations and managerial strategies in Sweden 1880 to 1930, on domestic Swedish politics during the 1930's and 1940's, and on Swedish neutrality during the Cold War. He is currently one of the coordinators of the research network, "Sweden during the Cold War".

Dr. Thorsten B. Olesen, lecturer Dept. of History, Aarhus University; associated researcher to the Danish Research Council project, "Danish Politics in Transition 1945-1985". His main fields of research include fascism during the inter-war period and topics related to Danish security policy and European integration after 1945. He is presently writing a book on Social Democracy and Security Policy in Denmark 1945-1949.

John Pinder is a visiting professor at the College of Europe, Bruges. He was Director of the Policy Studies Institute, London from 1964 to 1985. His books include *Britain and the Common Market* (1961), *The Economics of Europe* (1971), *Federal Union: The Pioneers - A History of Federal Union* (with Richard Mayne, 1990), *European Community. The Building of a Union* (2.ed. 1995). He is Chairman of the Federal Trust.

Dr. Thomas Rhenisch, Freiburg. He has conducted research on the history of European integration and on the economic policy of the Third Reich. He is currently preparing a research project on the history of "big technologies" in post-war Europe.

Dr. Vibeke Sørensen (†), Jean Monnet professor of International Organization and International Relations Dept. of History, University of Groningen. Major fields of specialization included 20th. Century economic history and the history of European integration with special reference to Denmark. She was working on a book on Danish and Dutch foreign economic policies after 1947.